A KISAMWAR GLOSSARY OF KANNADA WORDS

A KISAMWAR GLOSSARY
OF
KANNADA WORDS

ULLAL NARASINGA RAO

GYAN

Published by

Gyan Publishing House
5, Ansari Road
Daryaganj, New Delhi-110002
Phone: 011-47034999, 9811692060
E-mail: books@gyanbooks.com

Distribution Network
gyanbooks.com
India, USA, Canada, UK, Australia, France

ISBN : 978-81-212-4445-9 (PB)
First Published, 1891

2nd Impression 2020

Printed at: Gyan Press, Delhi.

PREFACE.

N the following Glossary I have tried, by means of classification, to produce a comprehensive and handy work of reference of *practical utility* for the Kanarese parts of India. An arbitrary but convenient plan of grouping together technical and other words under different heads has been adopted; and this arrangement will, I hope, be found suitable for purposes of ready reference by persons interested in a particular subject, by translators of official documents and the several Administrations. Official terms have been explained, and the use of words localised; information scattered in various works, inaccessible to many owing to their value or rarity, brought together and concentrated to effect a saving of time and labor. A general index has also been added.

I thought it beside my purpose to give the origin or derivation of words, or to indicate, as such, the foreign words which have by long use become naturalized in the Kanarese language.

Dr. Lepsius's system of transliteration, a key to which has been given, has been adopted; while such words as "Mysore" and "Canara" have been left undisturbed.

Among others, I have consulted Prof. Wilson's Glossary of Indian Terms, Chamier's Land Tenures of Canara, Mr. Rice's Mysore and Coorg, the Bombay Gazetteer Vol. XV. I must also gratefully acknowledge the valuable assistand received from Messrs. U. Raghunathaya and Bh. Shiva Rau in the preparation of the work for the press.

The usefulness of a work like this is a matter of trial and time. I am conscious that the work is capable of improvement both as to matter and execution. I trust, however, that the labor spent on the work will be duly appreciated by the public, and that friends and critics will enable me to enhance its practical usefulness by suggestions and corrections for a future edition.

MANGALORE,
July 1891.

U. N. R.

CONTENTS.

KEY TO TRANSLITERATION.

ಅ	a	*as in*	but.
ಆ	â	„	car
ಇ	i	„	pin.
ಈ	i	„	evil.
ಉ	u	„	put.
ಊ	û	„	rule.
ಋ	ṛi	„	terrific.
ಎ	e	„	set.
ಏ	ê	„	mate.
ಐ	ai	„	aisle.
ಒ	o	„	not.
ಓ	ô	„	ode.
ಔ	au	„	ounce.
ಂ	ṅ, ń, n, m.		
ಃ	h	*vocalised* h.	
ಕ	ka	*as in*	kin.
ಖ	kha	„	stockholder.
ಗ	ga	„	gun.
ಘ	gha	„	ghost.
ಙ	ṅa	„	sing.
ಚ	ča	„	church.
ಛ	cha	„	church-hill.
ಜ	ja, za	„	Japan or zeal.
ಝ	jha	„	hedge-hog.
ಞ	ńa	„	onion.
ಟ	ṭa	*as in*	time.
ಠ	ṭha	„	court-house.
ಡ	ḍa	„	done.
ಢ	ḍha	„	blood-hound.
ಣ	ṇa	„	send.
ತ	ta	„	with.
ಥ	tha	„	thigh.
ದ	da	„	there.
ಧ	dha	*the preceding aspirated.*	
ನ	na	*as in*	not.
ಪ	pa	„	pat.
ಫ	pha	„	uphold.
ಬ	ba	„	bud.
ಭ	bha	„	abhor.
ಮ	ma	„	man.
ಯ	ya	„	young.
ರ	ra	„	rat.
ಲ	la	„	luck.
ವ	va	„	vulgar.
ಶ	śa	„	sure.
ಷ	sha	„	bush.
ಸ	sa	„	sit.
ಹ	ha	„	hut.
ಳ	ḷa	*cerebro-palatal* l.	
ಕ್ಷ	ksha	*as in*	mixture.

ABBREVIATIONS.

Bel.	Belgaum.
C.	Canara.
Cg.	Coorg.
Ch.	Chamier's Land Tenures of Canara (1853).
Lit.	Literal.
My.	Mysore.
N. C.	North-Canara.
R.	Reeve's Dictionary.
Rwt.	Rupee-weight.
Rd.	Mr. Alexander Read (Collector of Canara in 1813).
S. C.	South-Canara.
S. M.	Southern Mahratta.
Vlg.	Vulgar.
W.	Wilson's Glossary.
—	denotes the repetition of a preceding word.

Other abbreviations have been explained in their proper place.

Additions and Corrections.

Page 11	*line*	5	*for* makki-bâṇabeṭṭn	*read* makki-bâṇabeṭṭu
» 12	»	28	» khuski	» khushki.
» 15	»	18	» baṭṭi	» bhaṭṭi
» 16	»	23	» seedings	» seedlings
» 28	»	5	» tennon	» tenon
» „	»	10	» wier	» weir
» 47	»	14	» *delete the word*	cannot
» 48	»	24	» Bhûtâḷa Pâṇḍya	» Dêva Pâṇḍya
» 57	»	19	» Some	» An
» „	»	21	» are	» is
» 175	»	1	» waters stand	» water stands

» 176 » 29 » *the definition given of* ಅಲಬುಸಲಬು *read* Trees, brushwood, jungle, etc.; also ಆಲ ಅಲಬು (âla alabu) (S. C.).

A KISAMWÂṚ GLOSSARY

OF

KANARESE WORDS WITH EXPLANATORY MEANING.

Accounts and Book-keeping.

ಅಡಾವಾ **aḍâvâ.** A balance-sheet (N. C., S. M.).

ಅಸುವರಿ, ಅಸ್ವರಿ **asuvari, asvari.** A miscellaneous cash account in which alms to beggars and other nondescript items are entered (S. C.).

ಇಟ್ಟಣಿ **iṭṭaṇi.** A total; —ಬರೆಯು (-bareyu) to put down the total.

ಊಳ್ವರಿ **ûlvari.** A cadjan-leaf book or any other paper given by a landlord to the tenant, or by a master to his servant or workmen for the purpose of entering the payments and receipts respectively (S. C.).

ಊಳಿಗ **ûḷiga.** Items of different accounts indiscriminately put down, and not entered under their proper heads in a journal (W.); 2, a day book or journal (S. C.). ನಿಜ— (nija-) a fair diary (S. C.); ಸಪ್ಪು— (sappu-) a rough diary (S. C.); ವರ್ಗ— (varga-) items of account entered under proper heads (W.); ledger and journal (S. C.).

ಕಡ **kaḍa.** A loan; 2, "credit" as opposed to "cash"; ಕೈ— (kai-) a temporary loan; ಕೈಲಾಸ— (kailâsa-) *lit.* a loan to be repaid in Kailâsa or the heaven, hence a loan which is irrecoverable or not meant to be repaid by the borrower, a "bad debt" (S. C.).

ಕಿರ್ದಿ **kirdi.** A day-book, journal, otherwise ರೋಜ್— (rôj-) (N. C., S. M.) —ನಗದಿ (-nagadi) cash account, account of money received.

ಖರ್ಚು **kharcu.** Expenditure, disbursements; ಚಿಲ್ಲರೆ— (chillare-) petty expenses; ಬಿಡು— (biḍu-) expenditure not to be taken into account (S. C.).

ಖತಾಯಿತಿ, ಖತ್ಯಾತಿ **khatâyiti, khatâiti.** An entry (S.C.).

ಖತಾವಣಿ **khatâvaṇi.** A ledger; a merchant's ಖತಾವಣಿ being made up from his ಖರ್ಡಾ (*q.v.*).

ಖರ್ಡಾ **khardâ.** A day-book or journal; ಹಾತ್- (hât-) a rough daily account of receipts and disbursements, an off-hand account; ಕಚ್ಚಾ- (kaččâ-) a rough day-book the same as the preceding; ಪಕ್ಕಾ- (pakkâ-) cash-book in which the entries of the former are copied fair.

ಖಾತಾಬಂದಿ **khâtâbandi.** An abstract account or ledger.

ಖಾತೆ **khâte.** An account current in a person's name (S. C.); a ledger (N. C., S. M.).

ಜಮೆ **jame.** Collections, receipts; -ಹಿಡಿಯು (-hiḍiyu) to credit.

ಜುಮ್ಲಾ **jumlâ.** Total; ಏಕೂನ್- (ekûn-) grand total.

ಠವಣಿಸು **ṭhavaṇisu.** To cast figures in a column for the purpose of adding them up on a page; ಠವಣೆ (ṭhavaṇe) compound and simple addition (S. C.).

ತಬಲಕು **tabalaku.** A bundle of accounts tied together; -ಮಾಡು (-mâḍu) to sort accounts; to tie up accounts by a string or a band of paper (S. C.).

ತಾಳೆ ನೋಡು **tâḷe nôḍu.** To compare, or check accounts (S. C.); ತಾಳಾ ಬಂದ (tâḷâ-band) comparison of two different ಖಾತೆಗಳು. of transactions carried on between two firms or persons (N. C., S. M.).

ತೇರಿಜು **têriju.** An abstract account compiled from other detailed accounts; an account specifying the particulars and afterwards the amount; the same as ಠವಣೆ (S. C.).

ದಾಖ್ಲೆ **dâkhle.** Vouchers (C.).

ನಗದ್ **nagad.** In cash, "cash" (C.).

ನಿಂದಾಯ **nindâya.** What remains due.

ನಿಲವು **nilavu.** Balance; balance standing against a tenant, customer or a person (S. C.).

ನೋಂದ್ **nônd.** A daily account of dead-stock (N. C.).

ಬಾಕಿ **bâki.** Balance; ಜಾತಾ- (jâtâ-) balance due; ಪ್ರಾಕು- (prâku-) former balance; ಶಿಲಕು-, ಸಿಲ್ಕು- (silaku-, silku-) cash-in-hand.

ಬಾರು ಮಾಡು **bâru mâḍu.** To make an entry in a journal; to post figures in a ledger, etc. (C.).

ಬೇರಿಜು **bêriju.** The total sum or aggregate of an account (N. C S. M.) *Cf.* ತೇರಿಜು.

ಮುಜ್ರೆ **mujre.** A set-off; –ಮಾಡು (-mâḍu) to set-off; –ಕೊಡು (-koḍu) to allow a deduction.

ಮೇಸ್ತಕ **mêstaka.** A heading, an item or head of account.

ರೋಕ್, ರೋಕಟಿ, ರೊಖಡಾ, ರೊಖ್ಡಾ **rôk, rôkaṭi, rokhaḍâ, rokhḍâ.** In cash or ready-money (C.).

ರೋಜು **rôju.** A journal or day-book.

ಲೆಖ್ಖ **lekhkha.** Accounts; –ಆಚಾರ (-âčâra) money dealings: ಉಚ್ಚಾಪತಿ– (uččâpati-) a current account, a running account; ಗೀಟಿಕ್ಕಿದ– (giṭikkida-) an account that is crossed or marked; ಚಲ್ಲಿದ– (čallida-) a settled-up account; ಚಲ್ಲುಬಾಕಿ– (čallubâki-) a gradually decreasing account; ಟೂಕಿ– (ṭûki-) mental account (from ಟೂಕಿ a guess); ಟೋಕ–, ಠೋಕ–) ṭôk-, ṭhôk-) an aggregate account; –ನೋಡು (-nôḍu) to refer to account, to calculate; ಸುಳ್ಳು– (suḷḷu-) a "cooked" up account.

ವರ್ಗ **varga.** A ledger; ವರ್ಗಿಸು (vargisu) to 'post' accounts (S. C.).

ವಜಾವಟ್ಟ **vajâvaṭṭa.** A balance sheet (S. C.).

ಹಸ್ತಾಂತರ **hastântara.** The total amount of money in hand at the close of a day, cash balance.

ಹಾತ್‌ಕಡಿ **hâtkaḍi.** Ready-money, money in hand.

ಹಾತ್‌ಖರ್ಡೆ **hâtkharḍe.** A rough daily account of receipts and disbursements, an off-hand account.

Affinity and Relationship.

ಅಕ್ಕ **akka.** An elder sister; -ತಂಗಿಯರು (-taṅgiyaru) elder and younger sisters, sisters; —ಚ್ಚಿ (-čči) a term of affectionately addressing a small sister, "sissy"; ಅವಳು ನನಗೆ ಅಕ್ಕ (avaḷu nanage akka) she is my sister; ಅವಳು ನನಗೆ ಅಕ್ಕನಾಗ ಬೇಕು (avaḷu nanage akkanâga bêku) she is *related* to me as sister, she is my "cousin-sister" (S. C.). Similarly with regard to other words as ಅಣ್ಣ etc.

ಅಜ್ಜ **ajja.** A grand-father; ಮುತ್ತ– (mutta-) a great grand-father.

ಅಜ್ಜಿ **ajji.** A grand-mother; ಮುತ್ತ– (mutta-) a great grand-mother.

ಅಣ್ಣ **aṇṇa.** An elder brother; –ತಮ್ಮಂದಿರು (tammandiru) brothers,

ಅತ್ತಿಗಿ, ಅತ್ತಿಗೆ **attigi, attige.** Sister-in-law, being elder brother's wife or husband's elder sister; wife's elder sister; female cousin by father's sister or mother's brother.

ಅತ್ತೆ **atte.** A mother-in-law, being wife's or husband's mother; 2, a maternal, or 3, a paternal aunt.

ಅನಾಥ **anâtha.** An orphan; friendless and destitute (S. C.).

ಅಪ್ಪ **appa.** A father; ಚಿಕ್ಕ– (čikka-) a paternal uncle, being father's younger brother; ದೊಡ್ಡ– (doḍḍa-) a paternal uncle, being father's elder brother.

ಅವ್ವ **avva.** A mother; ಚಿಕ್ಕ–, ದೊಡ್ಡ– (čikka- doḍḍa-) being maternal aunts younger or older than the mother respectively.

ಅಳಿಯ **aḷiya.** A son-in-law; 2, nephew, generaly termed ಸೋದರಳಿಯ.

ಇಲ್ಲಟ **illaṭa.** A son-in-law adopted by an issueless father-in-law.

ಕಕ್ಕ **kakka.** A paternal uncle, a father's younger brother.

ಕಕ್ಕಚ್ಚಿ **kakkačči.** An aunt being a father's younger brother's wife, also ಕಚ್ಚಿ.

ಕುಂಪಾದ್ರಿ **kumpâdri.** *lit.* Co-fathers; the term is used by the Roman Catholics of South Canara to denote the supposed affinity said to exist between the father and the god-father of a child; ಕುಂಮಾದ್ರಿ (kummâdri) co-mothers (S. C.).

ಖಾಸ, ಖಾಸಾ **kâsa, khâsâ.** *lit.* Own, uterine, "full", by the same mother, as ಖಾಸಾ ತಂಗಿ.

ಗಂಡ **gaṇḍa.** A husband.

ಚಿಕ್ಕ, ದೊಡ್ಡ **čikka, doḍḍa** are used in combination with almost all the words under this heading, to denote maternal or paternal relationship.

ತಂಗಿ **taṅgi.** A younger sister; *see* ಅಕ್ಕ.

ತಂದೆ **tande.** A father.

ತಮ್ಮ **tamma.** A younger brother; *see* ಅಣ್ಣ.

ತಾಯಿ **tâyi.** A mother; ಮಲ–, ಬಲ–, ಸವತಿ (mala-, bala-, savati) a step-mother.

ತೌರ **taura.** Akin or related to a woman; –ಮನೆ (-mane) a wife's parental house; –ಅವರು (-avaru) a wife's immediate relatives; –ಊರು (-ûru) a wife's native village.

ದಂಪತಿ **dampati.** A married couple, husband and wife.

ದಾಯಾದಿ **dâyâdi.** A distant relation, a descendant from the same original male stock, a coparcener; –ತ್ವ (-tva) consanguinity, coparcenership; also rivalry (S. C.).

ನಂಟ, ನೆಂಟ **naṇṭa, neṇṭa.** A relative.

ನನಂದೆ **nanande.** A sister-in-law, being a husband's sister.

ನಾದನಿ, ನಾದಿನಿ **nâdani, nâdini.** A wife's or husband's sister; 2, a younger brother's wife.

ನೆಗೆಣ್ಣಿ, ನೆಗೆಹೆಣ್ಣು **negeṇṇi, negeheṇṇu.** Sisters-in-law, being the wives of two uterine brothers.

ಪಿಜ್ಜ **pijja.** A great grand-father; *fem.* ಪಿಜ್ಜಿ (S. C.).

ಬೀಗ **bîga.** The relationship existing between the parents of the bride and the bridegroom; *fem.* ಬೀಗತಿ.

ಭಾವ **bhâva.** A husband's elder brother; 2, a wife's brother, also –ನೆಂಟ (-neṇṭa); 3, a cousin.

ಮಗ **maga.** A son; ಮೊಂ– (mom-) a grandson; ಮರಿ– (mari-) a great grandson; ಸಾಕುವ–, ಸಾಕು– (sâkuva-, sâku-) an adopted son; ಮಲ–, ಬಲ– (mala-, bala-) a step-son; ಚೊಚ್ಚಲು– (čoččalu-) a first born son; ಮಚ್ಚಿಲು– (maččilu-) a second son; *fem.* ಮಗಳು.

ಮಾವ **mâva.** A maternal uncle; 2, a father-in-law.

ಮೈದುನ **maiduna.** A cousin; 2, a brother-in-law, being wife's brother, or sister's husband.

ಸಡ್ಡಕ **saḍḍaka.** Brothers-in-law, being the husbands of two sisters.

ಸವತಿ **savati.** The relationship existing between the two wives of a person.

ಸೊಸೆ **sose.** A maternal niece; 2, a daughter-in-law.

ಸೋದರ **sôdara.** Co-uterine, maternal. The word is seldom used alone; it always precedes other words, as: ಅತ್ತೆ, ಅಳಿಯ, ಮಾವ, ಸೊಸೆ.

ಹೆಂಡತಿ **heṇḍati.** A wife; ಕಿರಿ– (kiri-) a second wife.

ಹೆತ್ತವರು **hettavaru.** Parents.

Agricultural and Rural.

ಅಕ್ಕಿ **akki.** Paddy deprived of its husk, rice; ಅವಲಕ್ಕಿ (avalakki) paddy beaten flat, beaten rice; ಹುರಿಯಕ್ಕಿ (huriyakki) parched rice. Varieties of rice in I, Coorg are:—1, ಕರ್ತನಕ್ಕಿ red unhusked rice; 2, ಕಳಮೆ ಅಕ್ಕಿ paddy used for parched rice; 3, ಕೂಸಲಕ್ಕಿ cooked rice; 4, ಕೂಸಲ ಸಣ್ಣಕ್ಕಿ cooked rice of a superior kind; 5, ಕೆಂಬಟ್ಟೆ red unhusked rice; 6, ಕಿಸಕ್ಕಿ coarse rice; 7, ದಪ್ಪಕ್ಕಿ coarse rice; 8, ಪುಲ್ಟಕ್ಕಿ medium rice; 9, ಸಣ್ಣಕ್ಕಿ superior rice. II, North Canara: ಪಾಂಡ್ಯಾ, ಕಾಗಾ, ಮೊತಾಳಗೊ, ಬೆಳ್ಕೊ, ಅಜ್ಗ, ಸಂಣ್ಕಲ್ಗಿ, ದಬಸ್ಸಾಲಿ, ಜೀರಿಗೆಸಾಲಿ, ಕೊತ್ತುಂಬರಿಸಾಲಿ, ಸೋರ್ತಿ, ಮುಡ್ಗೊ, ಬಳಾರಿ, ಪಕ್ಸಾಲೆ, ಚಿಂತಾಮಣಿ ಸಾಲಿ, ಕರ್ಗನಕ್ಕಿ, ಕೆಂಪು ಕುಂಕುಮಕೇಸರಿ, ಜೀಡಿ ಕುಂಕುಮಕೇಸರಿ, ಸೋಮಸಾಲಿ, ಚಪ್ರಾಲಿ. III, South Canara: ಬೆಳ್ತಿಗೆ, ಕುಚ್ಚಿಗೆ, ಮಸ್ಕತಿ, ಗಂಧಸಾಲೆ, ಜೀರಿಗೆಸಾಲಿ, ಸಮುಗ, ಅಮಟಿ, ಅಪ್ಪಸಾಲೆ, ಕಳಮೆ, ಗುಡ್ಡುಬಿಳಿದು. IV, Mysore: ದೊಡ್ಡ ಭತ್ತ, ಹೊಟ್ಟೆಕೆಂಬಟ್ಟೆ, ಅರಸಿನ ಕೆಂಬಟ್ಟೆ, ಸುಕದಾಸ, ಮುರಜಿಲ, ಯಾಲಕ್ಕಿರಾಜಾ, ಕೋಣವಲಿ, ಬಿಳಿ ಸಣ್ಣಭತ್ತ, ಪಟ್ಟಭತ್ತ, ಕರಿಕಲ್ಲು, ಕುಡುಪಾಲಕ್ಕಿ (boiled rice), ಹಸಿಯಕ್ಕಿ (unboiled rice).

ಅರ್ಕಲ್ ಸಾಗ್ವಳ್ಳಿ **arkal-sâgvaḷḷi.** Cultivation carried on in kumries two years after they are cleared, or a year after the first cultivation following kumri-clearing. This mode of cultivation is restricted only to the five southern mâgaṇes of the Kasargod Taluk. The cultivation is very lightly assessed only ⅛ of the previous year's assessment being charged. The derivation of the word is very obscure. Does the word come from the Malayalam ಆಱಕಲ್ಲ್ (âṟakall) which means "a channel from the river"? (S. C.).

ಅಗೆ, ಅಗೆಅಡಿ, ಅಗೇಡಿ, ಅಗಯದಿ **age, age-aḍi, agêḍi, agayadi.** A nursery; —ಹೊಯ್ಯು (-hoyyu) to sow seeds for plants.

ಅಟ್ಟ **aṭṭa.** A rural granary (S. C.).

ಅಡಿನೀರು ಕಟ್ಟು **aḍiniru kaṭṭu.** To store up water in a field after the second and third crop until rainfall.

ಅಡ್ಡಸಾಲು **aḍḍasâlu.** A transverse furrow in ploughing.

ಅದಿರಾಸು **adirâsu.** Remains of a heap of corn, gleanings.

ಅರುಬು **arubu.** Aridity.

ಅರೆಕೋರು **arekôru.** Half the produce of a field (My.).

ಅಲುಬು **alubu.** Weeds; —ಬಿದ್ದಹೊಲ (-bidda hola) a weedy field.

ಆಗಮೆ **âgame.** Cultivation; 2, a garden containing areca nut, cocoa-nut, plantain, limes, citrons (My.); —ದಾರ (-dâra) a cultivator; ಹೊಸ— (hosa-) land newly brought under cultivation.

ಆಡುರಿ **âḍuri.** A piece of cloth tied to the udder, generally of a cow or goat, to prevent the young ones from sucking.

ಆಯಮೇರ **âyamêra.** Portions of crop assigned at harvest-time to officers and servants (My.).

ಆಯಿದೆನೆ **âyidene.** The first crop.

ಆರಂಬ **âramba.** Cultivation, farming; ಕಾಡಾ—(kâḍâ-) dry cultivation; ಖಾಸಾ—(khâsâ-) cultivation by *owners* of land through their own servants; ನೀರಾ—(nîrâ-) wet cultivation; ಪತ್ತಿಗೆ—(pattige-) a joint farming concern; —ಸಾಮಾನು (-sâmânu) implements of farming.

ಆರುಕೋರು, ಏರುಕೋರು, **ârukôru, êrukôru.** A complete ploughing kit; ಒಂದಾರಿನ ಭೂಮಿ (ondârina bhûmi) as much land as can be tilled with one plough; ಮುಂದಾರು (mundâru) the front yoke of oxen.

ಆರೆತ್ತು **ârettu.** To winnow.

ಆಳ್ಧೊಲ **âḷdhola.** A field in one's possession.

ಇಜಾರೆ **ijâre.** A farm.

ಇಮ್ಮನು **immanu.** Land yielding two crops of rice per annum (W.).

ಇರಕಾರು **irakâru.** The early and latter crop.

ಈಚುಕೈ **îcukai.** The perpendicular staff in the shaft of a plough on which the ploughman presses.

ಉಂಡಿಗೆ **uṇḍige.** Hay, a sheaf of straw (S. C.).

ಉಕ್ಕಿ **ukki.** Ploughing; ಉಕ್ಕೆ ಹೊಲ (ukke hola) a ploughed field.

ಉಡು **uḍu.** The shaft of a plough, *written also* ಊಡು.

ಉಪ್ಪಳ **uppaḷa.** A salt marsh (S. C.).

ಉಬ್ಬಲು **ubbalu.** The husk of paddy.

ಉಲಮೆ **ulame.** Land given to a sub-cultivator (My.).

ಊಸೆಯು **ûseyu.** Rice growing wild.

ಊಳು **ûḷu.** To plough; ಊಳಿಕೆ (ûḷike) ploughing.

ಎಕಲು ಗದ್ದೆ **ekalu gadde.** A nursery for paddy.

ಎಬ್ಬು **ebbu.** To drive cattle, etc. (S. C.).

ಒಂಗಲು **oṅgalu.** An offering of corn before harvest.

ಒಂಡು **oṇḍu.** Alluvial deposit.

ಒಗ್ಗಾ **oggâ.** Seed for sowing.

ಒರವಿ **oravi.** Marsh or swamp.

ಔಟು **auṭu.** To winnow.

ಕಂಕಿ **kaṅki.** An ear of corn; —ಬಡಿಯು (-baḍiyu) to thrash out corn; —ಬಾಳು (-bâḷu) a sickle; —ಯೊಟ್ಟು, ಕಂಕೊಟ್ಟು (-yoṭṭu, kaṅkoṭṭu) to stack ears of corn; —ಬಾಣೆ (-bâṇe) a flial.

ಕಟಾವು **kaṭâvu.** Reaping; ಬೆಳೆ— (beḷe-) harvesting (C.).

ಕಡಂಗು **kaḍaṅgu.** A trench or ditch in a garden (My.).

ಕಡಿ, ಕಣಿ **kaḍi, kaṇi.** Broken rice, grit (S. C.).

ಕಣ **kaṇa.** A threshing floor; —ಡೌಲು (-ḍaulu) an estimate of corn on a threshing floor.

ಕಣ್ಣಿ **kaṇṇi.** A string to tie cattle with.

ಕರಡ **karaḍa.** Thatching-grass (S. C.); 2, a crusher (N. C.).

ಕರುವಗಲ್ಲು **karuvagallu.** A rub-stone for the cattle of a village.

ಕಳ್ಳು **karlu.** Salt land.

ಕಲ್ಗಚ್ಚಿ **kalgaċċi.** The fermented washings of rice given to cattle, swill, swillings. *Cf.* ಅಕ್ಕಚ್ಚಿ (akkaċċi) S. C.

ಕಶಿ **kaši.** Grafting; —ಡೆಗೆಯು (-degeyu) to weed out.

ಕಳುಬು **kaḷubu.** Weeds and grass standing in corn.

ಕಳಮೆ, ಕಳಮಿಗೆ **kaḷame, kaḷamige.** A paddy-field; a species of rice (S.C.).

ಕಾಬೂಜಿ **kâbûji.** A scare-crow in a field.

ಕಾರು **kâru.** A ploughshare; ಕಾಡಿಕೆ—(kâḍike-) the iron share of a plough

ಕಾಲಾವಧಿ **kâlâvadhi.** Season of cultivation, a term of cultivating season (S. C.).

ಕಾವಲು **kâvalu.** A grazing ground, *also called* ಹುಲ್ಲುಗಾವಲು: —ನಡಿಸು (-naḍisu) to allow or give a grazing ground (My.).

ಕುಡಗೋಲು **kuḍagôlu.** A sickle.

ಕುಪ್ಪೆಹಾಕು **kuppe hâku.** To stack hay.

ಕುರಿಗೆ **kurige.** A sowing machine and plough combined.

ಕುಸೂಲ **kusûla.** A granary.

ಕೃತ ಮಾಡು **krita mâḍu.** To improve, to make improvements (S. C.).

ಕೃಷಿ **krishi.** Husbandry, farming.

ಕೇಸು **kêsu.** Farming, tillage.

ಕೊಟ್ಟಣ **koṭṭaṇa.** Beating the husk from rice.

ಕೊತ್ತನೆ **kottane.** Clearing roots of trees for manuring them, root manuring.

ಕೊಯಲು **koyalu.** A rope tied to the leg and neck of a cow to prevent its going astray, a clog; 2, harvesting (S. C.).

ಕೊಯಿಕಿ **koyiki.** Reaping and mowing (My.).

ಕೊರಡು **koraḍu.** A clog; 2, a pollard.

ಕೋರು **kôru.** A mode of cultivation under which the produce is equally divided between the proprietor and the cultivator (My.).

ಕೋರ್ಮಾಗಿ **kôrmâgi.** A well-tilled field, the produce of which is equally divided between the cultivator and the proprietor (My.).

ಖಾಣಿಭೂಮಿ **khâṇibhûmi.** Very inferior and worthless land (from ಕಾಣಿ).

ಖುಷಿಗಿ **khushigi.** An untilled land; –ಜಿರಾಯತಿ (-jirâyati) cultivation of an untilled land; –ಹಕ್ಲು (-haklu) a dry crop-land (My.).

ಗಂಟಿ **ganṭi** Cattle (S. C.).

ಗಣ್ಣ **gaṇṇa.** A field-plot (S. C.).

ಗಚ್ಚಿ **gacci.** Swill, swillings.

ಗದ್ದೆ **gadde.** A paddy-field, a wet-land; –ಕಟ್ಟು (-kaṭṭu) a dike; 2, a ground fit to sow paddy in; –ಕಟ್ಟಿಕೊಳ್ಳು (-kaṭṭikoḷḷu) to lease out a farm on rent; –ಬದ, –ತೆವರು, –ಕಣಿಮೆ, –ಗುಣುಬು, –ಹುಣಿ, –ಮೇರೆ (-bada, -tevaru, -kaṇime, -guṇubu, -huṇi, -mêre) the ridge of a field; –ಮೇರೆ ಕೆತ್ತು (-mêre kettu) to pare down the ridges of a field; –ನೀರು ಬಿಡು (-nîru biḍu) to irrigate a field; –ಮಡಿ (-maḍi) a paddy-field. Different varieties of ಗದ್ದೆಗಳು are: I, ಕಾರು– (kâru-) wet land cultivated in wet season; 2, low fields along the river and salt water inlets, flooded during the height of the rains so that rice is planted after the water falls (N. C.). II, ಕಂ

ಬಳ—(kambaḷa-) A field in which a buffalo-race takes place. III, ಕೋಡೆ—(kôḍe-) Fields watered for cultivation of rice in the dry season (My.). IV, ಘಜ್ನಿ—(ghazni-) rice-lands in the salt tracts along the coast and yielding but one crop (N. C.). V, ಬಾಣಬೆಟ್ಟು—, ಮಕ್ಕಿಬಾಣಬೆಟ್ಟು—(bâṇabeṭṭu-, makki-bâṇabeṭṭu-) A field situated on the highest level and depending for its cultivation entirely on rain-water; these fields yield but very little produce. VI, ತಲೆನೀರ ಬೆಟ್ಟು— (talenîra beṭṭu-) Fields much like the foregoing but having the advantage of a tank or reservoir to supplement the help of the rain-water. VII, ಬೆಟ್ಟು— (beṭṭu-) Fields lying on a higher level than the next-mentioned, imperfectly irrigated, depending for water sometimes on the rains and sometimes on a reservoir called ತಲೆನೀರು and producing but one crop; termed in Coorg ಬೋರುಬೆಟ್ಟು (bôru-beṭṭu). VIII, ಬೈಲು—(bailu-) A plain open field best suited for rice cultivation, lying low, having abundance of water and producing two or three crops of rice, or two of rice and one of grain. IX, ಮಜಲ್—(majal-) Fields higher than ಬೈಲು but lower than ಬೆಟ್ಟು, in which a single crop of rice can be raised despite the deficiency in the periodical rains; sometimes two crops are also raised. X, ಪಟ್ಲ—(paṭla-) low-lying paddy-fields liable to be submerged during the height of the monsoon and therefore cultivated later on in the season; rice-land yielding an intermediate crop between the 1st and 2nd crops, being under water during the wet season (S. C.). XI, ಮೊಗರ— (mogara-) A field yielding two crops of grain and one of rice and as good as ಬೈಲುಗದ್ದೆ from which it differs in being close to the river (S. C.). XII, ಹೈನು— (hainu-) Wet land cultivated in hot season (My.).

ಗವತ **gavata.** A small ditch round a field.

ಗಲೇವು **galêvu.** A complete ploughing kit.

ಗಾರಿಸು **gârisu.** To garble grain.

ಗೀಚುವಳಿ **gîčuvaḷi.** Farming, tillage.

ಗುಂಜಿಗೆ **gunjige.** A weeding hook.

ಗುಂಟೆ, ಗುಂಟಿಕೆ **gunṭe, gunṭike.** A harrow or weeding machine; —ಮರ (-mara) an instrument for levelling ploughed fields.

ಗುಮ್ಮುರು **gumuru.** To chew cud.

ಗೂಗರಿ **gûgari.** A perquisite of the head of a village.

ಗೂಗು **gûgu.** The spear or beard of corn; —ಕಾಲ (-kâla) harvest-time

ಗೂಳಿ **gûḷi.** A bull.

ಗೇಯು **gêyu.** To plough, to till; —ದಾರ (-dâra) a cultivator; —ದಾಟ (-dâṭa) ploughing.

ಗೊಂಚಿ **goñči.** A field occupied by different tenants; —ಗಾರ (-gâra) the proprietor of such a field (My.).

ಗೊಟ್ಟ **goṭṭa.** A bamboo funnel for physicking cattle.

ಗೊಬ್ಬರ **gobbara.** Manure; ಕರಡ— (karaḍa-) manure of litter of dry-grass collected from November to February; ದ್ರೇಗಿನ —(drêgina-) manure of dry leaves of every kind collected from March to May; ಹುಡಿ— (huḍi-) manure of fresh leaves collected from June to October; ತಿಪ್ಪೆ—(tippe-) village manure; ಸುಡುಮಣ್ಣು or ಸುಡ್ಮಣ್ಣು (suḍumaṇṇu or suḍmaṇṇu) leaf-ash or refuse-ash manure; turf and litter burnt together (S. C.).

ಚಿಗರ **čigara.** A portion of wet and dry land, requiring fifty seers of seed grain (My.).

ಚಾಗೆ **ćâge.** Drought, failure of irrigation, want of rains.

ಚೆಲಕಿಸು **čelakisu.** To shell as almonds.

ಜತ್ತಿಗೆ **jattige.** A sowing-machine.

ಜುಬ್ಬಲು **jubbalu.** Boggy-land.

ಜಿರಾಯತಿ **jirâyati.** Farming, cultivation; ತರೀ—(tari-) wet cultivation: ಖುಷ್ಕಿ—(khuski-) dry cultivation.

ಡಾಕು ಹಾಕು **ḍâku hâku.** To brand cattle.

ಡೌಲು **ḍaulu.** An estimate; ಕುಪ್ಪೆ— (kuppe-) an estimate of the produce after the harvest is reaped and heaped; ನಿಲವು— (nilavu-) an estimate of the produce before the harvest is reaped and when the crop is standing. ಕಚ್ಚಾ— (kaččâ-) a rough estimate; ಪಕ್ಕಾ— (pakkâ-) a correct estimate.

ತಟ್ಟೆಕಾಳು **taṭṭe-kâḷu.** A plate of corn given to workmen for winnowing corn.

ತಲೆನೀರು **taleniru.** A reservoir of water or a tank at the top of a hill, and used to feed a beṭṭu field (S. C.).

ತಲೆವಾನಿ **talevâni.** Interest on the loan of grain.

ತಲೆಹಿಡಿ **talehiḍi.** The handle of a plough.

ತವಟು **tavaṭu.** To shake corn for separating chaff.

ತವಡು **tavaḍu.** Bran.

ತಳೆಹಾಕು, ತಳಿಕೆಹಾಕು **taḷehâku, taḷikehâku.** To train a wild ox by yoking it with a tame one.

ತುಂಡು **tuṇḍu.** A field plot varying in area from 15 kôls to 12 cawnies (Cg.).

ತೂರು **tûru.** To winnow.

ತೆನೆ **tene.** An ear of corn; ತೆನೆಹಾಲು ತುಂಬಿತು (tenehâlu tumbitu) the ear became plump and full.

ತೊಟ್ಟಿ **toṭṭi.** A trough.

ತೊಡಗುದನ **toḍagudana.** Stray cattle.

ತೊಳ್ಸಲು **toḷsalu.** Well-pounded and clean rice (S. C.).

ತೋಟ **tôṭa.** A garden.

ದಂಡಿಕಾಲ **daṇḍikâla.** Harvest time; ದಂಡಿಬೆಳೆ (daṇḍibeḷe) a plentiful crop, "a bumper" crop.

ದಡ್ಡು **daḍḍu.** Seedless paddy; otherwise ಚಟ್ಟೆ (caṭṭe) (S. C.).

ದನಕರ **danakara.** Live-stock.

ದಾವಣಿ **dâvaṇi.** A long rope to which cattle are tied in a row.

ದಿಣ್ಣೆ **diṇṇi.** Dry land; elevated or high land.

ದುಕ್ಕಿ ಮಾಡು **dukki mâḍu.** To prepare the ground for sowing.

ದೋಟಿ **dôṭi.** A plucking hook (S. C.).

ಧಾನಮಡಿ **dhânamaḍi.** Rice land, as opposed to ಬಾಗಾಯಿತು.

ನಟ್ಟಿ, ನಾಟಿ **naṭṭi, nâṭi.** A nursery, a seed-plot.

ನಲಿ **nali.** Noxious weeds and plants in a field.

ನಳಖಂಬ **naḷakhamba.** The pole in the middle of a hay-stack.

ನಾಯರು **nâyaru.** A plough (S. C.); ನೊಗ– (noga-) a yoke and plough.

ನಿಲವು **nilavu.** Any portion of rent outstanding as arrears and to be paid at the next crop (S. C.).

ನೀರಾವರಿಭೂಮಿ **nirâvaribhûmi.** Land under wet cultivation.

ನೀರ್ಪಾಲು **nîrpâlu.** Fixed hire for watering plants.

ನೆಲ **nela.** Soil; ಅಳ್ಳ-, ಜವಲಿ-, ಬುರುದೆ- (aḷḷa-, javali-, burude-) bog; ಕರಿ-(kari-) black cotton soil; ಕೆನ್ನೆಲ (kennela) red soil; ಕಟ್ಟಾಣಿ- (kaṭṭâṇi-) good soil; ಉಸುಬು- (usubu-) sandy soil.

ನೆಲ್ಲು **nellu.** Paddy.

ನೇಜಿನಡು **nêjinaḍu.** To transplant seedlings; ನೇಜಿ (nêji) seedlings.

ನೇಗಿಲು **nêgilu.** A plough; -ಕಟ್ಟು (-keṭṭu) to make a plough; -ಗುಳ (-guḷa) a ploughshare; -ಈಚು (-îcu) a plough-shaft; -ಸಾಲು (-sâlu) a furrow.

ನೊಗ, ನುಗ **noga, nuga.** A yoke; ಕರಿ- (kari-) and ಬಟ್ಟ- (baṭṭa-) are two varieties of yokes in S. C.

ಪಡ್ಪು **paḍpu.** A waste ground; ಮುಳಿಪಡ್ಪು (muḷi-paḍpu) a waste ground growing thatching-grass (S. C.).

ಪರಂಬೋಕು, ಪರಂಬು **parambôku, parambu.** Uncultivable land.

ಪುಲನ್ **pulan.** A valuable alluvial soil generally near the sea, covered with drift land; when the sand is cleared the ground is converted into rice-land and yields excellent rice; the place is suitable for cocoa- and cashew-nut plantations too; the maximum rate of assessment of such lands is about Rs. 2 per acre (N. C.). Also ಶಿಟ್ಟ (śiṭṭa).

ಪೇರಾವ **pêrâva.** Sowing of seed (My.).

ಪೈರು **pairu.** Standing crop or corn; ಅಕ್ಕಡಿ- (akkaḍi-) sowing different kinds of pulse at the fit season (My.); ಕೀಳು- (kîḷu-) fruit etc. growing on a lower level, as opposed to ಮೇಲು-; ಬೆದ್ದಲು- (beddalu-) corn growing on dry land; ಮುಂಗಾರು- (muṅgâru-) the earlier crop; ಹಿಂಗಾರು- (hiṅgâru-) the later crop.

ಪೊಸೆಹೊಯ್ಯುವದು **posehoyyuvadu.** A ceremony among the cultivators in Mysore at the beginning of tillage, when some seed is put in a vessel filled with earth placed on a plough and allowed to germinate.

ಬಂಜರು **bañjaru.** Waste land; ಅನಾದಿ- (anâdi-) an immemorial waste; ಶಾಮಿಲಾತ್- (śâmilât-) portions of common land.

ಬಟಾಯಿ **baṭâyi.** A mode of cultivation in which the farmer gives half the produce to the landlord (My.).

ಬಟ್ಟಬೈಲು **baṭṭabailu.** An open plain land; also ಬಟಾಬೈಲು.

ಬಡ್ಡಿಗೋಲು **baḍḍigôlu.** A flial or thrashing stick.

ಬಣಬೆ **baṇabe.** A stack.

ಬರ **bara.** Scarcity.

ಬಳಸು **baḷasu.** Husbandry, cultivation.

ಬಾಗಾಯಿತು **bâgâyitu.** A garden land as opposed to ಧಾನಮತಿ.

ಬಾರಿಕೆ **bârike.** Low swampy land adjacent to or below rice fields (Cg.).

ಬಿತ್ತುವ ಬೆದೆ **bittuva bede.** Sowing season.

ಬೀಜವರಿ **bijavari.** The amount of seed required for a portion of a field; the seed area of a field (S. C.). Different varieties are: 1, ಅಜ್ಲೆ (âjle) sixty seers (S. C.); 2, ಕೊಯ್ಲು (koylu) of five seers of 80 Rwt. (S. C.); 3, ಪೊಡಿಪಾಡ್ (podipâḍ) of Nileshwar, of about a mura and wanting about an acre of land (S. C.). 4, ಭಟ್ಟಿ (bhaṭṭi) of Coorg, of eighty seers of eighty Rwt.; as a fair average hundred batties of land may be assigned as equivalent to three acres; 5, ಮುಡಿ (muḍi) a measure supposed to be equal to half a baṭṭi, unlike which this is uniform in size being 30 × 4 Lingarâj poles and thus containing 3414 sq. yds.; oṇly used in Padinalknad and the western taluks of Mercara (Cg. See also Tables of weights etc. for S. Canara); 6, ಖಂಡುಗ (khaṇḍuga) a measure requiring 64000 sq. yds. of dry or 10000 sq. yds. of wet, land (My. See also Table ofmeasures etc.).

ಬೀಳು **biḷu.** Waste, uncultivated land; –ಬಿತ್ತಿ (-bitti) the quantity of seed required to sow a given extent of land. Waste lands in Dharwar are divided into six classes, viz: ಗೌತನ್ (gautan) the village site; ತುರ್ಮಂಡಿ (turmaṇḍi) a vacant site for cattle to stand in; ಗೈರನ್ (gairan) free-grazing ground; ಹುಲ್ಲುಭಾಮು (hullubhâmu) farmed grass-land; ಕುರನ್ (kuran) grazing land: ಖರಾಬ್ (kharâb) uncultivable land.

ಬುಡವೆತ್ತು **buḍavettu.** The strongest ox fixed nearest the plough-tail.

ಬೆಳೆ, ಬೆಳಸು, ಬೆಳವಿ **beḷe, beḷasu, beḷavi.** Crop. The different crops of S. Canara are ಏಣೆಲ, ಕಾರ್ತಿ (êṇel, kârti) the first crop of the season:

2, ಕೊಳ್ಕೆ (kolke) the 3rd crop obtained from the best sort of irrigated rice-land; 3, ಸುಗ್ಗಿ (suggi) the 2nd crop. In Mysore the two crops are ಕಾರ್ತಿಕ ಫಸಲ್, ವೈಶಾಖ ಫಸಲ್ (kârtika phasal, vaiśâkha phasal) the wet and dry crops; in Ashtagram, ಕಾರು (kâru) (wet) and ಹೈನು (hainu) (dry): and in the Malnad the former goes by the name of ಕೋಡು (kôḍu). In N. Canara there are but two crops ಕಾರ್ತಿ and ಸುಗ್ಗಿ.

ಬೆಳೆಕಾಣಿಕೆ beḷekâṇike. A present of fruits nuts and vegetables made by a tenant to his landlord when the crop is ready for the sickle and he asks permission to reap it (S. C.).

ಬ್ಯಾಣ, ಬ್ಯಾರ byâṇa, byâra. A pasturage in a village belonging to the head of the village and let out by him to the villagers.

ಬೊಗಸೆ bogase. Small perquisites granted to village servants and measured by handfuls.

ಬ್ಲಹ blaha. A small portion of land differing in extent from ಚಿಗರ (*q. v.* My.).

ಭತ್ತ bhatta. Paddy or rice not deprived of husk. The different modes of growing rice from paddy are the following. In N. Canara ಕುರಿಗೆ– (kurige-) from dry seeds. The seed is grown after the field is ploughed, manured and smoothed with ಕರಡ (*q. v.*). 2, ಮೊಳೆ– (moḷe-) from sprouted seed; in this, the soil is soaked thoroughly by keeping the field flooded; 3, ನಲ– (nala-) from planted seedlings; here the seed is thickly sown in nurseries and when the rains have fully set in the seedings are transplanted. In Mysore by ಪುಣಾಜಿ (puṇâji) or ಬರಭತ್ತ (barabhatta) the dry seed system, and ನಟ್ಟಿ (naṭṭi) transplanting system. The latter is of two kinds: 1, ನೀರಾಗಿ (nîrâgi) wet plants; 2, ಬರವಾಗಿ (baravâgi) dry plants. In S. Canara ಹುಡಿನೇಜಿ (huḍinêji) corresponds to ಬರವಾಗಿ of Mysore and ನೀರ್ನೇಜಿ (nîrnêji) to ನೀರಾಗಿ.

ಮಂಚಿಕೆ mañcike. A raised seat in a field for people to sit or sleep on while watching the crop.

ಮಣ್ಣು maṇṇu. Soil. Divided as regards its *position* into 1, ಅಡಿ– (aḍi-) low soil, the best because it receives nourishment from all about it; 2, ತಲೆ– (tale-) top-soil; 3, ನಡು– (naḍu-) middle soil, and hence moderately good. Divided as regards *color, quality, etc.* into ಅರಶಿನ– (araśina-) yellow; 2. ಉಸುಬು– (usubu-) sandy; 3, ಎರೆ– (ere-) black clayey; 4, ಕರಿ– (kari-) black; 5, ಕರಿಮಸುಬು– (karimasubu-) dark loam with sand; 6, ಕಲ್ಲು– (kallu-) gravelly; 7, ಕೆಂ– (kem-) red; 8, ಗೊಣಕಲ್– (goṇakal-) gravelly; 9, ಚೌಲ– (čaula-) saline and unproductive; 10, ಜೇಡಿ– (jêḍi-) glutinous white clayey; 11, ಬಿಳಿ– (biḷi-) white clayey.

ಮಕ್ಕಿ **makki.** The worst kind of rice-land yielding one crop and not attracting tenants (S. C.). 2, culturable land covered with thick brushwood (Cg.); ಬರೆ– (bare-) rice-fields in terraces on the side of a hill or slope (Cg.).

ಮಡಿ **maḍi.** A field; 2, a patch of ground dressed for planting vegetables (S. C.). –ಕಟ್ಟು (-kaṭṭu) an old rice-land; ಗದ್ದೆಯ– (gaddeya-) the bed of a field.

ಮಡಿಕೆ **maḍike.** *See* ಆರುಗೋಲು; –ಮೇಳಿ (-mêḷi) the handle of a plough; –ಸಾಲು (-sâlu) a furrow.

ಮಡೆಭೂಮಿ **maḍebhûmi.** Land in the bed of a river or tank; ಮಡೆ ಹೊಲ (maḍehola) a rich paddy-field.

ಮರಿಕೂಳೆ **marikûḷe.** A second crop from old stocks.

ಮಹಸ್ಸೂಲು **mahassûlu.** Crop.

ಮಾಗಾಣಿ **mâgâṇi.** An artificially irrigated land.

ಮಾಗಿಭೂಮಿ **mâgibhûmi.** Ploughed land.

ಮಾಡು **mâḍu.** A place under kumri cultivation (Cg.).

ಮುಗದಾಣ **mugadâṇa.** A cord put through the nose of an ox.

ಮುಗು **mugu.** Remuneration or hire paid to the owner for the hiring out of his workmen or ಮೂಲಿ ಹೊಲೆಯ (mûli holeya) (*q. v.*). Tulu ಬಿತ್ತಣೆ (bittaṇe) (S. C.).

ಮುಚ್ಚುಲು **muččulu.** A toy winnowing fan.

ಮುಸ್ತಾಜರ **mustâjara.** A farmer, a renter.

ಮೂಗಲು **mûgalu.** Impurities adhering to grain; –ಕೇರು (-kêru) to separate the impurities.

ಮೆದೆ **mede.** A stack of corn; –ಕೋಲು (-kôlu) a stacking stick.

ಮೇಣಿ **mêṇi.** The upright piece of a plough.

ಮೊರಭತ್ತ **morabhatta.** The established fees of village servants.

ಮೋತಿಖಾನೆ **môtikhâne.** A granary.

ರಹಿತ, ರೈತ **rahita, raita.** A ryot; ರೈತಾವಿ (raitâvi) husbandry.

ರೇಗಟೆ **règaṭe.** Cotton-soil.

ವಕ್ಕಲು, ವಕ್ಲು **vakkalu, vaklu.** A tenant; —ಇಡು (-iḍu) to tenant; —ಆಗು (-âgu) to occupy; —ಅಡಿ (-aḍi) sites of tenants' houses, hence holdings (S. C.). ಒಳ— (oḷa-) a sub-tenant; ಅಡ್ಡ— (aḍḍa-) a new tenant.

ವಡಿ, ಒಡಿ **vaḍi, oḍi.** A plot of rice-land, a field-plot (S. C.).

ವೊಡೆ **voḍe.** A cylindrical earthen pot to store paddy in.

ಶಿರುಲ **širula.** A rake-like tool made of wood (N. C.).

ಶ್ರಯ **šraya.** Improvement of land by cultivation.

ಸರ್ಗಿ **sargi.** A field composed of one to eight ತುಂಡುಗಳು (*q. v.*) (Cg.).

ಸದ್ದೆ **sadde.** A sowing machine with an aperture and used by one hand.

ಸಾಗು-ಬಡಿ, -ವಳ್ಳಿ, -ಸಂತು **sâgu-baḍi, -vaḷḷi, -santu.** Farming, tillage; ಸಾಗುಬಿದ್ದ ಹೊಲ (sâgubidda hola) a fallow-field (S. C.).

ಸಾಲು ಹೊಡಿಯು **sâlu hoḍiyu.** To harrow or level furrows.

ಹಕ್ಕಲು-, ಹಕ್ಲು -ಸಾಗುವಳ್ಳಿ **hakkalu-, haklu, -sâguvaḷḷi.** Cultivation on high-land without the aid of reservoirs (S. C.).

ಹಗೇವು **hagêvu.** A pit in which grain is stored.

ಹರ್ಟೆಕುಂಟೆ **harṭekuṇṭe.** A leveller, a levelling plank.

ಹಡ್ಲು **haḍlu.** A waste rice-field, fallow-land.

ಹರಗಣೆಚಿಪ್ಪು **haragaṇi-čippu.** A weeding plough.

ಹರಗುವರು **haraguvaru.** Co-farmers.

ಹರೆಕಾಳು **harekâḷu.** Gleanings, refuse.

ಹಲಿಗೆಮರ **haligemara.** A leveller; a plank used in levelling fields after the seed is sown.

ಹಲುವೆ, ಹಲುಬೆ **haluve, halube.** A rake.

ಹಲ್ಕ **halka.** A harrow.

ಹಶಿಗೆ **hašige.** Measuring of grain for the purpose of dividing it.

ಹಸರಾಣಿ (vlg. ಹಸ್ರವಾಣಿ) **hasarâṇi.** Vegetables given by tenants or farmers to their landlords prior to reaping corn or during festivals; vegetable-loads (S. C.).

ಹಾಳಿ **hâḷi.** A plot of field, a field-plot (S. C.).

ಹಿಕ್ಕಲು **hikkalu.** An outlet for water to run from one garden to another.

ಹುಗ್ಗಿ ಭತ್ತ **huggi bhatta.** Fees in grain.

ಹುದಿಲು **hudilu.** A marshy ground.

ಹುಲುಸು **hulusu.** The proper return or quantity, as in grain sown; out-turn.

ಹುಲ್ಲುಗಾವಲು **hullugâvalu.** Pasturage, grazing-ground.

ಹೊಲ **hola.** A field; ಹಿನ್ನೆ– (hinne-) land not easily watered but depending largely on rains; ಬೀಳುಬಿದ್ದ– (bîḷubidda-) a fallow field; ಸಾಗುಬಿದ್ದ– (sâgubidda-) a fallow field (S. C.); –ಗದ್ದೆ (-gadde) land for wet and dry cultivation; ಹೊಲೆ– (hole-) dry-land unfit for cultivation of rice; ಕೈಗಂಟು– (kaigaṇṭu-) a good field of which the produce is as sure as though it were already reaped; ಕೋಳಾಡ– (kôḷâda-) a field in which new corn springs from old stocks.

ಹೊಲಿ **holi.** Interest on grain lent to a person, or on arrears of rent in corn (S. C.).

Anatomy and Physiology.

ಅಂಗುಷ್ಠ, ಉಂಗುಟ **añgushṭha, uñguṭa.** The great toe; 2, the thumb.

ಅಂಗಳ **añgaḷa.** The palate, the roof of the mouth.

ಅಂಗಿಲು **añgilu.** The uvula.

ಅಂತರ್ವೇಷ್ಟನ **antarvêshṭana.** The peritonium.

ಅಂಸಫಲಕ **aṁsaphalaka.** The shoulder-blade.

ಅನ್ನಕೋಶ **annakôśa.** The stomach; –ಬಾಯಿ (-bâyi) the pylorus.

ಅಯಾಲ್ **ayâl.** The hair on the mane of a horse.

ಅಳ್ಳೆ **aḷḷe.** The "sides", the part between the abdomen and the diaphragm.

ಆಡ್ಚೆಪ್ಪೆ **âḍceppe.** The withers of a horse.

ಇಣಿ, ಹಿಣಿಲು **iṇi, hiṇilu.** The hump of an ox.

ಇಲಿ **ili.** The liver.

ಈಸಬುಡ್ಡಿ **isabuḍḍi.** The gall-bladder; ಈಸಗಾಯಿ (îsagâyi) the sounds of a fish.

ಉಗುರು **uguru.** The nail; 2, the claws; ಕಣ್ಣು (kaṇṇu) the quick of a finger-nail.

ಉಡಿ **uḍi.** The hip, waist or the haunch.

ಎದೆ **ede.** The thorax: –ಗುಂಡಿ, –ಹುರಿ (-guṇḍi, -huri) the sternum; –ಮುಗುಳು (-muguḷu) the pit of the stomach.

ಎಲುವು, ಎಲುಬು **eluvu, elubu.** A bone; ಕಾಲ್– (kâl-) the shin-bone; ಡುಬ್ಬ–, ಹೆಗಲು– (ḍubba-, hegalu-) the shoulder-blade; ಪಕ್ಕ– (pakk-) the ribs; ಛಪ್ಪ– (čhapp-) the hip-bone; ತಟ್ಟ– (taṭṭa-) the pelvis; ಬೆನ್ನ– (benn-) the spine; ಮಟ್ಟ– (maṭṭ-) the back-bone; ಮೆಟ್ರ– (meṭra-) the clavicle.

ಕಂಕಾಳ **kaṅkâḷa.** The skeleton.

ಕಂಕುಣಿ, ಕಂಕುಳಿ **kaṅkuṇi, kaṅkuḷi.** The socket of the eye.

ಕಂಕುಳ **kaṅkuḷa.** The axilla, armpit.

ಕಂಕೋಶ **kaṅkôśa.** The bladder.

ಕಂಠ, ಕತ್ತು, ಕುತ್ತಿಗೆ **kaṇṭha, kattu, kuttige.** The neck.

ಕಣ್ಣತಲೆ kaṇṇatale. The temples, also ಕಣ್ತಲೆ.

ಕಣ್ಣು kaṇṇu. The eye; ಎವೆ (eve) an eyelid; —ಗುಡ್ಡು (-guḍḍu) the eye-ball; ಗೀಚು (gîču) the eye-gum; —ಗನ್ನಡಿ (-gannaḍi) the retina; —ಗೊಂಬೆ, —ಕನೀನಕೆ, —ಪಾಪ (-gombe, -kanînake, -pâpa) the pupil; —ರೆಪ್ಪೆ (reppe) the eye-lash or the eye-lid; ಹುಬ್ಬು (hubbu) the eye-brow; ಬಿಳಿಗುಡ್ಡಿ (bile-guḍḍi) the white of the eye; —ಡೊಗರು (-dogaru) the hollow of the eye.

ಕಣ್ಣಿಮೆ kaṇṇime. The eyelid.

ಕಫಕೋಶ, ಶ್ವಾಸಕೋಶ kaphakôša, švâsakôša. The lungs.

ಕರಳು karaḷu. Intestines; ಕಿರಿ— (kiri-) smaller intestines.

ಕರಿಗುಡ್ಡು kariguḍḍu. The pupil of the eye.

ಕಳಿಜ kalija. The liver.

ಕಶೇರುಕ kašêruka. The spine; —ರಜ್ಜು (-rajju) the spinal cord.

ಕಾಲು kâlu. The leg; ಅಂ— (aṅ-) the sole of the foot; ಕಣ— (kaṇa-) "shank or cannon"; ಮುಂ— (muṅ-) the tarsus, foreleg; ಚುಂಚ— (čuṅča-) the pastern-joint; ಮೊಣ— (moṇa-) the knee; ಮೊಣಕಾಲಿನ ಸಂದು (moṇakâlina sandu) the hock of a horse; ಮೊಣಕಾಲಿನ ಚಿಪ್ಪು (moṇakâlina čippu) the patella or knee-pan; ಹಿಂ— (hiṅ-) the hind-leg.

ಕಾಳಿಜ kâḷija. *See* ಕಳಿಜ.

ಕಿವಿ kivi. The ear; —ಆನಕ or ಗರ್ಭಶ್ರವಣ (-ânaka or garbhašravaṇa) the tympanum or drum of the ear; —ಆಲೆ, —ಸೋನೆ, —ತಮ್ಮೆ (-âle, -sône, -tamme) lobe of the ear; —ಅರಗು (-aragu) rim of the ear; ಮೇಲ್— (mêl-) tip of the ear.

ಕೀಲು kîlu. A joint.

ಕುಂಕೆ kuṅke. The nape of the neck.

ಕುಂಡೆ kuṇḍe. The posteriors, also ಪಿರ್ರೆ (pirre); ಹೊರ— (hora-) the anus; ಒಳ— (voḷa-) the rectum.

ಕೆಚ್ಚಲು keččalu. An udder.

ಕೆನ್ನೆ kenne. The temples.

ಕೈ kai. The arm; —ಹರಡು (-haraḍu) the wrist; ಮೊಣ— (moṇa) the elbow; ಅಂಗೈ (aṅgai) the palm of the hand; —ರಟ್ಟೆ (-raṭṭe) the upper part of the arm, the shoulder; ಮುಂಗೈ (muṅgai) the fore-arm.

ಗಂಗೆತೊಗಲು **gange-togalu.** The dewlap of a cow or bull.

ಗಂಟ್ಲು **gaṇṭlu.** The throat; –ಮಣಿ (-maṇi) "Adam's apple"; –ನಾಳ (-nâḷa) the wind-pipe; –ಕೊಳವಿ (-koḷavi) the gullet.

ಗಜ್ಜಲು **gajjalu.** The groin; 2, the udder of a cow; –ಮುಲುಕು (-muluku) the cavity of the groin.

ಗಟ್ರು **gaṭru.** The hump of an ox.

ಗರ್ಭಕೋಶ **garbhakôśa.** The uterus; ಗರ್ಭಚೋಲ (garbha-ôla) the secundines.

ಗಲ್ಲ **galla.** The cheeks.

ಗಿರಿಗೆ **girige.** The ankle.

ಗುಲ್ಮ **gulma.** The spleen.

ಗೆಂಡೆ **geṇḍe.** The sphincter muscle of the anus, the rectum (S. C.).

ಗೆಜ್ಜೆ **gejje.** The groin.

ಗೆಣಿಕೆ **geṇike.** A knuckle.

ಗೊರಸೆ **gorase.** The hoof.

ಗೋಮಾಳೆ **gômâḷe.** The Adam's apple.

ಚಪ್ಪಿ **čappi.** The shoulder-blade.

ಚರಬಿ **čarabi.** Fat (S. C.).

ಚಿನ್ನಿ **činni.** The rump of an ox.

ಜತ್ರು **jatru.** The clavicle, collar-bone.

ಜಬ್ಬೆ **jabbe.** The outer side of the thigh; 2, the arm; 3, the liver.

ಜೂಗು **jûgu.** The mane of a horse.

ಟೊಂಕ, ನಡು, ಸೊಂಟ **ṭoṅka, naḍu, soṇṭa.** The loins; 2, the waist (S. C.).

ಡುಬ್ಬ, ಡುಬರಿ **ḍubba, ḍubari.** The hump of a camel.

ಡುಮಚಿ, ಪೃಷ್ಠ **ḍumači, prishṭha.** The haunch.

ತಲೆ **tale.** The head; ಕಣ್– (kaṇ-) the temporal bone, the temples; ಮುಂ– (mun-) the sinciput; ಹೆಡ– (heḍa-) the occiput; –ನೆತ್ತಿ (-netti) the crown of the head; –ಬುರುಡೆ (-buruḍe) the cranium; ಮೆದುಳು (meduḷu) the brain; –ಗಡ್ಡೆ (-gaḍḍe) the noddle.

ತೊಗಲು **togalu.** The skin, otherwise called ಪಿಸ್ಸಿ– (pissi-).

ತೊಡೆ **toḍe.** The thigh; –ಸಂದು (-sandu) the groin.

ತೊಳ್ಳೆ **toḷḷe.** Lungs, "lights".

ತೋಳು **tôḷu.** The arm; ಮೇಲ್— (mêl-) the forearm.

ತ್ವಚೆ **tvače.** A membrane.

ದವಡೆ **davaḍe.** The chin, the jaw.

ದುಗ್ಧವಾಹಿನಿ **dugdhavâhini.** The lactiferous glands.

ನಂಗಿಲು **naṅgilu.** The uvula.

ನಡ್ಡಿ **naḍḍi.** The spleen; 2, the milt of fish.

ನರ **nara.** A tendon; ಹೆರಕಲ— (herakala-) the tendon of the trapezi muscle forming the nape of the neck.

ನಳಿಗೆ **naḷige.** A duct.

ನಾಡಿ **nâḍi.** An artery; ಆದಿ— (âdi-) the aorta.

ನಾಲಿಗೆ **nâlige.** The tongue; ಕಿರಿ— (kiri-) the uvula.

ನಾಳ **nâḷa.** The wind-pipe.

ನಿರ್ಗಂಟು **nirganṭu.** The spleen.

ನೆಣ **neṇa.** The serum of the flesh; 2, the marrow of the bones.

ನೇತ್ರಜಾಲ **nêtrajâla.** The retina.

ಪಟ್ಟಡೆ **paṭṭaḍe.** The "girth" of an ox, also ಪಟ್ಟುಡಿ.

ಪರೆ, ಪೊರೆ **pare, pore.** A membrane.

ಪಿಂಡ **pinḍa.** The foetus; —ಪರೆ (-pare) the membrane enclosing the foetus.

ಪೃಷ್ಠವಂಶ **prishṭavamśa.** The spinal column.

ಫುಪ್ಪುಸ **phuppusa.** The lungs.

ಬಗಲು **bagalu.** The side from the arm-pit to the hip.

ಬಿಕ್ಕು **bikku.** The kidney.

ಬೀವು **bivu.** Catgut.

ಬೆನ್ನು **bennu.** The back; —ಹುರಿ (-huri) the chine.

ಬೆರಳು **beraḷu.** A finger; ಹೆಬ್ಬೆಟ್ಟು (hebbeṭṭu) the thumb; ತೋರ್—, ಮುಂ— (tôr-, mum-) the forefinger; ಪವಿತ್ರದ— (pavitrada-) the ring or annular finger; ಕಾಲ್— (kâl-) the toe.

ಮಂಡಿ **manḍi.** The knees.

ಮಗ್ಗಲು **maggalu.** A flank or side.

ಮಜ್ಜೆ **majje.** Marrow.

ಮಣಿಕಟ್ಟು **maṇikaṭṭu.** The wrist.

ಮಸ್ತಿಷ್ಕ **mastishka.** The brain.

ಮುಂಜುಟ್ಟು **muñjuṭṭu.** The forelocks.

ಮೂಗು **mûgu.** The nose; —ಸೊಳ್ಳೆ, —ಹೊಳ್ಳೆ (-soḷḷe, -hoḷḷe) a nostril; —ಕಂಭ, —ತೊಲೆ (-kambha, -tole) the ridge of the nose; ಮೂಗಿನ ಶಿಲೆ (mûgina śile) sides of the nose.

ಮೂತ್ರಕೋಶ **mûtrakôśa.** The kidney; —ದ್ವಾರ (-dvâra) the urethra.

ಮೀನಖಂಡ **mînakhaṇḍa.** The calf of the foot.

ಮೋದು **môdu.** Coagulation of blood.

ರಕ್ತ **rakta.** The blood.

ರಸ **rasa.** *Lit.* juice; a secretion or humour; ಅನ್ನ— (anna-) the chyle; ದುಗ್ಧ— (dugdha-) the lymph; ಪಾಚಕ— (pâčaka-) the gastric juice; ಶ್ವೇತ— (svêta-) the pancreatic juice.

ರೊಂಡಿ **roṇḍi.** The hip.

ಲಾಲಾಕೋಶ **lâlâkôśa.** The salivary glands.

ವಂಶಗ್ರಂಥಿ **vaṁśagranthi.** The vertibræ; ವಂಶರಜ್ಜು (vaṁśarajju) the spinal cord.

ವಸೆ **vase.** Serum, fat.

ವಕ್ಷ **vaksha.** The chest or thorax.

ಶಿರೆ **śire.** A vein.

ಶ್ವೇತರಸಾಶಯ **svêtarasâśaya.** The pancreas.

ಹಡ್ಡ, ಹರಡು **haḍḍa, haraḍu.** The ankle.

ಹಣೆ **haṇe.** The forehead.

ಹಲ್ಲು **hallu.** A tooth; ಛೇದಕ—, ಎದುರಿನ—, ಮುಂಬಲ್ಲು (čhêdaka-, edurina-, mumballu) the incisors; ದವಡೆ— (davaḍe-) the molars; ಸೂಲದ— (sûlada-) the eye-tooth; ಶೂಲದ— (śûlada-) the canine tooth or the cuspid; ದಂತ್ಯ (dantya) dentine; ವಜ್ರಗಾರೆ (vajragâre) the enamel of the teeth; ಕೋರೆ (kôre) a fang; ವಸಡು (vasaḍu) the gums; ಹಳಸೆ, ಹಲ್ಲುಗಾರೆ, ಪಾಚು (haḷase, hallugâre, pâču) tartar of the teeth.

ಹಿಂಗುದಿ **hiṅgudi.** The heel of the foot, also called ಹಿಮ್ಮಡಿ (himmaḍi).

ಹಿಂತೊಡೆ **hintoḍe.** The hamstring of a horse.

ಹಿಡಿಕಿ hiḍiki. The pasterns of a horse.

ಹಿರಳು hiraḷu. The hump of an ox.

ಹಿರಿ hiri. The liver.

ಹುಣಿಕೆಜವೆ huṇikejave. Piamater (R.).

ಹೃತ್ಕೋಶ hṛitkōśa. The pericardium.

ಹೃತ್ಪಟಲ hṛitpaṭala. The diaphragm.

ಹೆಗಲು hegalu. The shoulders.

ಹೆಗ್ಗತ್ತು heggattu. The nape of the neck.

ಹೆಡಕು heḍaku. The clavicle.

ಹೊಕ್ಕಳು hokkaḷu. The navel; –ಹುರಿ (-huri) the navel cord, the umbilical cord.

ಹೊಟ್ಟೆ hoṭṭe. The belly; ಕಿಬ್ಬೊಟ್ಟೆ (kibboṭṭe) the abdomen.

Architecture, Carpentry, Engineering, Joinery, etc.

ಅಂಕಣ **aṅkaṇa.** The space between two cross-beams; square partitions in the ceiling of a room or veranda of a native house (S. C.); ಪಾತಾಳ– (pâtâḷa-) the lower veranda of a temple.

ಅಂತಸುರ್ಣ್ಣ **antarsuṇṇa.** A purlin (S. C.).

ಅಟ್ಟೊಳಿಗೆ **aṭṭoḷige.** A temporary gallery, a scaffolding (S. C.).

ಅಡ್ಡಕತ್ತರಿ, ಕತ್ತರಿ **aḍḍakattari, kattari.** A collar-beam (S. C.).

ಅಡ್ಡಣಿಗೆ **aḍḍaṇige.** A tripod, trevet.

ಅಡ್ಡತೋಳು, ಅಡ್ಡದೋಲು **aḍḍatôḷu, aḍḍadôlu.** A cross-beam, transverse beam; 2, a tie-beam (S. C.).

ಅಡ್ಡನಾಲಿಗೆ **aḍḍanâlige.** A stone across a well.

ಅಡ್ಡಪಟ್ಟಿಗೆ **aḍḍapaṭṭige.** The upper and lower parts of a door-frame.

ಅಣೆಕಟ್ಟು **aṇekaṭṭu.** A dam, an anicut.

ಅಪ್ಸೇಟು **apsêṭu.** *Anglice:* Off-set, set-off (S. C.).

ಅರಚಟ್ಟೆ **aracaṭṭe.** A channel for irrigation.

ಆಣೆಕಲ್ಲು **âṇekallu.** The key-stone of an arch.

ಆಯ **âya.** The form of the basement of a building, also "the style" of a building; there are said to be ten styles of ಆಯ (S. C.).

ಇಮಾರತು **imâratu.** A building (N. C.).

ಐಮೂಲೆ **aimûle.** The obliquity in the rectangle of a building (S. C.).

ಒಪ್ಪಾರು **oppâru.** A pent-roof.

ಕಂಕಣ **kaṅkaṇa.** A cornice work; –ಬೋದಿಗೆ (-bôdige) the architrave; –ಕಟ್ಟಿಗೆ (-kaṭṭige) the "brace" of a building.

ಕಂಭ **kambha.** A post, a pillar; ಕಾಲು– (kâlu-) the pillars at each end of a beam; –ಗದ್ದಿಗೆ (-gaddige) the base of a pillar; –ಬೋದಿಗೆ (-bôdige) the chapiter; ಗುಂಡು– (guṇḍu-) a round pillar; ಚದರ್– (cadar-) a square pillar; –ಕಂಕಣ (-kaṅkaṇa) the cornice of a pillar, the uppermost entablature of a column; ಸಾಲು– (sâlu-) a colonnade, an arcade.

ಕಚ್ಚರಿ **kaččari.** The fluting of a column.

ಕಚ್ಚು **kaččn.** A notch.

ಕಟ್ಟಕಾಲಿವೆ **kaṭṭakâlive.** A feeding channel of a tank.

ಕಟ್ಟಪುಣಿ, ಕಟ್ಪುಣಿ **kaṭṭapuṇi, kaṭpuṇi.** An embankment; a revetment (S.C.).

ಕಟ್ಟು **kaṭṭu.** To build; ಕಟ್ಟಡ, ಕಟ್ಟೋಣ (kaṭṭaḍa, kaṭṭôṇa) a building (S.C.); ಮುಂಗಟ್ಟು (muṅgaṭṭu) interior work (My.); ಸರ– (sara-) centring, centering (My.); ಹೆಪ್ಪು– (heppu-) turfing; ಹೊರಳೆ– (horaḷe-) stone-work of class stream (My.); ಸೂಜಿ– (sûji-) needle-stone revetment (My.); ಏರಿ– (êri-) stone-work in a tank (My.).

ಕಟ್ಟೆ **kaṭṭe.** A mound round a tree (S.C.); a veranda (S.M.).

ಕಡಗು **kaḍagu.** A mound round a tree; a drain or gutter (My.).

ಕಡೆಕಟ್ಟು **kaḍekaṭṭu.** A double cross-beam.

ಕಪೋತ **kapôta.** A cornice (My.).

ಕಬೆಕೋಲು **kabekôlu.** A post forked at the top and used to rest a rafter on (S.C.).

ಕಮಾನು **kamânu.** An arch; ಅಂತರ್– (antar-) the span of an arch; –ಒಲವು (-oḷavu) the inclination of an arch (S.C.).

ಕಲ್ಗಟ್ಟಣೆ **kalgaṭṭaṇe.** A stone embankment to prevent the washing away of the ground near a river (S.C.).

ಕಲ್ಪಡುವು **kalpaḍuvu.** A stone buttress.

ಕಲ್ಹಾಸಿಗೆ **kalhâsige.** Pavement (My.).

ಕಳ್ಳಿವಾಸ **kaḷḷivâsa.** A canopy, an awning; otherwise ಮೇಲ್ಗಟ್ಟು (mêlgaṭṭu) (S.C.).

ಕಾಮಗಾರಿ **kâmagâri.** Public works, repairs.

ಕಾಲಟ್ಟ **kâlaṭṭa.** A trestle.

ಕಾಲುಗುಂಜೆ **kâlugunje.** A pole with a forked top to receive a rafter; *cf.* ಕಬೆಕೋಲು.

ಕಾಲಿವೆ **kâlive.** An aqueduct, a channel.

ಕಿಟಿಕಿಗೂಡು **kiṭikigûḍu.** A window-frame.

ಕುಂದ **kunda.** A stone pillar (S.C.).

ಕುಂಬೆ **kumbe.** The ridge of a roof (S.C.).

ಕುತ್ತಿಕೋಲು **kuttikôlu.** A king-post (S.C.).

ಕುದುಮೆ **kudume.** The side-roof of a house (S. C.).

ಕುಬಾಳು, ಕುಬಲ **kubâḷu, kubala.** The ridge of a roof (Tuḷu) (S. C.).

ಕೂಟ **kûṭa.** A roof-frame, the structure formed of wall-plates, beams, and joists over which the roof or the second floor is fixed (S. C.).

ಕೂರು, ಕೂಲು **kûru, kûlu.** "Dovetail, tennon"

ಕೆಸರ್ಪಟ್ಟಿ **kesarpaṭṭi.** A lintel.

ಕೈಚಿ **kaiči.** A truss.

ಕೊಗಳ **kogaḷa.** A roof-top; a house-top; the ridge of a roof (S. C.); also ಕೊಬಲ.

ಕೋಡಿ **kôḍi.** The wier of a tank; an outlet for the surplus water of a tank (My.).

ಕೋಣಕಲ್ಲು **kôṇakallu.** The wier of a tank.

ಕೋಲ್ಬಂದಿ **kôlbandi.** Renewing a building (S.C.); old stone revetment (My.); also ಬೋಲ್ಬಂದಿ.

ಗಂಡವಟ್ಟಿಗೆ **gandavaṭṭige.** A piece of wood nailed across a door to strengthen the planks of it.

ಗಡಂಚೆ **gaḍañče.** A trestle.

ಗದ್ದಿಗೆಕಲ್ಲು **gaddigekallu.** A pedestal, a plinth.

ಗಾಬಡಿ **gâbaḍi.** Patches; —ಹಾಕು (-hâku) to tongue (S. C.).

ಗಾರೆ **gâre.** Lime plaster, mortar; ಮಡ್ಡಿ—, ಒರಟು—, ಬೋಳ—, ಚಕ್ಕಸುಣ್ಣ (maḍḍi-, oraṭu-, bôḷa-, čakkasuṇṇa) coarse plaster; ವಜ್ರ— (vajra-) hard plaster, 'concrete and brickbat'; ನಯ— (naya-) fine plaster; ರಸವರ್ಗ (rasavarga) cementing water (My.).

ಗುಜ್ಜು **gujju.** A queen-post, a strut (My.).

ಗುಶಿ, -ಗೂಟ **guši, -gûṭa.** A pin connecting the horizontal and perpendicular beams together.

ಗೋಲು **gôlu.** A moulding.

ಘೂಡು **ghûḍu.** A circular frame of wood constructed in a river to divert the current of water washing away land; a revetment (N. C.).

ಚಂದಾಯ **čandâya.** A gable-roof.

ಚಡಿ **čaḍi.** A groove (S. C.).

ಚಪರಾಸ ಹಾಕು **caparâsa hâku.** To set a saw.

ಚಾವಣಿ **câvaṇi.** A lintel.

ಚೌಕಟ್ಟು **čaukaṭṭu.** A door-frame.

ಜಂತಿ, ಜಂತೆ **janti, jânte.** A joist, generally of cocoanut or palmyra tree (S. C.); a rafter crossing another.

ಜಡಮೊಳೆ **jaḍamoḷe.** A rivet.

ಜಾಲಾಂದ್ರ **jâlândra.** Lattice-work.

ಜೀರ್ಣವಾಗಿದೆ **jirṇavâgide.** Is out of repairs, or has gone into decay or disrepair (S. C.); ಜೀರ್ಣೋದ್ಧಾರ ಮಾಡು (jirṇôddhâra mâḍu) to reconstruct a building out of repairs, to renew a building (S. C.).

ಜೋಡಿಗೆ **jôḍige.** A carpenter's joint, a rabbet.

ತಖ್ತಬಂದಿ **takhtabandi.** Wainscotting; ceiling, planking; also ತಖ್ತಪೋಷ್.

ತರಣಿ **taraṇi.** The cornice of a wall below the upper moulding.

ತರಾಯಿ **tarâyi.** A joist (My.).

ತಲಪಿರಿಗೆ **talapirige.** Channel conducted from springs (My.).

ತಲೆಕಟ್ಟು **talekaṭṭu.** An anicut.

ತಾಳವಾರ **tâḷavâra.** A shelving roof supported by pillars.

ತಿರ್ಕಾಸು **tirkâsu.** Oblique, slanting (S. C.).

ತ್ರಾಸು **trâsu.** *Anglice* "Truss".

ತೂಬು, ತೂಂಬು **tûbu, tûmbu.** A flood-gate, a drain, a gutter, a sluice.

ತೊಲೆ, ತೋಳು **tole, tôḷu.** A beam (S. C.); ದೊಡ್ಡ– (doḍḍa-) a main beam; ಗೋಡೆ– (gôḍe-) a wall-plate; ಕಂಭ– (kambha-) a pillar plate.

ತೋಳು **tôḷu.** A door-post, a jamb.

ದಾಶೆ, ದಾಸಿ **dâše, dâsi.** A wall-plate.

ದಾರವಂದ **dâravanda.** A door-frame; –ಪಟ್ಟೆ (-paṭṭe) the lintel of a door-frame (S. C.).

ದಾಲುಚಕ್ಕೆ **dâlučakke.** Ornamental work on a door-frame.

ದಿಮ್ಮಿ, ದಿಮ್ಮೆ **dimmi, dimme.** A wedge; ಪಕ್ಕಾ– (pakkâ-) abutment (My.); ಮಧ್ಯ– (madhya-) a pier (My.); ಮೂಲ– (mûla-) the point of a pier (My.).

ದುರಾಕಿ, -ಮೊಳೆ **durâki, -moḷe.** A dowel-pin, a dowel.

ದೂಲ **dûla.** A beam (My.).

ನ್ಯಂಬು **nyambu.** A "tenon"; –ಕಳಚು (-kaḷaču) to take out a tenon; –ಬಿಗಿಯು (-bigiyu) to put in or fasten a tenon.

ಪಕಾಶೆ **pakâše.** Rafters (S. C.); ಮೂಲೆ– (mûle-) hip-rafters (S. C.).

ಪಟಿ, ಪಟ್ಟಿ **paṭi, paṭṭi.** Rafters of cocoa or palmyra palm (S. C.).

ಪಡೆ **paḍe.** A mortise; –ಕೂಡಿಸು (-kûḍisu) to dovetail, to join a mortise and tenon; –ತೋಡು (-tôḍu) to make a mortise.

ಪಣಬು **paṇabu.** A platform bridge (My.).

ಪರಸ್ಬಂದ **parasbanda.** Pavement.

ಪಾಟಿಕೆಲಸ **pâṭikelasa.** Work done by the P. W. D. in which a party of coolies is engaged, party-work (S. C.).

ಪಾದಟ್ಟಿಗೆ **pâdaṭṭige.** The pedestal of a column (S. C.).

ಪಾವಟಿ **pâvaṭi.** The steps of a tank.

ಪಿಂಜಿ **piñji.** The outer part of a window or door-wall.

ಪಿದರ **pidara.** The tie-beam in a roof (S. C.).

ಪಿಳ್ಳೆಕಾಯಿ **piḷḷekâyi.** A pent roof joined at equilateral triangles.

ಪುಸ್ತಬಂದಿ **pustabandi.** A buttress (My.).

ಪೆರಮಾಳುಚೆಟ್ಟಾ **peramâḷučeṭṭâ.** The inner cornice of a door or window.

ಪೆರಿಕಿ **periki.** A paling-board.

ಪೋರೊಟು **pôroṭu.** Side-planks, planks sawn off from a log of wood to give it a rectangular appearance (S. C.); side-slips of timber (S. C.).

ಫರಸ್ತಬಂದಿ **pharastabandi.** A stone apron (My.); *cf.* ಪರಸ್ಬಂದ.

ಬಣ್ಣಟ್ಟಿಗೆ **baṇṇaṭṭige.** A piece of wood driven through the rafters to keep them fast (S. C.).

ಬಳೆ **baḷe.** The rapiers of bamboos fastened crosswise to the rafter of a roof (S. C.).

ಬಲಗು **balagu.** The ridge pole.

ಬಲಿಪು **balipu.** (Tulu). A rope fastened over a thatched roof to keep thatching compact (S. C.).

ಬಾಂದು **bându.** An embankment (N. C.).

ಬಾಗುಮಾಳಿಗೆ **bâgumâḷige.** A gable roof.

ಬಾಗಲು **bâgalu.** A door; —ದಾರಬಂಧ (-dârabandha) the lintel; —ನಿಲವು (-nilavu) door-posts, jambs; ನೆಲ— (nela-) a trap-door (S. C.); —ಪಡಿ (-paḍi) a sill; ಹೊಸ್ತಲು (hostalu) threshold, a sill; —ಗಡಿ (-gaḍi) a fastening to a native door; ಗುಬ್ಬುಗೂಡು (gubbugûḍu) a pivot hole on which a door turns.

ಬಾವಡಿಪಟ್ಟಿ **bâvaḍipaṭṭi.** A pole-plate (S. C.)

ಬುರುಜು **buruju.** A revetment (S. C.).

ಬಿಗಿಕಲ್ಲು **bigikallu.** The keystone of an arch.

ಬೆಂಗಟೆ **beṅgaṭe.** A ceiling; —ಹೆಡೆ (-heḍe) a ridge-pole.

ಬೆಣೆ **beṇe.** A wedge (S. C.).

ಬೆರಸೋಳು **berasôḷu.** A ridge-piece, a ridge-pole (S. C.).

ಬೋದಿಗೆ **bôdige.** An architrave, head-piece couple (My.); ಗಡಿಗೆ— (gaḍige-) the imposts or capitals of a pillar; ದೊಂತೆ— (donte-) a double architrave.

ಭೇರಿ **bhêri.** A tunnel (My.).

ಮಟ್ಟು **maṭṭu.** The measurement of a given area, 2, level; ಒಳ— (oḷa-) the internal measurement of a given area (S. C.); ಹೊರ— (hora-) the external measurement (S. C.); ನೀರಿನ— (nîrina-) the water-level or perfectly level; ರಾಶಿ— (râśi-) an inclined plane; ಕಡ್ಡಿ— (kaḍḍi-) perpendicularity; —ಹಲಿಗೆ (-halige) a level.

ಮರಕಟ್ಟು **marakaṭṭu.** A wooden wall of a tank constructed when the earth is not firm.

ಮರಸುತ್ತು **marasuttu.** A screw; —ತೆಗಿ (-tegi) to unscrew.

ಮರಹಮ್ಮತ್ **marahammat.** Repairing; —ಇಲಾಖೆ (-ilâkhe) D. P. W.

ಮಾಡ್, ಮಾಡು **mâḍ, mâḍu.** A roof; ಅಂತರ್— (antar-) an under-roof, a side-roof (S. C.); ಕಳ್ಳ— (kaḷḷa-) an under-roof; ಪೆನೆ— (pene-) a pent roof (S. C.); ಚೌಮೂಲೆ— (čaumûle-) a hip-roof; ಚಟ್ಟೆ— (čaṭṭe-) a flat roof; ಕತ್ತರಿ— (kattari-) a roof having collar-beams (S. C.).

ಮುದಲೆಕರು, ಮುದಲೆಗರು **mudalekaru, mudalegaru.** A lateral rafter supporting a ridge-piece.

ಮೀಟು **mîṭu.** To unrivet.

ಮೇಕು **mêku.** A peg or nail; —ಹೊಡಿಯು (-hoḍiyu) to nail down.

ಮೇಲ್ಪುರೆ **mêlpure.** The superstructure of a house (S. C.).

ಮೊಕಸರ **mokasara.** A beam from pillar to pillar, a pillar-plate.

ಮೊಗುಳು **moguḷu.** The wall at the gable end of a house-roof.

ಮೊಳೆ **moḷe.** A nail; ಆಣಿ (âṇi) a small nail (S. C.). ಹೆಡೆ— (heḍe-) a boss.

ರಿಪೀಸ್ **ripis.** Collar rafters (My.).

ರೀಪು **ripu.** Wooden laths (S. C.).

ಲದಾವು **ladâvu.** An arch (My.).

ಲೋವೆ **lôve.** The eaves of a roof; 2, the frame-work of a thatch.

ವಾರಿಚಪ್ಪರ **vârićappara.** A shelving roof supported by rafters.

ವಾಸಕಾಲು **vâsakâlu.** A door-frame (My.).

ಶಲಾಟುಕ **śalâṭuka.** A cross-beam holding together rafters joined at an equilateral triangle.

ಶಿಪಾಯಿ **śipâyi.** Struts (S. C.).

ಸಂದು ಹಾಕು, -ಮಾಡು **sandu hâku, -mâḍu.** To rabbet.

ಸರ **sara.** A rafter; ಮೇಲ್— (mêl-) a centre-beam.

ಸಾರ **sâra.** Scaffolding; also ಸಾರವೆ (My.).

ಸುಣ್ಣ **suṇṇa.** A wall-plate (S. C.).

ಸೂತ್ರಪಟ್ಟಿ **sûtrapaṭṭi.** An outer frame of a door; 2, see ಗಂಡಪಟ್ಟಿಗೆ.

ಸೂರು **sûru.** Eaves of a roof; —ಅಂಚಿನ ಹೊಡೆ (-añćina hoḍe) the beam under the eaves of a roof; —ಪಟ್ಟೆ (-paṭṭe) a slip of board nailed on the edge of eaves.

ಹಗರು **hagaru.** The main-beam supporting a thatch.

ಹಣೆಮಣಿ **haṇemaṇi.** Capitals of a pillar.

ಹುಗುಲು **hugulu.** A mortise.

ಹುತ್ತಿ **hutti.** Raised turf channel (My.).

ಹುದಿ **hudi.** The fold of a door.

ಹೆಕ್ಕಟ್ಟು **hekkaṭṭu.** The lath-work on the roof of a house.

ಹೆಟ್ಟಿಗೆ **heṭṭige.** The centre-beam of a roof.

ಹೊಡೆ **hoḍe.** The principal beam of a roof; ಬೆಂಗಟೆ— (beṅgaṭe-) the ridge pole.

Astronomy and Astrology.

(*Note.* Words Astrological are marked Al., the arbitrary signs are placed in brackets.)

ಅಂಶ **aṁśa.** "Degree"; –ಚಕ್ರ (-čakra) a table consulted by astrologers in casting horoscopes, an astrological diagram to determine the degree of the sun in any sign; –ತ್ವ (-tva) the degree of the sun in the zodiac at one's birth.

ಅಧೋಬಿಂದು, ಅಧೋಭಾಗ **adhôbindu, adhôbhâga.** The nadir.

ಅನುಮತಿ **anumati.** The 15th day of the moon's age on which she rises one digit less than full.

ಅಭಿಜಿತ್ತು **abhijittu.** The space of 48 minutes—24 immediately before midday and 24 immediately after; 2, Vega, *a* Lyra.

ಅಯನ **ayana.** Precession of the ecliptic; ಉತ್ತರ–, ದಕ್ಷಿಣ– (uttara-, dakshiṇa-) the sun's course through the northern and southern constellations respectively; ಗ್ರಹ– (graha-) planetary precession; –ಅಂಶ (-aṁśa) the precession of Spica Virginis (ಚಿತ್ರಾ) which according to Sûryasiddhânta is 180° from the first point of Aries and is the starting point of Libra; –ಸಂಧಿ (-sandhi) the solstitial point, otherwise called ಅಯನಾಂಶ.

ಅಸ್ತ **asta.** Disappearance, setting, also ಅಸ್ತಮಯ; ಪೂರ್ವ–, ಪಶ್ಚಿಮ– (pûrva-, paščima-) disappearing in the east and west respectively.

ಅಕ್ಷ **aksha.** Axis, latitude; ನಿರ್– (nir-) the equator; –ಉತ್ತರ, –ದಕ್ಷಿಣ (-uttara, -dakshiṇa) parallels of north and south latitude respectively.

ಆಕಾಶಗಂಗೆ, ಮಂದಾಕಿನಿ **âkâśagaṅge, mandâkini.** The milky way, Via lactea.

ಇಳಿತ **iḷita.** Neap tide.

ಉಚ್ಚ **učča.** The zenith; –ದಶೆ (-daśe) good fortune (Al.); –ಸ್ಥಾನ (-sthâna) the ascending node.

ಉಪಗ್ರಹ **upagraha.** A satellite.

ಉನ್ನತಿ **unnati.** Altitude; 2, culmination.

ಉಲ್ಕ, ನಿರ್ಘಾತ **ulka, nirghâta.** A meteor, a shooting star.

ಕಂದು kandu. The black spots in the moon.

ಕತ್ತಲೆ kattale. Darkness; ಮುಂ—, ಹಿಂ— (muṅ-, hiṅ-) are respectively darkness in the first and latter part of the night.

ಕದಂಬ kadamba. Pole of the ecliptic.

ಕರಣ karaṇa. Half of the moon's age. Each lunar day is divided into two karaṇas; there are, according to astrology, eleven karaṇas, of which four are constant; these are 1, ಶಕುನಿ (śakuni) which occupies the latter part of the 14th day of the dark fortnight; 2, ಚತುಷ್ಪಾದ and ನಾಗವಾನ (čatushpâda, nâgavâna) which occupy the new-moon-day; 3, ಕಿಂಸ್ನಿಗ್ಧ (kiṁsnigdha) occupying the first part of the first lunar day of the bright fortnight. The variables are ಬವ (bava) occupying the latter part of the first lunar day (bright fortnight), ಬಾಲವ and ಕೌಲವ (bâlava, kaulava) the second lunar day. ತೈತಲೆ and ಗರಿಜೆ (taitale, garije) the third; ವಣಿಜೆ and ಭದ್ರೆ (vaṇije, bhadre) the fourth day, and again from ಬವ till the fourteenth day of the dark fortnight when ಶಕುನಿ recurs.

ಕರ್ಣ karṇa. Distance; ಚಲ—, ಮಂದ— (čala-, manda-) "Radius-vector" or the distance from the sun to a planet (ρ. or R.); ಶೀಘ್ರ— (śîghra-) the distance from the earth to a planet.

ಕಲೆ, ಕಳೆ kale, kaḷe. A digit; 2, $\frac{1}{12}$ part of the sun or moon's diameter; 3, $\frac{1}{16}$ part of the moon's diameter which is constant, the other 15 parts revolve round the moon and correspond to a "tithi" or a lunar day; ವಿ— (vi-) the second of an arc.

ಕಿರಿಗ್ರಹ, ಸೂಕ್ಷ್ಮಗ್ರಹ kirigraha, sûkshmagraha. Asteroids revolving between Mars and Jupiter.

ಕೇಂದ್ರ kêndra. A "center"; ವಿಷಮ— (vishama-) eccentricity (*e.*).

ಕೋಟಿ kôṭi. Cosine.

ಕ್ರಾಂತಿ krânti. Declination (δ.); —ವೀಧಿ (-vîdhi) the ecliptic; —ಪಾತ (-pâta) the equinoctial point.

ಖಮಧ್ಯ khamadhya. The zenith, the vertical point.

ಗಂಡ gaṇḍa. One-twenty-seventh part of the ecliptic; ಅತಿ— (ati-) the time at which the sun is in one of the signs of the zodiac.

ಗಣ gaṇa. A series of asterisms classed into three heads: 1, ನರ (nara) human; 2, ರಾಕ್ಷಸ (râkshasa) inhuman; 3, ದೇವ (dêva) divine (Al.).

ಗುಡಿ **guḍi.** The ring round the sun or moon in damp weather, halo.

ಗುಳಿಕ **guḷika.** The fictitious son of the sun (S. C.); —ಉದಯ (-udaya) an inauspicious time for marriage, extending over an interval of $3\frac{3}{4}$ ghaḷiges (S. C.); —ಕಾಲ (-kâla) a somewhat auspicious time (My.).

ಗ್ರಹ **graha.** A planet; ನವ— (nava-) the nine planets of Hindu astronomy, viz: 1, ಸೂರ್ಯ (sûrya) the sun, denoted by ☉; 2, ಚಂದ್ರ (čandra) the moon by ☾; 3, ಮಂಗಳ (maṅgaḷa) Mars, ♂; 4, ಬುಧ (budha) Mercury, ☿; 5, ಬೃಹಸ್ಪತಿ (bṛihaspati) Jupiter, ♃; 6, ಶುಕ್ರ (śukra) Venus, ♀; 7, ಶನಿ (śani) Saturn, ♄; 8, ರಾಹು (râhu) the ascending node or Caput draconis, ☊; 9, ಕೇತು (kêtu) the descending node or Cauda draconis, ☋; —ಕೂಟ (-kûṭa) conjunction of planets (Al.); —ಬಲ (-bala) the "equilibrium" or equality of two horoscopes (Al.); —ಪತಿ (-pati) the sun; —ಕಕ್ಷೆ, —ವೀಧಿ (-kakshe, -vîdhi) an orbit.

ಗ್ರಹಣ **grahaṇa.** An eclipse; ಸೂರ್ಯ—, ಚಂದ್ರ— (sûrya-, čandra-) are solar and lunar eclipses respectively; ಅರ್ಧ—, ಅಪೂರ್ಣ—, ಖಂಡ—, ಪಾರ್ಶ್ವ— (ardha-, apûrṇa-, khaṇḍa-, pârśva-) a partial eclipse; ಕಂಕಣ— (kaṅkaṇa-) an annular eclipse; ಪೂರ್ಣ—, ಸರ್ವ— (pûrṇa-, sarva-) a total eclipse; ಪಾತಾಳ— (pâtâḷa-) an eclipse below the horizon; ತಾರಾ— (târâ-) occultation; ಪ್ರತ್ಯಕ್ಷ—, ಅಪ್ರತ್ಯಕ್ಷ— (pratyaksha-, apratyaksha-) are visible and invisible eclipses respectively.

ಗ್ರಾಸ **grâsa.** The "greatest phase", the portion eclipsed.

ಚಂದ್ರ **čandra.** The moon; —ಖಂಡ (-khaṇḍa) phases of the moon; —ಬಿಂಬ, —ಮಂಡಲ (-bimba, -maṇḍala) disc or orb of the moon; —ಪರಿವರ್ತನ (-parivartana) lunation; ಬಿದಿಗೆ— (bidige-) the crescent moon; ಅಮಾವಾಸ್ಯೆ (amâvâsye) "new moon"; ಪೂರ್ಣಮಿ, ಹುಣ್ಣಿಮೆ (pûrṇami, huṇṇame) full moon ☺; ಶುಕ್ಲಾರ್ಧ— (śuklârdha-) the first quarter ☽; ಕೃಷ್ಣಾರ್ಧ— (krishṇârdha-) the last quarter, ; ನಷ್ಟ— (nashṭa-) a waning moon; ಖಂಡ— (khaṇḍa-) the gibbous moon.

ಚಕ್ರವಾಳ **čakravâḷa.** The horizon.

ಛಾಯೆ **čhâye.** Umbra; ಅಪೂರ್ಣ— (apûrṇa-) penumbra.

ತಾರಾ **târâ.** A star; —ಗಣ (-gaṇa) nebula.

ತಿಂಗೊಡೆ, ತಿಂಗಳೋಡು, ತಿಂಗಳುಗಡು **tiṅgoḍe, tiṅgaḷôḍu, tiṅgaḷugaḍu.** The first day of the solar month considered to be unlucky (Al.).

ತಿಥಿ **tithi.** "Age of the moon", a lunar day.

ದಶೆ **daše.** The reign of a planet; ದುರ್– (dur-) misfortune (Al.).

ದಿಗಂತ, ದಿಶಾಂತ **diganta, dišânta.** The horizon.

ದೇಶಾಂತರ **dêšântara.** Longitude in time.

ದೃಕ್ಸಿದ್ಧಾಂತ **driksiddhânta.** Apparent calculation.

ಧನಿಷ್ಠಾಪಂಚಕ **dhanishṭhâpañčaka.** *Lit:* five stars commencing from ಧನಿಷ್ಠಾ (dhanishṭhâ). Astrologers say that when a death takes place on a day when the moon is in one of these stars five more deaths will take place on that day.

ಧೂಮಕೇತು, ಬಾಲಚುಕ್ಕಿ, ಬಾಲನಕ್ಷತ್ರ **dhûmakêtu, bâlačukki, bâlanakshatra.** A comet.

ಧ್ರುವಮಂಡಲ **dhruvamaṇḍala.** Ursa minor.

ನಂದೆ **nande.** The 1st, 6th, and 11th day of either lunar fortnight.

ನತ, ನತಿ **nata, nati.** Zenith distance.

ನಕ್ಷತ್ರ **nakshatra.** A star; 2, an interval of 13° 20′ corresponding to 13 days odd, otherwise called ಮಹಾ– (mahâ-); ನಿತ್ಯ– (nitya-) the star occupied by the moon on each day (Al.); ಜನ್ಮ– (janma-) the star under which a man is born (Al.); ಶುಕ್ರ– (šukra-) the evening-star. The Hindu astronomy recognizes but 40 stars, 27 of which are astrological. The latter are believed to exercise certain meteorological influences, such as heat, rain, etc. The intervals, generally 13 days odd during which such weather lasts, are named after the respective stars. In giving therefore what may be called a 'stellar calendar', it will not be out of place to note the various agricultural operations carried on during the occupation of the sun on the star, with some rural expressions embodying the observations of the cultivators. The *astrological* stars are:—1, ಅಶ್ವಿನಿ (ašvini) β. Arietis, (*b*) rain from the 11th to the 24th April when the ground is tilled (My.); 2, ಭರಣಿ (bharaṇi) 35 Arietis, (*b*) rain from 25th April to 4th May when various kinds of grain are sown; 3, ಕೃತ್ತಿಕಾ (krittikâ) ε. Tauri, (*b*) the height of summer, when "not even 10 drops of rain should fall" so that the earth may be rendered fertile (S. C.); this star with the preceding goes by the name of ಭರಣಿಕೃತ್ತಿಕಾ, and when that happens to be a ನಿತ್ಯ ನಕ್ಷತ್ರ no new work is to be commenced (Al.); 4, ರೋಹಿಣಿ (rôhiṇi) Bull's eye, Aldebaran, *a* Tauri, (*b*) rain from 22nd May to 4th June, when paddy and cotton is sown; 5, ಮೃಗ ಶಿರಾ (mṛigaśirâ) 116 Tauri, (*b*) rain from the 5th to 18th June, the harbinger of the S. W. monsoon, is believed to confine the wild beasts to their dens: ಮೃಗಶಿರಾ ಮಳೆ ಮೃಗಗಳಿಗೆ ಸೆರೆ; this rain is so excellent for cultivation that "even a slight scratching" of the fields is believed to ensure a plentiful crop, and the rice plants planted during this rain are supposed to be strong enough to defy the ravages of wild beasts, and despite them, will grow healthy in Ârdrâ at least: ಮೃಗಶಿರೆಯಲ್ಲಿ ನಟ್ಟರೆ ಮೃಗ ತಿಂದರೂ ಅಳಿಯದು, ಆರ್ದ್ರೆ ಬಳಗೆ ಆಗುತ್ತದೆ (S. C.); 6, ಆರ್ದ್ರಾ (ârdrâ) [Sans: wet] Betelguese, (*b*) the entry of the sun into the mansion of this star —ಆರ್ದ್ರಾಪ್ರವೇಶ— lasting from the 19th June to the 2nd July, marks the outburst of the S. W. monsoon, the rain being so excessive as to redden river-water. And it is a matter of faith with the Hindus that if it rains well during this star, it will continue doing so for six more stars. This and the four to be mentioned below, go by the name of ಆರ್ದ್ರಾಪಂಚಕ (ârdrâpañcaka) and denote the interval during which the S. W. monsoon lasts; paddy is sown, and the rain strengthens the plants. Two expressions illustrating the importance of this rain are:—ಆರ್ದ್ರಾ ಮಳೆ ಬಂದರೆ, ಆದಷ್ಟು ನೋಡೇನು (If it rains in Ârdrâ, I shall see what I can do); ಆರ್ದ್ರೆಯಲ್ಲಾದರೆ ಆಯಿತು, ಹೋದರೆ ಹೋಯಿತು (All is well if it rains in Ârdrâ, if not all is lost) (S. C.); 7, ಪುನರ್ವಸು (punarvasu) Pollux, β. Geminorum, (*b*) rain from 3rd to 16th July; paddy is sown (My.). A bad time for sowing paddy—the plants will grow 'as thin as a cat's hair'; this rain is said to be destructive to cattle (S. C.); 8, ಪುಷ್ಯ (pushyâ) δ. Centauri, (*b*) rain from the 17th to the 30th July; gram is sown and mango seeds (My.); "If seed is sown in Pushyâ, it will be attacked by insects, and even cats will get no rice"; but for existing crop the rain is good (S. C.); 9, ಆಶ್ಲೇಷಾ (âślêshâ) 49 Centauri, (*b*) rain from 31st July to 12th August; gram is sown, mango seeds germinate (My.); sunshine is preferable in Âślêshâ—

ಆಶ್ಲೇಷೆಯಲ್ಲಿ ಬಿಸಲೇ ಲೇಸು— for the tender ears of corn may rot if it rains (S. C.); 10, ಮಘಾ (maghâ) Regulus, *a* Leonis, (*b*) rain from 13th to 16th August; the entrance of the sun into the mansion of this star marks the outburst of the N. W. monsoon. The various sayings in connection with this star best illustrate the usefulness of this rain to the agricultural classes—ಮಘಾ ನೀರು ಮಗನಿಗೂ ಬಿಡೆ [I will not allow Maghâ water even to my son]; ಮಘಾ ನೀರು ಮೊಗ್ಗೆಯಲ್ಲಿಡ ಬೇಕು (Maghâ water is worth being stored up in a pot); ಮಘಾ ಮಳೆ ಬೆಳೆಗೆ ಲೇಸು (Maghâ rain is good for the crop); this rain is said to develope "milk" in the ears of corn (S. C.). This and the four mentioned below, go by the name of ಮಘಾಪಂಚಕ (maghâpañčaka) and denote the interval during which the N. W. monsoon lasts (S. C.); 11, ಹುಬ್ಬಾ (hubbâ) *a*. Leonis, (*b*) rain from the 26th August to 8th September, said to strengthen the paddy by hardening the "milk" into grain. ಹುಬ್ಬಾಮಳೆ ಅಬ್ಬೆ ಹಾಲು (Hubbâ rain is mother's milk to the crop) (S. C.); 12, ಉತ್ತರಾ (uttarâ) Deneb, (*b*) rain from 9th to 22nd September, the harvesting season: ಉತ್ತರೆಯಲ್ಲಿ ಒತ್ತರೆ (Harvesting in uttarâ) (S. C.); 13, ಹಸ್ತಾ (hastâ), δ. Corvi, (*b*) rain from 23rd September to 7th October when millet and gingelly seed is sown (My.); 14, ಚಿತ್ರಾ (čitrâ) Spica Virginis, (*b*) rain from the 8th to 21st October, when millet and gingelly seed is sown (My.); "If it rains in Čitrâ, it will work wonders" (S. C.); 15, ಸ್ವಾತಿ (svâti) Arcturus Bootis, (*b*) rain from 21st October to 4th November, and supposed to stimulate the growth of pearls (S. C.); 16, ವಿಶಾಖಾ (viśâkhâ) 24 Libra, (*b*) rain from 4th to 17th November, when paddy is sown for the 2nd crop, and said to breed venomous reptiles (S. C.); 17, ಅನುರಾಧಾ (anurâdhâ) β. Scorpio, (*b*) rain from 18th to 30th November, said to be favorable to the 2nd crop (S. C.); 18, ಜ್ಯೇಷ್ಠಾ (jyêshṭhâ) Antares, *a* Scorpii, (*b*) rain from 1st to 13th December, when paddy is sown for the 3rd crop (S.C.); 19, ಮೂಲಾ (mûlâ) 34 Scorpio, (*b*) rain from 14th to 27 December, when cummin and coriander seed is sown (My., C.); 20, ಪೂರ್ವಾಷಾಢಾ (pûrvâshâḍhâ) δ Sagittarius, (*b*) rain from 14th to 27th December, when cummin and coriander seed is sown (My., C.); 20*a*. ಅಭಿಜಿತಾ (abhijitâ) Vega, *a* Lyra—a star occupying 19 ghaḷiges between

Nos. 20 and 21; 21, ಉತ್ತರಾಷಾಢಾ (uttarâshâḍhâ) *a* Sagittarius; 22, ಶ್ರವಣಾ (śravaṇâ) Altair, *a* Aquilae; 23, ಧನಿಷ್ಠಾ (dhanishṭhâ) *a* Delphinii; 24, ಶತಭಿಷಾ (śatabhishâ) λ. Aquarii; 25, ಪೂರ್ವಾಭಾದ್ರಾ (pûrvâbhâdrâ) Markab, *a* Pegasi; 26, ಉತ್ತರಾಭಾದ್ರಾ (uttarâbhâdrâ) Alpheratz; 27, ರೇವತಿ (rêvati) ξ. Piscium, *(b)* rain from 28th March to 11th April when the land is ploughed (My.). The other stars are ಸಪ್ತಋಷಿ (saptaṛishi) Ursa major containing seven stars; ತ್ರಿಶಂಕು, ಲುಬ್ಧಕ (triśaṅku, lubdhaka) the dog-star, Sirius, Cannis major; ಅಗಸ್ತ್ಯ (agastya) Canopus; ಬ್ರಹ್ಮಹೃದಯ (brahmahṛidaya) Auriga capella; ಅಪಾಂವತ್ಸ (apâṁvatsa) Procion; ಅರುಂಧತಿ (arundhati) the star nearest the Ursa major; ಧ್ರುವನಕ್ಷತ್ರ (dhruvanakshatra) the pole-star.

ನಾಡಿ **nâḍi.** A line (Al); —ಕೂಟ (-kûṭa) the planetary conjunction consulted by astrologers before a matrimonial alliance is fixed upon (Al.).

ಪಂಚಾಂಗ **pañcâṅga.** An almanac consisting of five ಅಂಗಗಳು—ತಿಥಿ, ವಾರ, ನಕ್ಷತ್ರ, ಯೋಗ, ಕರಣ (*q. v.*).

ಪದಮಧ್ಯ **padamadhya.** The nadir.

ಪರಮಾಪಮ **paramâpama.** The inclination of a planet; ವಿಕ್ಷೇಪಧ್ರುವ (vikshêpadhruva) the greatest inclination of a planet.

ಪರಸ್ಪರ **paraspara.** Opposition (☍).

ಪರಿಧಿ **paridhi.** The sun or moon's disc; 2, the corona of the moon —ಪಾದಾಂತರ (-pâdântara) quadrature (□).

ಪಕ್ಷ **paksha.** A fortnight; ಶುಕ್ಲ— (śukla-) the bright fortnight; ಬಹುಳ— (bahuḷa-) the dark fortnight.

ಪಾತಸ್ಥಿತಿ **pâtasthiti.** The descending or ascending node.

ಬಲ **bala.** Influence; ಗ್ರಹ— (graha-) planetary influence (Al.); ತಾರಾ— (târâ-) the aspect of the stars (Al.).

ಭರ್ತ **bharta.** Spring tide.

ಭಾನುಮಧ್ಯ **bhânumadhya.** The position of the sun between Mercury and Venus, which according to astrology is a sign of the cessation of rain, 'the heat being so much as to dry up the ocean' (Al.).

ಭುಕ್ತಿ **bhukti.** The ministry of a planet (Al.).

ಭುಜ **bhuja.** A sine.

ಭೂವಿಪ್ರಕರ್ಷಣ bhûviprakarshaṇa, Apogee.

ಭೂಸನ್ನಿಕರ್ಷಣ bhûsannikarshaṇa. Perigee.

ಮಂಡಲ maṇḍala. The disk of the sun or the moon; ಶುದ್ಧ— (śuddha-) lit: the clean disk of the moon or the sun after an eclipse, the last contact.

ಮಾಂದಿ mândi. The fictitious son of the sun, also ಗುಳಿಕ (Al.).

ಮಾಸ mâsa. A month, usually lunar, of 30 days called ತಿಥಿ; ಚಾಂದ್ರ— (čândra-) a lunar or synodic month; ಸೌರ— (saura-) a solar month; ನಾಕ್ಷತ್ರ—(nâkshatra-) a sidereal month; ಅಧಿಕ— (adhika-) an intercalar month; ಸಾವನ— (sâvana-) a month consisting of 30 risings and settings of the sun (see ಸೌರ); ಬಾರ್ಹಸ್ಪತ್ಯ— (bârhaspatya-) a month depending on the motions of the planet Jupiter.

ಮೇರು mêru. The poles.

ಮೋಕ್ಷ môksha. "Last contact"; 2, emersion; 3, egress.

ಯಾಮ್ಯೋತ್ತರಾಂತರ yâmyôttarântara. (ಯಾಮ್ಯ south, ಉತ್ತರ north, ಅಂತರ space) The distance from north to south; hence azimuth.

ಯೋಗ yôga. An interval of 13° 20′ of an arc or the ecliptic; the 27th part of a great circle, measured as the plane of the ecliptic, and used in calculating the longitudes of the sun and the moon; 2, the total of the degrees, minutes of the sun and moon, etc. from the first point of "Aries"; astrologers enumerate 27 yôgas corresponding with the 27 stars (supra) or the divisions of the moon's path, but varying according to the day of the week.

ರಾಶಿ râśi. A sign of the zodiac; these are 1, ಮೇಷ (mêsha) Aries, the ram, (o or ♈); 2, ವೃಷಭ (vṛishabha) Taurus, the bull, (I or ♉); 3, ಮಿಥುನ (mithuna) Gemini, the twins (II or ♊); 4, ಕರ್ಕಾಟಕ (karkâṭaka) Cancer, the crab, (III, ♋); 5, ಸಿಂಹ (simha) Leo, the lion (IV, ♌); 6, ಕನ್ಯೆ (kanye) Virgo, the virgin (V, ♍); 7, ತುಲಾ (tulâ) Libra, the scales, (VI, ♎); 8, ವೃಶ್ಚಿಕ (vṛiśčika) Scorpio, the scorpion, (VII, ♏); 9, ಧನು (dhanu) Sagittarius the archer, (VIII, ♐); 10, ಮಕರ (makara) Capricornus, (IX, ♑); 11, ಕುಂಭ (kumbha) Aquarius, the water-pot bearer, (X, ♒); 12, ಮೀನ (mîna) Pisces, the fishes, (XI, ♓). —ಚಕ್ರ (-čakra) an astrological diagram; ಸ್ಥಿರ— (sthira-) the 2nd, 5th, 8th, and 11th constellations (Al.); ಚರ— (čara-) the 1st,

4th, 7th, and 10th constellations (Al.); ಉಭಯ— (ubhaya-) the 3rd, 6th, 9th, and 12th constellations (Al.); ಅಷ್ಟಮ— (ashṭama-) enmity, hatred; ನೀಚ— (nîča-) an unfortunate natal sign (Al.); ಉಚ್ಚ— (učča-) a fortunate natal sign (Al.).

ರೇಖಾ **rêkhâ.** The meridian.

ಲಂಬನ **lambana.** Parallax; ವಿಷಮ—ತ್ವ (vishama—tva) parallactic inequality.

ಲಗ್ನ **lagna.** The rising of a sign, its appearance above the horizon, the oblique ascension; the divisions of the equator which rise in succession, with each sign in an oblique sphere; 2, the ascendant of a star; the 1st, 4th, 7th and 10th signs of the zodiac (Al.); ಲಗ್ನಾಧಿಪತಿ (lagnâdhipati) a reigning star in the constellation (Al.).

ವಕ್ರೋಸ್ರ **vakrôsra.** Refraction.

ವಲಯ, ಭೂ— **valaya, bhû-.** A zone; ಉಷ್ಣ— (ushṇa-) the torrid zone; ಮಧ್ಯ— (madhya-) the temperate zone; ಶೀತ— (śîta-) the frigid zone.

ವರ್ಷದ ಫಲ **varshada phala.** "The astrological fruit of the year" (Al.).

ವರ್ಷಯೋಗ **varshayôga.** The position of the sun apart from Venus and Mercury, which, according to astrology, is the commencement of rain—'enough to cause a deluge'—Used in contradistinction to ಭಾನುಮಧ್ಯ (p. 39.) (Al.).

ವಿಷುವತ್ **vishuvat.** The equinox; ಮೇಷಾ— (mêshâ-) the vernal equinox; ತುಲಾ— (tulâ-) the autumnal equinox.

ವಿಷುವಾಂಶ **vishuvâṁśa.** Right ascension (α, A.R.).

ಶನಿ **śani.** The Saturn; —ವಲಯ (-valaya) Saturn's ring.

ಶರ **śara.** The latitude of a planet; 2, curtate distance.

ಶೃಂಗ **śṛiṅga.** The cusps of a planet, *e.g.* the moon.

ಸಂಕ್ರಮ **saṅkrama.** The transit of the sun or other planetary bodies from one sign of the zodiac to another.

ಸಂಕ್ರಾಂತಿ **saṅkrânti.** The solstice; ಕರ್ಕಾಟಕ— (karkâṭaka-) the summer solstice; ಮಕರ— (makara-) the winter solstice; —ವೃತ್ತ (-vṛitta) a tropic.

ಸಂದುಕಟ್ಟು **sandukaṭṭu.** A crisis (Al.); three crises supposed to be "bad" for children are mentioned. These are ಗ್ರಹಣದ— (grahaṇada-)

the interval between the first and the last contact in an eclipse; ಅಮಾವಾಸ್ಯೆ— (amâvâsye-) between the change and the new moon; ಹುಣ್ಣಿಮೆ—(huṇṇame-) between the full moon and the wane (Al.).

ಸಂಧಿ sandhi. "Conjunction" (☌); ನೀಚ— (nîča-) inferior conjunction; ಉಚ್ಚ— (učča-) superior conjunction; —ಮಧ್ಯ (-madhya) "synodic" period; —ಮಧ್ಯಪರಿವರ್ತನ (-madhyaparivartana) synodic revolution; ದಶಾ— (daśâ-) the conjunction between the reigns of two planets (Al.).

ಸಂಪಾತ sampâta. A node.

ಸಮಸಪ್ತ samasapta. Opposition (☍).

ಸಾಮಾನ್ಯ sâmânya. An astrological term to denote an inauspicious moment; otherwise called ವಿಷಘಳಿಗೆ (vishaghaḷige).

ಸಾಯನಭೋಗ sâyanabhôga. Longitude.

ಸಾಲಾವಳಿ sâlâvaḷi. The favorableness or agreement of two horoscopes (Al.).

ಸಾವನ sâvana. A solar day.

ಸ್ಥಾನ sthâna. "A mansion or house in a horoscope"; astrologers say there are 12 "houses", each having a certain influence. These are 1, ಜನ್ಮ (janma) house of life; 2, ಧನ (dhana) of wealth; 3, ಭ್ರಾತೃ (bhrâtṛi) of brothers or heroism; 4, ಸುಖ (sukha) of happiness; 5, ಬುದ್ಧಿ, ಪೂರ್ವಪುಣ್ಯ (buddhi, pûrvapuṇya) of wisdom; 6, ಶಷ್ಠ, ಶತ್ರು, ರೋಗ (śashṭha, śatru, rôga) of disease; 7, ಕಳತ್ರ (kaḷatra) of wife or husband; 8, ಮೃತ್ಯು (mṛityu) of death; 9, ಭಾಗ್ಯ (bhâgya) of prosperity; 10, ಕರ್ಮ (karma) of action; 11, ಲಾಭ (lâbha) of profit; 12, ವ್ಯಯ (vyaya) of waste or loss (Al.); 2, the position of a heavenly body; ಸ್ಫುಟ— (sphuṭa-) 'apparent place'; ಮಧ್ಯ— (madhya-) mean place; —ಭೇದ (-bhêda) parallax.

ಸ್ಪರ್ಶ sparśa. "First contact"; 2, immersion; 3, ingress.

ಸ್ಫುಟ sphuṭa. The apparent place of a heavenly body; ಮಂದ— (manda-) the heliocentric position of a planet; ಶೀಘ್ರ— (śîghra-) the geocentric position of a planet; ಜಾತಕ—ಮಾಡು (jâtaka—mâḍu) to calculate the most accurate point in which the centre of a planet remains at a given time and by that means to prophesy coming events (Al.).

ಸ್ಪ್ರಗ್, ಸ್ಪ್ರುಗ್ಜ sprug, sprugja. A tangent; ಕೋಟಿ— (kôṭi-) a cotangent.

Botany.

ಅಂಕಣ aṅkaṇa. A cell.

ಅಂಕುರ aṅkura. A bud; a sprout.

ಅಂಡ aṇḍa. The ovum; –ಕ (-ka) an ovule; –ಆಧಾರ (-âdhâra) the placenta; –ಆಶಯ (-âśaya) an ovary.

ಅಡರ್ aḍar. A twig, a switch (Tu., S. C.).

ಅಡ್ಡಲಾಕು aḍḍalâku. A sprout from the side of the stem or root.

ಉಪಪತ್ರ upapatra. A stipule.

ಊಡೆ, ಬೀಳು ûḍe, bilu. The aerial roots of the banyan.

ಊಬು ûbu. The arista or awn of grasses.

ಎಸಳು esaḷu. A petal.

ಓಟೆ ôṭa. The stone of a fruit.

ಕಣುಲು kaṇulu. The first germ springing from a seed; 2, the top and tender part of a bamboo, used for curry or pickles, by the Hindus.

ಕಲಾಪ kalâpa. A catkin.

ಕಾಂಡ kâṇḍa. A culm or stalk.

ಕಾಯಿ kâyi. A fruit; 2, a capsule; ಕಸು– (kasu-) an unripe fruit· ಬಣ್ಣಂಗಾಯಿ (baṇṇaṅgâyi) an unripe cocoanut (S. C.).

ಕುಡಿ kuḍi. An eye, bud or germ; ಬಳ್ಳಿ– (baḷḷi-) a tendril.

ಕುತ್ತಿ kutti. A stump, a pollard (S. C.).

ಕುರ್ಲೆ kurle. A young plantain stalk (S. C.)

ಕುಸುಮ kusuma. The corolla; –ದಳ (-daḷa) a petal.

ಕುಸುರಿ kusuri. The pulp of a fruit.

ಕೆಚ್ಚು keččü. Core-wood.

ಕೆತ್ತೆ kette. The bark of a tree.

ಕೇಸರ kêsara. A stamen; –ತಂತು (-tantu) a filament.

ಕೊಂಗೆ koṅge. An offshoot.

ಕೊಂಬೆ kombe. A branch; ಕವಲು– (kavalu-) a forked branch: ಅಟ್ಟ– (aṭṭa-) the main branch; ಕೊಟ– (koṭa-) the uppermost branch of a tree; ನಡು– (naḍu-) the central branch.

ಕೋಡು kôḍu. A pod; 2, a legume (S. C.).

ಗಡ್ಡೆ gaḍḍe. A bulb.

ಗದೆ gade. A spadix.

ಗರಿ gari. A frond, the leaf of a fern or a palm.

ಗಿಟಕು giṭaku. The kernel of a cocoanut.

ಗಿಡ giḍa. A plant.

ಗುಸಿ gusi. The superfluous shoots of a tobacco plant.

ಗೆಲ್ಲು gellu. A bough; ಅಡ್ಡ— (aḍḍa-) a lateral branch.

ಗೊನೆ gone. A bunch of flowers or fruits; also ಗೊಂಚಲು.

ಗೊರಟು goraṭu. The putamen or stone of a fruit.

ಚಕ್ಕೆ čakke. The bark.

ಚಿಗುರು čiguru. A bud, a sprout; —ಕುಡಿ (-kuḍi) the point of a bud.

ಚೆಂಡು čeṇḍu. A capitulum.

ಛದ čhada. A bract.

ಛೇಗು, ಸೇಗು čhêgu, sêgu. The heart, core, or close grain of wood.

ಜಡೆ jaḍe. An aerial root, generally of the banyan.

ತಂತು tantu. A filament.

ತಿಗುಡು tiguḍu. The external coat or bark of a tree.

ತಿರುಳು tiruḷu. The core of a tree.

ತುಂಬು tumbu. The foot-stalk or pedicel of a flower or leaf.

ತುಷ tusha. A glume, palea, the bract of grain; also ಬುಷ.

ತೊಂಡೆ toṇḍe. The upper, insipid part of a sugar-cane (My.).

ತೊಟ್ಟು toṭṭu. A petiole or a stalk.

ತೊಡಮೆ toḍame. A fruit-stalk.

ದಂಟು danṭu. A culm, a stalk; ಎಲೆ— (ele-) a petiole.

ದಳ daḷa. A petal; ಫಲ— (phala-) a carpel.

ದಿಂಡು dinḍu. The round stalk inside a plantain tree.

ನಳ naḷa. A tube, an air vessel.

ನಾಭಿ nâbhi. The hilum; —ಬಂಧ (-bandha) the funicle.

ಪಟ, ಪಟಲ paṭa, paṭala. An involucre.

ಪತ್ರ patra. A leaf; ಅಖಂಡ— (akhaṇḍa-) an undivided leaf; ಗರಿಯ— (gariya-) a pinnate leaf; ಪಾಣಿ— (pâṇi-) a palmate leaf.

ಪನ್ನಾಡೆ **pannâḍe.** The net-like substance at the top of a cocoanut tree.

ಪರಾಗ **parâga.** Pollen grain; —ಕೇಸರ (-kêsara) the stamen; —ಕೋಶ (-kôśa) an anther.

ಪಲ್ಲವ **pallava.** A leaf-bud.

ಪೀಸು **pîsu.** The fibres or villi of plants or fruits.

ಪೊಂಬಾಳೆ **pombâḷe.** The flower of a cocoa or areca nut tree.

ಪೋಟ್ರೆ **pôṭre.** The hollow of a tree.

ಫಲ **phala.** A fruit; ಅಷ್ಟಿ— (ashṭi-) a drupe; ಆವೃತ— (âvṛita-) an achene; ಕೋಶ— (kôśa-) a capsule; ಗುಲಿ— (guli-) a berry; ದೃಢ— (dṛiḍha-) a nut; ಸಮಾಸಿಕ— (samâsika-) a collective fruit; ಸ್ಯೋತ— (syôta-) a follicle.

ಬಳ್ಳಿ **baḷḷi.** A creeper.

ಬೀಜ **bîja.** Seed; —ಪತ್ರ (-patra) a cotyledon.

ಬೆಂಡು **beṇḍu.** The pith of wood.

ಬೇರು **bêru.** The root; ಕೂಗಟ—, ತಾಯಿ— (kûgaṭa-, tâyi-) the tap root; ಜಡೆ (jaḍe) the adventitious roots of the banyan; ಭ್ರೂಣದ— (bhrûṇada-) the radicle; ಶಡೆ (śaḍe) the loose roots (My.).

ಭಿತ್ತಿ **bhitti.** Dissepiments.

ಭ್ರೂಣ **bhrûṇa.** The embryo.

ಮಟ್ಟೆ **maṭṭe.** The branch or frond of any palm tree; called ಮಡಲು (maḍalu) (S. C.).

ಮರ **mara.** A tree; ಚಾಗಿನ— (câgina-) a close grained tree; ಚೋಕ— (côk-) a tree past bearing (S. C.); ಜೋಡ— (jôḍ-) a tree branching out into two from the stem (S. C.); ಬಿಳಿ— (biḷi-) sap-wood; ದದ್ದು— (daddu-) touch-wood; ಚಾಬಿನ— (câubina-) a timber tree; ಕುಂಬು— (kumbu-) touch-wood (S. C.); ಮನ್ನಾಜಾತಿ— (mannâjâti-) a reserved tree (S. C.); ಕಾಡು— (kâḍu-) a wild tree; ಜಂಗ್ಲಿ— (jangli-) forest timber.

ಮಿಡಿ **miḍi.** A fruit-bud.

ಮುಳ್ಳು **muḷḷu.** A thorn, spine.

ಮೊಗ್ಗೆ, ಮುಗ್ಗಿ **mogge, maggi.** A flower-bud.

ಮೊಳ್ಕೆ **moḷke.** Germination; 2, a sprout.

ಮೋಟು **môṭu.** A pollard.

ಲೋಳೆ lôḷe. Albumen.

ಶಂಕು šaṅku. The claw or stalk of a petal; 2, the trunk of a lopped tree.

ಶಮಿ šami. A siliqule.

ಶಲಾಕೆ šalâke. The style; —ದ್ವಾರ (-dvâra) the stigma.

ಸಂದು sandu. A node.

ಸಸಿ sasi. A young plant, sapling; ಗುಳಿ— (guḷi-) a plant in a pit (S. C.). ಯಡೆ— (yaḍe-) a plant about to bear (S. C.); the two foregoing words are generally applied to cocoanut plants (S. C.).

ಸೊನೆ sone. The milky juice exuding from the stem, or a twig broken off a tree.

ಹಗಿನು haginu. The close grain of a tree; 2, the gum or resin of a tree.

ಹಾಲು hâlu. The milky juice of a plant.

ಹಾಳೆ hâḷe. A spathe, generally of the areca-nut tree.

ಹಿಪ್ಪಿ hippi. The pith of wood.

ಹೀಚು hiču. Young unripe fruit.

ಹೊಟ್ಟು hoṭṭu. A bract.

Civil and Judicial.

ಅಡವು, ಅಡಮಾನ **aḍavu, aḍamâna.** A mortgage; –ಚೀಟು, –ದಸ್ತೇವಜು (-cîṭu, -dastêvaju) a mortgage-deed; ತೋರ್– (tôr-) a species of mortgage of real property, in which some land or part of an estate is pointed as security for the repayment of a loan (Ch.); a mortgage without possession, an hypothecated mortgage (S. C.); ಭೋಗ್ಯಾದಿ– (bhôgyâdi-) a mortgage of real property in which the land itself is made over to the mortgagee, a usufructuary mortgage; –ಯದುರುನುಡಿ (-yadurunuḍi) a receipt obtained by the mortgager of property from the mortgagee for things left as security for the debt (W.); a counterpart of a mortgage-deed (S. C.); ಮೇಲ್– (mêl-) a second mortgage (S. C.).

ಅನ್ಯತ **anyata.** (This Tulu word of Sanskrit origin is found in the Aḷiyasantâna text and means:) 'A gift to others than those who cannot inherit, *e. g.* a son' (S. C.).

ಅನಾದಿಭೂಮಿ **anâdibhûmi.** Land transferred by mortgage (My.).

ಅನ್ವಾದಿ **anvâdi.** Re-mortgage of lands (My.); –ದಾರ (-dâra) a re-mortgagee, the mortgagee who holds the property from the proprietor called ಭೋಗ್ಯದಾರ (*q. v.*).

ಅನುಭವ **anubhava.** Enjoyment (My.); experience (S. C.); –ಕೊಡು (-koḍu) to instruct, as a Vakil (S. C.).

ಅನುಭೋಗ **anubhôga.** Enjoyment; –ದಾರ (-dâra) a possessor, an owner (S. C.).

ಅಮಲಜಾರಿ, ಅಮಲ್ಜಾರಿ **amalajâri, amaljâri.** The execution of the decree of a court; –ಅರ್ಜಿ (-arji) an 'execution-petition'.

ಅಮಾನತು, ಅನಾಮತು **amânatu, anâmatu.** A deposit; 2, a trust.

ಅರ್ಜಿ **arji.** A petition; –ದಾರ, –ದಾಸ್ತು (-dâra, -dâstu) a petitioner; ಯದ್ರು– (yadru-) a counter-petition; ತಳ್ಳಿ– (taḷḷi-) an anonymous or pseudonymous petition (S. C.); ನಿನಾವಿ–, ನಿನಾಮಿ– (ninâvi-, ninâmi-) an anonymous petition (S. M.); ಅಸಲ್– (asal-) a plaint (S. M., N. C.).

ಅರ್ಥ **artha.** Consideration; –ದ ಹಣ (-da haṇa) consideration-money (S. C.).

ಅವಧಿ **avadhi.** A period; 2, the term stipulated for payment; —ಆರವಾರ (-âravâra) a usufructuary mortgage with a stipulation that the mortgagee shall not be dispossessed before a certain time (S. C.); —ಬಾಧಕ (-bâdhaka) the bar of time (S. C.).

ಅಶನಾರ್ಥ (vlg. ಅಶಿನಾರ್ಥ) **aśanârtha.** Maintenance; —ಕೈಫೇತು (-kaiphêtu) a suit for maintenance (S. C.).

ಅಷ್ಟಭೋಗ **ashṭabhôga.** A term used in deeds of conveyance of land, to signify the free and unrestricted enjoyment of the eight products of the property alienated, viz: ಸಿದ್ಧಿ (siddhi) land cultivated; ಸಾಧ್ಯ (sâdhya) the produce of land; ಪಾಷಾಣ (pâshâṇa) minerals; ನಿಕ್ಷೇಪ (nikshêpa) property deposited in the land; ನಿಧಿ (nidhi) treasure-trove; ಜಲಾಮೃತ (jalâmṛita) water and its products; ಅಕ್ಷಿಣಿ (akshiṇi) actual privileges; ಆಗಮಿ (âgami) future rights and privileges (W.); *vide* ಸರ್ವಾಧಿ.

ಅಳವಿ **aḷavi.** An instalment; —ಪತ್ರ (-patra) an instalment-bond. For —ಗೇಣಿ *see* Land Tenures.

ಅಳಿಯಸಂತಾನ **aḷiyasantâna.** The name of the law of inheritance supposed to have been introduced into S. Canara about the beginning of the 13th century. Under this, landed property is managed by a senior male member of the family, called ಯಜಮಾನ (yajamâna) although the property descends in the female line. Thus, an aḷiya or sister's son succeeds to an estate in preference to the son of a proprietor. This unnatural law is said to have originated from the whim of Bhûtâḷa Pâṇḍya, a former ruler of Canara, who is said to have demanded of his wife, for sacrificial purposes, his own son. The wife refused, but the sister readily yielded. Bhûtâḷa Pâṇḍya therefore laid down his law of inheritance or regulations called ಕಟ್ಟು ಕಟ್ಟಳೆ (kaṭṭu kaṭṭaḷe) for his subjects and since then Aḷiyasantâna custom has become a law among the Śûdrâs (with certain exceptions) of Canara. The rules are 14 in number: ಜಾತಿ ನೀತಿ (jâti nîti) the rules for the guidance of castes following the law; ಮಾನ ಮರ್ಯಾದೆ (mâna maryâde) the rights and privileges of certain families; ಹುಟ್ಟು ಕಟ್ಟು (huṭṭu kaṭṭu) the *abolition* of the original Makkaḷasantâna law and the introduction of the new Aḷiyasantâna law; ಹಿಂದೆ ಮುಂದೆ (hinde munde) the different degrees of superiority consisting in the ಪಟ್ಟ ಪಟ್ಟಾವಳಿ (paṭṭa paṭṭâvaḷi) honors held by certain families; ಬಳಿ ಬಣ್ಣ (baḷi baṇṇa) the rules and regulations to be followed by people not having status or respectability; ಅಳಿ ಉಳಿ (aḷi uḷi) death and devolution of property; ಹೆಚ್ಚು ಕಮ್ಮಿ (hečču kammi) the honors appropriate to each caste (S. C.).

ಅಡಳತೆ, ಅದ್ಯಳಿತೆ **âḍaḷate, âdyaḷite.** Management; –ಗಾರ (-gâra) a manager (C.).

ಆದಾಯವೆಚ್ಚ, ಆದಾವೇಚ **auayavečča, âdâvêča.** *Lit.* Profits and expenses: management; –ನೋಡು (-nôḍu) to manage the affairs of a concern (C.).

ಆಧಾರ **âdhâra.** An exhibit; 2, means (S. C.); 3, a security, mortgage (My., Cg.); –ಸ್ಥ (-stha) a man of means, a substantial man (S. C.); ನಿರಾಧಾರಿ (nirâdhâri) a pauper; ದೃಶ್ಯ– (dṛiśya-) a hypothecated mortgage, mortgage without possession (My., Cg.).

ಆಧೀನ **âdhîna.** Control, possession; ಪರಾಧೀನ (parâdhîna) alienation; ಸ್ವಾಧೀನ (svâdhîna) taking into possession of one's self, possession (C.).

ಆಬ್ರು **âbru.** Honor, good name; –ಲುಕ್ಸಾನು (-luksânu) loss of honor, defamation (S. C.).

ಆಯ, –ಸಾಯ **âya, -sâya.** Payment in kind, corn given from the threshing floor to hereditary servants of the village (My., S. M.).

ಆರವಾರ **âravâra.** A mortgage, generally usufructuary; ಅವಧಿ– (avadhi-) *see* ಅವಧಿ; ಇಳದ– (iḷada-) a mortgage of property in which the land itself is made over to the mortgagee, a usufructuary mortgage (S. C.).

ಆರ್ಜಿತ **ârjita.** Acquired, obtained, hence acquisition; ಪಿತ್ರಾರ್ಜಿತ (pitrârjita) ancestral property; ಸ್ವಾರ್ಜಿತ, ಕಷ್ಟಾರ್ಜಿತ (svârjita, kashṭârjita) self-acquired, acquired by one's labor (C.).

ಆಸ್ತಿ **âsti.** Property, moveable or immoveable (S. C.); 2, personal property; ಚರ– (čara-) moveable or personal property (S. C.); ಸ್ಥಿರ– (sthira-) real property (S. C.).

ಇಜಾರೆ, ಇಜಾರಿಗೆ **ijâre, ijârige.** Rent; 2, a contract.

ಈಟಸರ್ತಿಚೀಟು **iṭasartičiṭu.** A deed in writing by which two people mutually agree to the exchange of lands, an instrument of exchange of immoveable property. This word is used in the Kundapur Taluk (S. C.).

ಈಡು iḍu. Security; —ಆಗು (-âgu) to become a security for.

ಉಪಭೋಗ upabhôga. Enjoyment (S. M.); —ದಾರ (-dâra) a sub-proprietor one enjoying land under another (C.); 2, a tenant enjoying only the right to the produce of fruit-trees (Bby.).

ಎದುರುಚೀಟು eduručiṭu. A document executed by the purchaser of land engaging to give it back to the vendor on repayment of the money within a certain time (W.); the counterpart of 2, a conditional sale-deed (C.), or 3, a lease executed by the landlord to his tenant. *See* ಎದುರುವಳ್ಳಿ (S. C.).

ಎದುರುನುಡಿ edurunuḍi. The counterpart of a deed (S. C.); —ಕ್ರಯಚೀಟು (-krayačîṭu) a conditional sale-deed (S. C.).

ಎದುರುವಳ್ಳಿ eduruvaḷḷi. A counter-agreement executed by the tenant to the proprietor on the receipt of a gêṇičîṭu (Ch.).

ಏಲಂ êlam. A court-sale, sale by public auction held by an officer.

ಒತ್ತಿ, ಒತ್ತೆ otti, otte. Pledge, security, mortgage; ತೋರ- (tôr-) a mortgage without possession, a hypothecated mortgage (S. M.); ಕಬ್ಜಾ- (kabjâ-) a usufructuary mortgage (S. M.); ಇಳು- (iḷu-) a usufructuary mortgage to be redeemed within a stipulated time, a conditional sale-deed (S. M.).

ಒಪ್ಪಿತ oppita. Signature; 2, admission.

ಒಪ್ಪಿದ oppida. Relating to, forming a part of (S. C.).

ಒಳಸಂಚು oḷasañču. Collusion (S. C.).

ಕಂತು kantu. An instalment (S. C.); 2, stipulation of payment; —ದಸ್ತೇವಜು (-dastêvaju) an instalment-bond (S. C.).

ಕಟ್ಟಡಕ kaṭṭaḍaka. A written agreement (My.).

ಕಟ್ಟಳೆ ಕಂದಾಚಾರ kaṭṭaḷe kandâcâra. *Lit.* The fixed amount payable to the militia, customary ceremonies (S. C.).

ಕಟ್ಟುತ್ತರ kaṭṭuttara. A paper of settlement between the disputants.

ಕಟ್ಟುಕಟ್ಟಳೆ kaṭṭukaṭṭaḷe. Rules and regulations (S. C.); *see* ಅಳಿಯ ಸಂತಾನ.

ಕಡ kaḍa. A debt, loan; ಕಡನಪತ್ರ, ಕಡಬಿ (kaḍanapatra, kaḍabi) a debt-bond, a note of hand.

ಕಪಟ kapaṭa. Collusion (S. M., N. C.).

ಕಬೂಲಾಯತ್ kabûlâyat. The counterpart of a lease given by the tenant to his landlord, a lease (S. M.).

ಕಬೂಲಿ kabûli. Consent, satisfaction; –ಯಾತ್ (-yât) an agreement.

ಕರಾರು karâru. An agreement; a contract (S. C.); ಗೇಮೆ–, ಗೇಗೇ– (gême-, gêgê-) a contract for the performance of some work, a labour-contract (S. C.); ಜಾಮಿನ್– (jâmin-) a security-bond (C.); –ವಾಕ್ (-vâk) an accurate estimate (My.).

ಕರ್ತ karta. A proprietor (My.); ಮೂಲ– (mûla-) an original proprietor, a mûlagâr (My.).

ಕಕ್ಷಿ kakshi. Contention, a party; –ಗಾರ (-gâra) a party, vakil's client (S. C.).

ಕಾರಣ kâraṇa. Right, title; 2, reason, ground.

ಕಾಲಬಣ್ಣಿಗೆ kâlabaṇṇige. A fixed term, a vâyidâ (S. C.).

ಕುದುವು kuduvu. A pawn, pledge.

ಕ್ರಯ kraya. Purchase; –ಗಾರ (-gâra) a purchaser, a buyer (S. C.); *cf.* –ದಾರ (-dâra. My.); –ಚೀಟು, –ಪತ್ರ, –ಸಾಧನ (-cîṭu, -patra, -sâdhana) a deed of sale, a sale-deed; ಅವಧಿ–ಚೀಟು (avadhi—cîṭu) a conditional sale-deed stipulating the time within which to redeem the property (S. C.); ಖಂಡಿತ–ಚೀಟು (khaṇḍita—cîṭu) an absolute sale-deed (S. C.); –ಚೀಟಿನ ಎದುರುನುಡಿ (-cîṭina edurunuḍi) the counterpart of a sale-deed (S. C.).

ಕೃತ kṛita. The improvements effected on property; hence the value of improvements (S. C.).

ಕೈಕಡ kaikaḍa. A temporary loan; otherwise ಕೈಗಡ, ಕೈಸಾಲ, ಮೈಗಡ.

ಕೈಫೇತು kaiphêtu. A plaint (S. C.); *see also* "Criminal"; the written statement of a defendant (S. M.); a deposition (My.).

ಕೈವಶ kaivaśa. Actual possession.

ಖಂಡಪತ್ರ khaṇḍapatra. A deed of settlement; 2, deed of aquittance (S. M.).

ಖಟ್ಲ khaṭla. A suit, a case (N. C.).

ಖರೀದ್‌ಪತ್ರ kharidpatra. A deed of sale, a sale-deed (S. M.).

ಖುಲಾಸಪತ್ರ khulâsapatra. A deed of release (S. C.).

ಗಿರವು, ಗಿರವಿ **giravu, giravi.** A mortgage (Cg., My.); —ಸೊತ್ತು (-sotta) mortgaged or pledged property (Cg., My.).

ಗೇಣಿ **gêṇi.** The rent paid by the tenant to the landlord or owner (S. C.); 2, tenancy (S. C.); *cf.* ಕೇಣಿ (My.). *See* "Land Tenures" *for the varieties of* gêṇis.

ಗೊಂಚುಪತ್ರ **goñćupatra.** A supplemental mortgage-deed (S. C.).

ಜಂಟೆಬದಕು **jaṇṭebadaku.** A joint concern.

ಜಪ್ತಿ **japhti.** A distraint or attachment under the orders of a Court; —ವಾರಾಂಟು (-vârâṇṭu) a warrant for attachment or distraint; —ಹುಕುಂ (-hukum) an order for distraint.

ಜಾಮೀನು **jâminu.** Security, bail; —ದಸ್ತೇವಜು (-dastêvaju) a security-bond (S. C.); ರೊಖ್ಖ— (rokkha-) a bond for the payment of another's debt (My.); ಹಾಜರ್— (hâjar-) a surety for the personal appearance of any one, when required by the Court to attend.

ಜಾರಿ **jâri.** In force; —ಮಾಡು (-mâḍu) to enforce; *see* ಅಮಲ್—.

ಜಿಂದಗಿ, ಜಿಂದಿಗಿ **jindagi, jindigi.** Personal property; ಅಮವಾಲ್—, ಬೇವಾರಿಸ— (amavâl-, bêvârisa-) the property of a person dying intestate or heirless, unclaimed property.

ಜಿಮ್ಮೆ **jimme.** Possession; —ಹಚ್ಚು. —ಮಾಡು (-haćću, -mâḍu) to give in charge of.

ಜೀವನಾಂಶ **jivanâmśa.** Alimony, maintenance (S. C.).

ಠರಾವು **ṭharâvu.** Judgment, decision (S. C.).

ಠಸ್ಸೆ **ṭhasse.** Stamp; —ತೀರ್ವೆ (-tîrve) stamp-duty (S. C.).

ಡಂಗಾ **ḍaṅgâ.** Sitting down at a creditor's door with a determination not to move till the payment of the sum due.

ತಕರೀರು **takariru.** Objection; —ಅರ್ಜಿ (-arji) an appeal (S. M.); 2, a counter-petition (My., C.).

ತನಖಾ **tanakhâ.** An assignment (My.).

ತಪಾಸಣೆ **tapâsaṇi.** Review of a judgment (N. C., S. M.).

ತಮಸೂಕ್ **tamasûk.** A bond, a written agreement (My.).

ತಹ, ತಾಹಾ **taha, tâhâ.** Consent, agreement; —ಬಂದಿ, —ನಾಮೆ (-bandi, -nâme) a written agreement, a karâr.

ತಾಕಟ್ಟು **tâkaṭṭu.** Pledge or pawn; 2, means (S. M.).

ತಾಕು **tâku.** A certain portion of land (My.).

ತೀರ್ಪು **tirpu.** Judgment, decision (S. C.).

ದಂಡನೆ **daṇḍane.** A penalty, fine; —ಶರ್ತ (-śarta) a penalty-clause in a document (S. C.).

ದಕ್ಕು **dakku.** A species of usufructuary mortgage lapsing on the failure to pay the mortgage-amount within the stipulated time (S. M.).

ದತ್ತ **datta.** Adoption; —ಸ್ವೀಕಾರ (-svîkâra) making an adoption.

ದಸ್ತೇವಜು **dastêvaju.** A document, a bond; ಕಂತು— (kantu-) an instalment bond (S. C.); ಕರಾರ— (karâra-) a contract (S. C.); ಮೂಲ— (mûla-) a title-deed (S. C.); ಮೈಸಾಲ— (maisâla-) a simple bond, an I. O. U. (S. C.); ಅದಲಾಬದಲಿ—, ಅದಲ್‌ಬದಲ್— (adalâbadali- adalbadal-) a deed of exchange, generally of lands (S. C.); ಪೋಕಳ್— (pôkaḷ-) *lit.* a hollow document, a document without consideration (S. M.).

ದವಣಿ **davaṇi.** A fixed term of payment; —ಚೀಟು (-čîṭu) an instalment bond.

ದಾವೆ **dâve.** A claim; —ದಾರ (-dâra) a claimant.

ದಿವಾಳಿ **divâḷi.** Insolvency; —ಅರ್ಜಿ (-arji) an insolvency-petition.

ದೀಡಿ **diḍi.** A penalty-clause in a lease or mortgage-deed (N. C.).

ದುರಾಯಿ **durâyi.** Citation, summons.

ದೈವಸ್ಯ **daivasya.** Temple-lands or property, endowments to a temple.

ನಂಬ್ರ **nambra.** A cause, a suit; ದಿವಾಣಿ— (divâṇi-) a civil suit (N. C.); ಫೌಜದಾರಿ— (phaujdâri-) a criminal suit (N. C.); ಮೂಲ— (mûla-) an original suit (S. C.).

ನಗ **naga.** Moveable property; also —ನಾಣ್ಯ (-nâṇya) (Cg.).

ನಿರ್ಧಾರಣಾಂಶ **nirdhâraṇâmśa.** The issues in a suit (S. C.).

ನಿಶೂದಿ, ನಿಶುದ್ಧಿ **niśûdi, niśuddhi.** A bill of acquittance, a release-deed.

ನೋಂದಣಿ **nôndaṇe.** Registration by the Registrar of Assurances (N. C., S. M.).

ಪಂಚಾಯತ **pañčâyata.** *Lit.* Gathering of five, an arbitration, the "panch"; —ಫೈಸಲು (-phaisalu) an award by an arbitration (S. C.); ಆಪಸ್— (âpas-) arbitrators *inter se,* arbitrators selected by the parties themselves in private; also ಆಪಸ್ಪಂಚಹಸ್ಥರು (My.).

ಪತ್ತಿಗೆ **pattige.** Partnership, joint-concern.

ಪರಭಾರೆ **parabhâre.** Assignment, transfer (S. C.).

ಪಕ್ಷ **paksha.** A side, part; —ಗಾರ (-gâra) a party (S. M.).

ಪಾಲು **pâlu.** A share; —ಗಾರ (-gâra) a co-sharer, a co-parcener (S. C.); —ಗಾರಿಕೆ ದಸ್ತೈವಜು (-gârike dastêvaju) an instrument of partnership (S. C.); —ಪಟ್ಟಿ (-paṭṭi) a partition-deed (S. C.); —ನಿಶಾದಿ (-niśâdi) a deed of release under a partition-deed (S. C.).

ಪುದವತ್ **pudavat.** Investment of money made by persons for the up-keep and maintenance of temples or charitable institutions; religious money-endowments (My.).

ಪುನರಾಲೋಚನೆ **punarâlôčane.** Review of a judgment (S. C.).

ಪುನರ್ವಿಚಾರಣೆ **punarvičâraṇe.** Re-trial or re-hearing of a case.

ಪೆಣ್ಣುಮೂಲ **peṇṇumûla.** *Lit.* settlement on, or assignment of property to, a female; succession in the female line, *e.g.* from mother to her daughter. The incidents of Peṇṇumûla seem to be much the same as those of Aḷiyasantâna, except that the former is followed by the Moplas. This may perhaps evidence that the followers of this law of inheritance were Šûdra converts who still adhere to the Aḷiyasantâna law (S. C.).

ಪೈಂಟು **paiṇṭu.** *Anglice* point, the issues in a suit (S. C.).

ಪೋಟ್ಗಿ **pôtgi.** Maintenance (S. M.); —ದಾವೆ (-dâve) a suit for maintenance (S. M.).

ಪ್ರತಿಫಲ **pratiphala.** The consideration for a document or bond; —ಮೊಬಲಗು (-mobalagu) consideration-amount (S. C.).

ಪ್ರಮಾಣ **pramâṇa.** Oath, swearing, affirmation; —ಮಾಡು (-mâḍu) to take oath, to swear (S. C.); —ಮುಚ್ಚಳಿಕೆ (-muččaḷike) an 'oath-paper' (S. C.); —ಪತ್ರ (-patra) an affidavit (S. C.).

ಪ್ರಾಯಸ್ಥ **prâyasta.** An adult, a major, a person who has attained majority (S. C.); ಅ— (a-) a minor (S. C.).

ಫಾರಿಖತ್ತು **phârikhattu.** Dissolution of partnership; 2, divorce; 3, paying off, liquidation; —ಪತ್ರ (-patra) a deed of dissolution of partnership.

ಫೈಸಲು **phaisalu.** Judgment; ರಾಜಿ— (râji-) a râzi-decree.

ಬಜಾವಣಿ **bajâvaṇi.** Execution of a decree (N. C., S. M.); —ದರಖಾಸ್ತು (-darakhâsta) an execution-petition (N. C., S. M.).

ಬದುಕು **baduku.** Property (S. C.); 2, succession by an heir to the property of one following the Aḷiyasantâna law (S. C.); —ಭತ್ತೆ (-bhatte) maintenance (Cg.).

ಬಳವಳಿಪತ್ರ **baḷavaḷipatra.** A deed of dower.

ಬಾಧ್ಯ **bâdhya.** Claim or right to possession; —ಸ್ಥ (-stha) an heir; —ತೆ (-te) a claim.

ಬಾಳು **bâḷu.** Succession by an heir to Aḷiyasantâna property (S. C.): see ಬದುಕು.

ಬೇನಾಮಿ **bênâmi.** *Lit.* without name, fictitious, as a purchase under a false name (C.).

ಭೋಗವಟೆ **bhôgavaṭe.** Occupancy, enjoyment; also ಭೋಗೋಟೆ.

ಭೋಗ್ಯ **bhôgya.** Enjoyment (S. C.); 2, a usufructuary mortgage (My., Cg.); -ದಾರ (-dâra) the owner or occupier of land, the proprietor (S. C.); a usufructuary mortgagee (My., Cg.); ಏಕ– (êka-) undivided possession held only by one.

ಮಕ್ಕಳಸಂತಾನ **makkaḷasantâna.** The ordinary law of inheritance under which sons succeed to the property of the father; used in contradistinction to ಅಳಿಯಸಂತಾನ (S. C.).

ಮಹಾಜರ್ **mahâjar.** A document signed by the chief persons of a village in attestation of the truth of the circumstances mentioned in it; —ದಾರ (-dâra) one signing such a document; *see also* 'Criminal'.

ಮಿಗುತೆ, ಮಿಗ್ತೆ **migute, migte.** *Lit.* Balance, leavings; mesne profits (S. C.).

ಮುಟಮುರ್ದಿ **muṭamurdi.** Unjust seizure (My.).

ಮುದ್ದೆ **mudde.** The issues in a suit (S. M.).

ಮೂಲಗಾರ **mûlagâra.** The original proprietor or holder of a permanent lease obtained from the government, or his assignee (C.).

ಮೇಲ್ **mêl.** A particle denoting superiority, excess, etc.; —ಚೀಟು (-cîṭu) an assignment (S. C.); 2, a deed of transfer; —ಚಿಟ್ಟಾ (-ciṭṭhâ) a temporary lease of rice-land (W.); —ಸಾಧನ (-sâdhana) a conditional mortgage-deed, the pledge being forfeited on failure to pay the amount within the stipulated time; —ಹಕ್ಕು (-hakku) an assignment, and when the word is used in connection with an 'edurunuḍi', the equity of redemption (S. C.); —ವಾಶಿ (-vâśi) *see* 'Revenue'.

ಮೊಖ್ತ್ಯಾರ **mokhtyâra.** An agent; —ನಾಮೆ (-nâme) a power of attorney.

ಯೋಗ್ಯತೆ **yôgyate.** The 'merits' of a case (S. C.).

ರಜಬಂದಿಗೆ, ರಜವಂತಿಗೆ **rajabandige, rajavantige.** A compromise (S. C.); a composition-deed (N. C.).

ರಾಜಿ **râji.** A compromise, an amicable settlement; —ನಾಮೆ (-nâme) a deed of compromise.

ಲಾಗುಲಿಗಾಡು **lâguligâḍu.** Compensation for damages.

ಲಾಗುವಾಡು **lâguvâḍu.** Expenses; improvements effected on an estate, hence the value of improvements.

ಲಾವಣಿ **lâvaṇi.** A lease executed by the landlord to his tenant (S. M.).

ವರ್ಗದಾರ **vargadâra.** A proprietor; *see* ವರ್ಗ *under* 'Revenue' (S. C.); 2, a lease-holder (Nagar Div., My.); 3, a transferee (My.).

ವಾಗ್ದಾನಪತ್ರ **vâgdânapatra.** A promissory note.

ವಾದಿ **vâdi.** A plaintiff; ಎದುರು—, ಪ್ರತಿ— (eduru-, prati-) a defendant.

ವಾಯಿದೆ **vâyide.** A term, an instalment, a term of payment; —ಚೀಟು (-cîṭu) a promissory note.

ವಾರ **vâra.** Rent paid by the tenant to his landlord (My.).

ವಾರಸು, ವಾರಿಸು **vârasu, vârisu.** Heirship; —ದಾರ (-dâra) an heir; —ಅರ್ಜಿ (-arji) an application for a certificate of heirship (S. C.); ಬೇ— (bê-) ownerless, unclaimed.

ವಾರಸಪತ್ರ **vârasapatra.** An assignment.

ವಿಮೆಪತ್ರ **vimepatra.** A policy of insurance.

ವಿವಾದ **vivâda.** Dispute; —ಅಂಶ (-amśa) the points in dispute, issues (S. C.).

ವ್ಯವಸ್ಥಾಪತ್ರ **vyavasthâpatra.** A deed of settlement (S. C.).

ವ್ಯಾಜ್ಯ **vyâjya.** A suit; ಅಕಾರಣ— (akâraṇa-) a groundless suit; —ದ ಹೇತು (-da hêtu) the cause of action (S. C.).

ವ್ಯವಹಾರ **vyavahâra.** A law-suit; ವ್ಯವಹರಣ (vyavaharaṇe) proceedings.

ಶರಾಟದ ಪತ್ರ **śarâṭada patra.** A deed of exchange of lands (N. C.).

ಶಾಯಿದಿ **śâyidi.** An attestor, a witness; —ಹಾಕು (-hâku) to attest; —ಬರೆಯು (-bareyu) to cite (S. C.).

ಶಾಸನ **śâsana.** A deed, an 'instrument'; ಕ್ರಯ— (kraya-) a sale-deed; ಕ್ರಯದಾನ— (krayadâna-) a sham deed of gift which is really a sale (W.); ತಾಂಬ್ರ— (tâmbra-) a deed on copper plate; ದಾನ— (dâna-) a deed of gift (S. C.); ಮರಣ— (maraṇa-) a will (S. C.); ನಿಧಾನ— (nidhâna-) a deed of settlement in the form of a will (S. C.).

ಶ್ರಾಯ **śrâya.** Fit season, proper time (S. C.).

ಸಂದಾಯ **sandâya.** Payment (of a debt), liquidation; —ಮಾಡು (-mâḍu) to pay off, liquidate.

ಸಂಪಾದನೆ **sampâdane.** Gains, earnings; illegal or unauthorized gains; ಸ್ವ— (sva-) self-acquisition.

ಸಂಸೃಷ್ಟ **saṁsṛishṭa.** *Lit.* United or joined, property acquired by a family divided but re-united.

ಸರ್ವಾಧಿ **sarvâdhi.** A word used in sale-deeds or transfers to denote "all". This word is seldom used by itself, it is preceded by alliterative, reiterative or rhyming words to denote the things and objects included in "all". Some obsolete expressions to denote the incidents of, and the liabilities, charges, etc. attached to, the property sold are: ಆಯದಾಯ, ಅಲಫಲ, ನೆಲಹೊಲ, ನೆಕ್ಕಿತುಂಬೆ, ಜಲಪಾಷಾಣ, ನಿಧಿ ನಿಕ್ಷೇಪ, ನೀರ್ಧಾರೆ, ಮಾನಮರ್ಯಾದೆ, ಹಕ್ಕುತೊಕ್ಕು, ತಾಕುತೊಡರು, ಬಿಟ್ಟಿಬೇಗಾರಿ, ವೀಳ್ಯಬೂಳ್ಯ, ಪಾವುಸೈಚಿಲ್, ಊರು ಸಂದಸ್ಪಂತಾ, ವಂತಿಗೆ ವರಾಡ, ಮುಂತಾಗಿ ಸರ್ವಾಧಿ ಆಚಂದ್ರಾರ್ಕ ಪರಿಯಂತರ etc., which can be explained as follows: ಆಯದಾಯ (âyadâya) profit and loss, or income and expenditure, ಅಲಫಲ (alaphala) leaves and fruits, ನೆಲಹೊಲ (nelahola) soil and fields, ನೆಕ್ಕಿತುಂಬೆ (nekkitumbe) the "chaste-tree" and *Phlomis indica* (trees large and small), ಜಲಪಾಷಾಣ (jalapâshâṇa) water and minerals, ನಿಧಿನಿಕ್ಷೇಪ (nidhinikshêpa) treasure and property deposited in land, ನೀರ್ಧಾರೆ (nîrdhâre) water-shed and springs, ಮಾನಮರ್ಯಾದೆ (mânamaryâde) rights and privileges, ಹಕ್ಕುತೊಕ್ಕು (hakkutokku) rights and restrictions [from ತೊಕ್ಕು to trample upon?], ತಾಕುತೊಡರು (tâkutoḍaru) defects [ತಾಕು contact, collision; ತೊಡರು obstruction, impediments], ಬಿಟ್ಟಿಬೇಗಾರಿ (biṭṭibêgâri) compulsory labor, ವೀಳ್ಯಬೂಳ್ಯ (vîlyabûlya) the right of precendence in taking

ವೀಳ್ಯ betel-leaf (or the holy-fig leaf?) and ಬೂಳ್ಯ sandal-paste (used at a demon-worship), ಪಾವುಪೈಚಿಲ್ (pâvupaicil) the subscriptions due to demons, ಊರು ಸಂದಪ್ಪಂತಾ (ûru sandappantâ) according to the local usages, ವಂತಿಗೆ ವರಾಡ (vantigevarâḍa) scot and lot of the village (ವರಾಡ being the subscription from the villagers on public occasions), ಮುಂತಾಗಿ (muntâgi) etc., ಸರ್ವಾಧಿ (sarvâdhi) all, ಆಚಂದ್ರಾರ್ಕ (âcandrârka) as long as the sun and moon endure, ಪರಿಯಂತರ (pariyantara) till, ಆಳಿ (âḷi) having ruled, ಬಾಳಿ (bâḷi) having prospered, ಬಾಹಾದು (bâhâdu) you shall continue (to enjoy). The whole expression thus means: "subject to the payments due, the defects in the land, you shall rule and enjoy for ever etc." The above expression is now abbreviated into 1, ನೆಲ ಹೊಲ ನೀರು ನಿಧಿ ವಸ್ತೈರೆ ಸರ್ವಾಧಿ soil and fields, water and treasure, etc. all; 2, ಕಾಡು ಕೆರೆ ಜಲ ಹೊಲ ಸರ್ವಾಧಿ jungles, tanks, water, soil, etc. all; 3, ಮನೆ ಹಟ್ಟಿ ಕೊಟ್ಟಿಗೆ ವಸ್ತೈರೆ ಸರ್ವಾಧಿ house, cowpen, out-house, wooden things, etc. all (S. C.). A similar expression in use in N. C. is ಬಾಳೆ ಬಳ್ಳಿ, ಹಲಸು ಮಾವು ಕಂಚಿ ನಿಂಬೆ, ವಾಟೆ ಮುರ್ಗಲು, ತೆಂಗು ಶಿಂಗಾರ, ನಟ್ಟು ತೇಜಪೂಜೆ ಮಾನಮರ್ಯಾದೆ, ನಿಧಿನಿಕ್ಷೇಪ, etc. ಅನುಭವಿಸಿ, which means: ಬಾಳೆ ಬಳ್ಳಿ (bâḷe baḷḷi) plantains and creepers, ಹಲಸು ಮಾವು (halasu mâvu) jack and mango trees, ಕಂಚಿ ನಿಂಬೆ (kañci nimbe) limes of different sorts, ವಾಟೆಮುರ್ಗಲು (vâṭemurgilu) mate mangosteen, ತೆಂಗು ಶಿಂಗಾರ (tengu śiṅgâra) cocoa and areca palms, ನಟ್ಟು (naṭṭu) having planted, ತೇಜಪೂಜೆ (tējapûje) the worship of the local deities, etc.; and the whole expression means: "you shall enjoy the land alienated by effecting agricultural improvements, and conforming to the local duties etc." *Cf.* ಅಷ್ಟಭೋಗ.

ಸಾಕಲ್ಯವಾಗಿ **sâkalyavâgi.** In full, entirely (S. C.).

ಸಾಧನ **sâdhana.** A document, a deed, an exhibit.

ಸಾಧನೆ **sâdhane.** Contention, plea (S. C.).

ಸಾಲ **sâla.** Debt; ಕೈ—, ಸುಖ— (kai-, sukha-) a loan without interest, a temporary loan; ಜಂಗಮ— (jaṅgama-) an urgently demanded debt; —ಮೂಲ (-mûla) assets and liabilities (S. C.); ಮೈ— (mai-) a debt not secured by any mortgage (S. C.); —ಸಮ್ಮಂಧ (-sammandha) pecuniary obligation.

ಸಾಕ್ಷಿ **sâkshi.** Evidence; 2, a witness; —ಪಟ್ಟಿ (-paṭṭi) a list of witnesses; ಎದುರು— (eduru-) a defence witness (S. C.); ಗುರ್ತದ— (gurtadu-)

an identifying witness (S. C.); ಸುಳ್ಳು— (suḷḷu-) false evidence, perjury; ಪಟ್ಟೆದಾರ (pattedâra) a witness accompanying the bailiff to point out the defendant against whom a suit is brought, an identifying witness (S. M.).

ಸುಫರ್ದಿ **suphardi.** Possession; 2, possession by delivery.

ಸ್ತ್ರೀಧನ **stridhana.** Jointure, a woman's private property.

ಸ್ಥಿತಿ **sthiti.** Estate, property; ಚರ— (čara-) moveable property (My.).

ಸೊತ್ತು **sottu.** Property; ಚರ—, ಸ್ಥಿರ— (čara-, sthira-) moveable and immoveable property respectively.

ಸ್ವಾಸ್ತಿ **svâsti.** Lands endowed to temples (S. C.).

ಹಕ್ಕು **hakku.** Right; ಮೂಲಿ— (mûli-) the right of a mûlagâr, proprietary right; ವಾರಸಿ— (vârasi-) right of heirship; ಮಾಮೂಲ— (mâmûla-) a prescriptive right, an easement (S. C.); ವಹಿವಾಟದ— (vahivâṭada-) a prescriptive right, an easement (N. C.).

ಹಫ್ತೆ **haphte.** An instalment (S. M.); —ಬಂದಿ, —ಪತ್ರ (-bandi, -patra) an instalment-bond (S. M.).

ಹರಾಜಿ **harâji.** An auction by sale.

ಹವಾಲತೆ **havâlate.** Trust, charge; 2, transfer, change; generally the transfer of a debt from the original debtor to one who becomes responsible for it to the creditor (W.); assignment of a debt (S.C.).

ಹಶಿಗೆ, ಹಸುಗೆ **haśige, hasuge.** A share; —ಪಟ್ಟಿ (-paṭṭi) a partition-deed.

ಹಿಶೆ **hiśe.** A share; —ದಾರ (-dâra) a sharer, a coparcener (S. C.).

ಹೆಣ್ಣುಬಾಳು **heṇṇubâḷu.** A woman's estate.

ಹೊನ್ನಬಡ್ಡಿ **honnabaḍḍi.** The interest on money lent by a temple.

ಹೊಣೆಗಾರಿಕೆಪತ್ರ **hoṇegârikepatra.** An indemnity bond (S. C.).

ಹೊರಸ್ವಸ್ಥಿ **horasvasthi.** The private lands held by a temple as their own property, in contradistinction to assignment of produce or money from lands retained in the possession of the donor (My.).

ಹೊಲದಸರ, ಹೊಲಗಡಿವ್ಯಾಜ್ಯ **holadasara, holagaḍivyâjya.** A field-boundary dispute or suit (W.).

Colors and Dyeing.

ಅದ್ದಣ **addaṇa.** The act of dyeing or dipping.

ಅರಶಿನ **arašina.** Yellow; *also* ಅರಸಿನ.

ಅಳಗ **aḷaga.** A *white* cow or bull having black or red spots (S. C.).

ಅಸ್ಮಾನಿ **asmâni.** Sky-blue, azure.

ಇಂಗಲೀಕ **iṅgalika.** Vermilion.

ಉಬ್ಬೆ **ubbe.** Steaming dirty linen in lye water.

ಊದಾ **ûdâ.** Blue, sky-blue; 2, violet.

ಕಂದು **kandu.** Livid; 2, tawny, brown, chocolate color.

ಕಪ್ಪು **kappu.** Black; ಎಣ್ಣೆ– (eṇṇe-) dark black (S. C.); ಕಾಗೆ– (kâge-) jet-black.

ಕಪಿಲ **kapila.** Tawny; *cf.* ಕಬ್ಲ್ತಿ (kablti) (S. C.).

ಕಪಿಶ **kapiša.** Brown, tawny.

ಕಿರಿಮಂಜಿ **kirimañji.** Vermilion.

ಕುಸುಂಬೆ **kusumbe.** Rouge.

ಕೆಂಚ, ಕೆಂಜ **keñča, keñja.** Bay (S. C.).

ಖಾಕಿ **khâki.** Drab.

ಗಂಜಿ **gañji.** Starch; –ಇಕ್ಕು (-ikku) to starch.

ಗುಲಾಬಿ **gulâbi.** Pink (S. C.).

ಗುಲಾಲಿ **gulâli.** Pink (S. C.).

ಗುಲೆನಾರಿ **gulenâri.** Dark-red.

ಗೆಂದ **genda.** Auburn (S. C.).

ಗೆರಿ, ಗೆರೆ **geri, gere.** Light-gold color.

ಗೋರೋಚನ **gôrôčana.** Tawny.

ಚಲವೆ **čalave.** Bleaching of clothes; –ಮಾಡು (-mâḍu) to bleach.

ಚಿಂಚ **činča.** Roan.

ಜಂಗಾಲ್ **jaṅgâl.** Green.

ಜರ್ದಾಣ್ **jardâṇ** Light-brown, bay.

ಜುಂಜ **juñja.** Brown; ಕಪ್ಪು– (kappu-) dark brown.

ಜೋಗಿ **jôgi.** Yellowish red, orange color; *also* ಕಿತ್ತಳೆ ಬಣ್ಣ.

ದುರಂಗಿ **durangi.** Differently colored on *both* sides, as clothes worn by Hindu ladies (S. C.).

ಧೂಮ್ರ **dhûmra.** Purple.

ನರೆ **nare.** Gray.

ನಾಪರ್ಮಾನಿ **nâparmâni.** Chocolate.

ನೀಲ **nila.** Indigo-blue; ಅಚ್ಚ- (ačča-) ultramarine.

ಪಚ್ಚೆ **pačče.** Green (S. C.).

ಪಾಂಡರ **pâṇḍara.** Pale-yellow.

ಪಾಟಲ **pâṭala.** Pale red.

ಬಟ್ಟ **baṭṭa.** Piebald, as a horse.

ಬಣ್ಣ **baṇṇa.** A color; ಗಚ್ಚಿ-, ನಿಲ್ಲದ- (gačči-, nillada-) a fading color; ಘಟ್ಟಿ- (ghaṭṭi-) a fast-color; ಹೂ- (hû-) a light color; ಜೊತ್ತು- (jottu-) a durable color; ಪಕ್ಕಾ- (pakkâ-) grain-dyeing; ಬೂದಿ- (bûdi-) iron-gray (S. C.); -ಕಟ್ಟು (-kaṭṭu) the fixing of a colour; 2, to tie up the colored border of a cloth, such as is worn by the Hindus, so as to preserve it; -ಹಾಕು (-hâku) to dye.

ಬಿಳಿ, ಸಫೇದು **biḷi, saphêdu.** White.

ಬೂದಿ **bûdi.** Gray, ash-color.

ಮಂಗಳ **mangaḷa.** Spotted, dapple, as an ox (S. C.).

ಮಡಿ **maḍi.** Faint red.

ಮಲ್ಲ **malla.** Blackish white—applied only to bulls or cows (S. C.).

ಮಸಕು **masaku.** Dark, dusky.

ಮೈರೆ **maire.** Tawny—applied to bulls and cows (S. C.).

ರಂಗು **rangu.** A color, a pigment; -ಹಾಕು (-hâku) to color; -ಹಿಡಿ (-hiḍi) color to stand (washing).

ಲಾಖಿ **lâkhi.** Lake, lac dye.

ಹಂಡ, ಹುಂಡ **haṇḍa, huṇḍa.** *See* ಅರಗ (S. C.).

ಹಸುರು **hasuru.** Green.

ಹಳದಿ **haḷadi.** Yellow.

ಹುನಗ **hunaga.** Reddish white—applied to bulls having white spots on a red surface (S. C.).

ಹುರುಮಂಜಿ **hurumanji.** Dark or brown red.

Commercial.

ಅಂಗಡಿ **aṅgaḍi.** A shop, a mart; –ಮಂಡ (-maṇḍa) a shop-stall, counter; –ಮಂಡಿಸಿಕೊಳ್ಳು (-maṇḍisikoḷḷu) to spread out wares for sale.

ಅಡ್ಡಗೆರೆ **aḍḍagere.** An erasure on a coin in consequence of which it is depreciated (S. C.); –ಮುಕ್ಕಾಲು (-mukkâlu) an old quarter-anna piece having the figure of scales on its obverse (S. C.).

ಅಣಿಪಾಡು **aṇipâḍu.** A trade-secret.

ಅಸಲು **asalu.** Principal; –ಬಡ್ಡಿ (-baḍḍi) principal and interest (S. C.).

ಉಂಡಾಳಿತ **uṇḍâḷita.** Buying in lots; *also* ಹುಂಡಾಳಿತ (huṇḍhâḷita).

ಉಚ್ಚಾಪತಿ, ಉದರಿ **uččâpati, udari.** Dealings on credit, buying on tick.

ಉದಿಕಾಸು **udikâsu.** Ready-money.

ಊಚಿ **ûči.** Superior, A-1 (S. C.).

ಎಡೆನಾಣ್ಯ **eḍenâṇya.** Paper-money.

ಕರಗು **karagu.** To sell (My.); –ಪಡಿ (-paḍi) sale (My.).

ಕಸರು **kasaru.** Profit or loss on the exchange of coin, surplus (S. C.).

ಕಸಾಕಶಿ **kasâkaši.** Higgling.

ಕಿಫಾಯಿತು **kiphâyitu.** Profit (S. C.).

ಕುಸರಿ, ಕೊಸರು **kusari, kosaru.** Something into the bargain, an additional quantity given by shop-keepers to buyers.

ಕೇಕ **kêka.** Custom, dealings on credit (S. C.); –ದವ, ಕೇಕಿ (-dava, kêki) a customer (S. C.).

ಖರೀದಿ **kharidi.** Net price; –ಪಟ್ಟಿ (-paṭṭi) an invoice.

ಗಿರಾಕಿ **girâki.** A customer (S. C.); saleable, in request (My.).

ಗೈರ **gaira.** Above par, dear (S. C.).

ಚಂಡಿವಳ **čaṇḍivaḷa.** Hansel; 2, something given to dissolve a bargain.

ಚಿಲುವಾನ **čiluvâna.** The odd or broken money over a round sum, *called* ಚಿಲ್ಲರೆ (S. C.).

ಚಿಲ್ಲರೆ, ಚಿಲ್ರೆ **čillare, čilre.** Change for coin (S. C.); 2, the odd or broken money over a round sum (S. C.).

ಚುಂಗಡಿ **čuṅgaḍi.** Retail (S. C.); 2, change for money (S. C.); 3, interest amount (My., Cg.).

ಚುಕಾಯಿಸು čukâyisu. To settle a price.

ಚೌಕಶಿ čaukaši. Cheapening the price, higgling.

ಜಂತ್ರಿ jaṇtri. A table of interest.

ಜೋಕುಂ jôkum. Risk (S. C.).

ಠೋಕ್ ṭhôk. Cash, ready-money; 2, wholesale.

ಡೌಲು ḍaulu. Appraisement; —ಕಟ್ಟು (-kaṭṭu) to appraise, estimate.

ತಗ್ಗು taggu. Dearness, high price (My.); cheap (S. C.).

ತರಗು taragu. Brokerage; the deduction made from all payments and termed in India, custom (W.).

ಥೇಟಪಟ್ಟಿ thêṭapaṭṭi. An invoice.

ದರ್ಖಾಸ್ತ darkhâsta. A bid (My.); ಚಡ- (čaḍ-) the highest bid (My.).

ದಬಾದುಬಿ dabâdubi. An unfair dealing.

ದರ dara. Price, rate; —ವಾರು (-vâru) detail of prices.

ದಲಾಲ dalâla. A broker; ದಲಾಲಿ (dalâli) brokerage.

ದಿವಾಳಿ divâḷi. Bankruptcy, insolvency (C.).

ದೇಣೆ dêṇe. Lending; ಲೇಣೆ- (lêṇe-) borrowing and lending, money dealings; *also* ಲೇವಾದೇವಿ (S. C.); —ದಾರ (-dâra) a debtor.

ಧಾರಣೆ dhâraṇe. Rates, market price, *also* ಪೇಟೆ- (pêṭe-); ಕಸರು- (kasaru-) below par; ಗೈರು- (gairu-) above par; ಹುಂಡಿ- (huṇḍi-) 'exchange'.

ನಫೆ, ಮುನಾಫೆ naphe, munâphe. Profit, gains.

ನಿಧಿ nidhi. A bank (My.).

ನಿರಖು nirakhu. Fixed price; —ನಾಮೆ (-nâme) price-current of market rates (My.).

ನೀವಿ nivi. Capital, stock.

ನೋಟ nôṭa. Examination of money, assaying, *also* —ಸಲಿಗೆ (-salige). This is ordinarily done by striking the coin aganist the ground, or by testing it by the ring, or by looking for any depreciatory marks, called ಅಡ್ಡಗೆರೆ (in S. C.), or by looking at its wear and tear, or by tossing, termed ಮೀಟು (mîṭu); ದಿವಾ- (divâ-) day-light assaying (My.).

ಪಾರ್ಖಾವಣೆ pârkhâvaṇi. Shroffing; 2, assaying money.

ಪಾಡಿ **pâḍi** *See* ಕಸರು.

ಪೇಚೆ ಮಾಡು **pêče mâḍu.** To endorse a hunḍi.

ಪೋಟಿ **pôṭi.** Out-bidding, competition; *also* ಪೋಟಾ– (pôṭâ-).

ಬಕ್ರಿ ಮಾಡು **bakri mâḍu.** To sell.

ಬಡ್ಡಿ **baḍḍi.** Interest; –ಗಂಟು (-ganṭu) interest and principal; ಮಾರ್– (mâr-) compound interest; –ಗೆ– (-ge-) compound interest (S. C.); ಸರಳ– (saraḷa-) simple interest; ಕಾಯಿದೆ–, ಚಾಲು– (kâyide-, čaulu-) $12\frac{1}{2}$ per cent interest (S. C,); ಚಕ್ರ– (čakra-) compound interest; 2, $6\frac{1}{4}$ per cent interest (S. C.); ಪೈಸೆ– (paise-) $5\frac{5}{7}$ per cent interest (S. C.); ಕಾಯಿಕ– (kâyika-) interest on money paid at stated periods (W.); ಕಾಲಿಕ– (kâlika-) the usual interest on money left to accumulate (W.); ವಾಸ್ತವಿಕ– (vâstavika-) customary or established interest (W.); ಉತಾರ್– (utâr-) interest calculated on payments made by a debtor (S. C.); ಕಾರಿತಾ– (kâritâ-) the rate of interest agreed upon between the parties irrespective of any law or regulation; ಹೊಲಿ (holi) interest in kind (S. C.), *see p.* 19.

ಬೀಮ **bîma.** Insurance; *also* ಬೀಮು, ವಿಮೆ, ಭೀಮಾ; –ಉತ್ರಾಯಿಸು (-utrâyisu) to effect insurance on; –ಪತ್ರ (-patra) a policy of insurance.

ಬುಜ್ರಿಕೆ, ಬುದ್ರಿಕೆ **bujrike, budrike.** *Lit:* Dignity, a person's solvency or worth.

ಬೇಪಾರ, ವ್ಯಾಪಾರ, ಬೇರ **bêpâra, vyâpâra, bêra.** Trade. (In Tulu ಬೇರ is a term to denote the necessaries for a 'chew'—betel, arecanut, tobacco and lime).

ಬೋಣಿ **bôṇi.** Handsel, hansel, the first money a seller receives in the morning; –ಮಾಡು (-mâḍu) to take hansel.

ಭಂಡ, –ವಾಳ **bhaṇḍa, -vâḷa.** The capital of a firm; –ಸಾಲೆ (-sâle) a ware-house (S. C.).

ಮಂಡಿ, ಮಾಂಡ **manḍi, mânḍa.** A shop-stall, 2, a ware-house; –ಪೂಜೆ (-pûje) the pûjâ to a shop-stall performed the day after the Dîpâvaḷi festival (S. C.); –ಗಿರಾಕಿ (-girâki) a wholesale dealer.

ಮದಿಪು **madipu.** Valuàtion, appraisement.

ಮುಂಗಡ **muṅgaḍa.** Earnest money, advance.

ಮುಬಾದಿಲೆ **mubâdile.** A temporary loan.

ಮುರಿಸು **murisu.** To cash, to 'change' a coin (S. C.).

ಮೇಲಾಡು **mêlâḍu.** To out-bid; ಮೇಲಾಟ (mêlâṭa) competition.

ಮೋಸಂ **môsam.** The trading-season; *also* ಮೊಹಸಂ, ಮೊಸಂ, ಮುಸುಂ.

ರಖಂ **rakham.** Wholesale.

ರೊಖ್ಖ **rokhkha.** The change for a coin; cash in hand (S. C.).

ಲೇಣೆ **lêṇe.** Borrowing; —ದಾರ (-dâra) a creditor.

ಲೇವಾದೇವಿ **lêvâdêvi.** Money dealings, transactions.

ಲೈಲಾಮ್ **lailâm.** Sale by public auction (C.).

ವಟ್ಟ **vaṭṭa.** The agio or difference in the exchange of money, premium or discount.

ವಟಾಯಿಸು **vaṭâyisu.** To cash, as a currency note, a bill of exchange.

ವಾರು **vâru.** A bid; —ಕರೆಯು (-kareyu) to cry out a bid, to sell by auction; ಒಂದು— (ondu-) the first bid; ಮೂರು— (mûru-) the highest bid (S. C.).

ವಾರ್ಜಿಕ, ವಾರ್ಜಿಗೆ **vârjika, vârjige.** Higgling, haggling (S. C.).

ವಿಳಾಸ **viḷâsa.** The figures marked on cloth by the Navâyats to indicate its cost price, net price (S. C.).

ಸಂಚಕಾರ **sañcakâra.** Earnest-money.

ಸರಕು **saraku.** Goods, articles, things, ware.

ಸರಾಫ **sarâpha.** A jeweller (S. C.); 2, a banker; 3, a shroff.

ಸಹಾಯ **sahâya.** Profits; 2, cheap.

ಸಾಟೆ **sâṭe.** Barter, truck; 2, a contract to buy; —ಹಣ (-haṇa) contract-money.

ಸಾಲ **sâla.** (*see p.* 58); —ಗಾರ, —ದವ (-gâra, -dava) a creditor; —ಎತ್ತು, —ತೆಗಿ, —ಮಾಡು (-ettu, -tegi, -mâḍu) to borrow, to take a loan; —ಪರಿಹರಿಸು, —ಸಂದಾಯ ಮಾಡು (-pariharisu, -sandâya mâḍu) to clear or pay off a debt; —ವಸೂಲು ಮಾಡು, —ಬರ ಮಾಡು (-vasûlu mâḍu, -bara mâḍu) to recover a debt; —ಮುಳುಗಿಸು (-muḷugisu) to defraud a creditor of his debt.

ಸುತ್ತಿಗೆ **suttige.** A surety or security for the payment of money (S. C.).

ಸೂಟು, ಸೂಟ **sûṭu, sûṭa.** Rebatement.

ಹರಗೆ **harage.** Partnership.

ಹುಂಡಿ **huṇḍi.** A bill of exchange, a huṇḍi. This is either ದರ್ಶನಿ or ಖಡಾ (darśani, khaḍâ) payable at sight, or ಮುದತ್ (mudat) payable within a specified time; both kinds of bills are either ನಾಮಜೋಗ್ (nâmajôg) payable to the drawee, or ಶಾಹಾಜೋಗ್ (śâhâjôg) payable to order (C.).

ಹುದುವು **huduvu.** A partnership, a joint concern.

ಹುಲ್ಲುಕಡ್ಡಿ, ಹುಲ್ಕಡ್ಡಿ **hullukaḍḍi, hulkaḍḍi.** A handful of hay given by the vendor of cattle to the purchaser in token of the ratification of the bargain (S. C.).

Criminal and Police.

ಅಂಕೆ **aṅke.** Restraint, control, authority.

ಅಂಗಶೋಧನೆ **aṅgaśôdhane.** Search of person (S. C.).

ಅಕ್ರಮ **akrama.** Illegal, unlawful; 2, irregularities, illegality (S. C.); –ಕೂಟ (-kûṭa) an unlawful assembly; –ಕೈದು (-kaidu) wrongful confinement; –ತಡೆ (-taḍe) wrongful restraint; –ಸ್ತ್ರೀಸಂಗ (-strîsaṅga) rape.

ಅತಿಕ್ರಮ **atikrama.** Violation, infringement; –ಪ್ರವೇಶ (-pravêśa) criminal trespass.

ಅನುಮಾನ **anumâna.** Suspicion; 2, doubt; –ದ ಫಲ (-da phala) the benefit of doubt (S. C.).

ಅನ್ಯಾಯಾರ್ಜಿತ **anyâyârjita.** Wrongful gain.

ಅಪರಾಧಿ **aparâdhi.** An accused, an offender, a defendant (Cg., My.); ಹಳೆ– (haḷe-) an old offender (S. C.).

ಅಪ್ರಮಾಣಿಕತೆ **apramâṇikate.** Dishonesty.

ಅಬಂದರೆ, ಅಬಂದರ **abandare, abandara.** Irregularities (My.).

ಅಲೆ **ale.** An accused person (contraction of ಮುದ್ದೈಅಲೆ); *also* ಆರೆ (S. C.).

ಆತ್ಮಹತ್ಯ **âtmahatya.** Suicide.

ಆಧಾರ **âdhâra.** Recognizance, bail.

ಆಪಾದನೆ **âpâdane.** Accusation, charge; *also* ಅಪಾದನೆ; –ಪಟ್ಟವ (-paṭṭava) an accused person (S. C.).

ಆರೋಪಿ **ârôpi.** An accused person (S. M., N. C.).

ಆಸಾಮಿ **âsâmi.** An individual, a party; –ಚೋರಿ (-côri) kidnapping (S. C.); –ಹೊರಳಿಕೆ (-horaḷike) false personation; –ಹೊರಳಿಕೆ ದಗೆ (-horaḷike dage) cheating by personation.

ಇರಾದೆ **irâde.** Intention; ಕೆಟ್ಟ– (keṭṭa-) dishonest intention.

ಉಟಾರಣೆ, ಉಠಾರಣೆ **uṭâraṇe, uṭhâraṇe.** Fabrication.

ಉರ್ಡಾಡು **urḍâḍu.** To struggle (S. C.); ಉರ್ಡಾಟ (urḍâṭa) struggle (S. C.).

ಉರುಳು ಹಾಕು **uruḷu hâku.** To hang.

ಎಕರಾರು ಪಡು **ekarâru paḍu.** To confess, admit.

ಒದೆ, ತುಳಿ **ode, tuḷi.** To kick.

ಕಟ್ಟು **kaṭṭu**. To bind or secure; ರಟ್ಟೆ– (raṭṭe-) to bind the arms from behind (S. C.); ಹೆಡಮುಡಿ–, ಹೆಡಮುರಿ– (heḍamuḍi-, heḍamuri-) to pinion.

ಕಡಿ **kaḍi**. To cut, to stab; ಕಡಿದಾಡು (kaḍidâḍu) to fight, to wrestle; –ತ (-ta) a stab, a cut.

ಕತರ್ಚು **katarču**. Contention, strife (My.).

ಕತಬೆ **katabe**. A bail-bond, a recognizance.

ಕನ್ನ **kanna**. Burglary, housebreaking; –ಹೊಡಿಯು (-hoḍiyu) to break into a house.

ಕನ್ನೋಜಿ **kannôji**. *Lit.* Of Canouj; a knave, an artful, deceitful ma (S. C.); 2, a pickpocket (S. C.).

ಕಬೂಲಿ **kabûli**. Confession.

ಕಲಹ **kalaha**. An affray.

ಕಲೆ **kale**. A mark, a scar; ಕನದ–, ಕಂದ– (kanada-, kanda-) a livid mark, ecchymosis (S. C.); ಗೀರಿದ– (gîrida-) a scratch-mark (S. C.).

ಕಸೂರಿ **kasûri**. Negligence, oversight, carelessness (My.).

ಕಳವಿ **kaḷavi**. Counterfeit; –ನಾಣ್ಯ. –ಹಣ (-nâṇya, -haṇa) a counterfeit coin.

ಕಳವು **kaḷavu**. Theft; ಕಟ್ಟದ– (kaṭṭaḍa-) theft in a building (S. C.); ದರೋಡೆ– (darôḍe-) dacoity (S. C.); ಜಬ್ರಿ– (jabri-) robbery (S. M.).

ಕಳ್ಳ **kaḷḷa**. A thief; 2, counterfeit; –ಮುದ್ರೆ (-mudre) a false seal; –ನಾಣ್ಯ (-nâṇya) a counterfeit coin.

ಕಾಣೆಯಾಗು **kâṇeyâgu**. To miss (S. C.).

ಕಾಯಲ್ ಸವಾಲ್ **kâyal savâl**. Questioning the accused point-blank if he is guilty or not (My.).

ಕೆಡಕು **keḍaku**. Mischief.

ಕೆಡಿಸೋಣ **keḍisôṇa**. *Lit.* spoiling; seduction.

ಕೈದಿ **kaidi**. An accused; ಹಳೆ– (haḷe-) an old offender (My., Cg.).

ಕೈದು **kaidu**. Confinement; ಬರಿ– (bari-) simple imprisonment (S. C.); ಕಠಿಣ– (kaṭhiṇa-) rigorous imprisonment; –ಮಾಡು (-mâḍu) to arrest, to apprehend.

ಕೈಫೇತು **kaiphêtu**. The statement of an accused (S.C.).

ಕೊಲೆಪಾತಕ **kolepâtaka**. Culpable homicide not amounting to murder.

ಕೋಳ **kôḷa**. Stocks; ಕೈ– (kai-) hand-cuffs; ಕಾಲ್– (kâl-) stocks.

ಖಬರದಾರ್ **khabaradâr.** Beware! take care! (S. C.).

ಖೂನಿ **khûni.** Murder; –ಗಾರ (-gâra) a murderer.

ಗರ್ಭಸ್ರಾವ **garbhasrâva.** Abortion.

ಗಲ್ಲುಮರ **gallumara.** The gallows, gibbet; ಗಲ್ಲಡಾವ್ (galĉadâv) hanging.

ಗಸ್ತಿ **gasti.** Patrole; –ಬರು (-baru) to patrole.

ಗುನೆ **gune.** An offence; –ಗಾರ (-gâra) a culprit; –ಗಾರಿ (-gâri) a fine.

ಗುಮಾನು **gumânu.** Suspicion; ಗುಮಾನಿ ಮನುಷ್ಯ (gumâni manuśya) a suspicious character, a suspected person.

ಘಾಯ **ghâya.** A wound.

ಚಪಾವ ಮಾಡು **čapâva mâḍu.** To conceal, hide, screen, suppress.

ಚಿತಾವಣಿ **čitâvaṇi.** Instigation (My.).

ಚೋರಿ **čôri.** Theft; 2, robbery (S. C.); ರಹಜನ್– (rahajan-) highway robbery; ಮಶಾಲ್– (maśâl-) torch-light robbery; –ಮಾಲು (-mâlu) stolen property.

ಜಖಂ **jakham.** Injury, hurt (S. C.).

ಜಬರ್ದಸ್ತಿ **jabardasti.** Violence, oppression.

ಜರಬು ಮಾಡು **jarabu mâḍu.** To exercise undue authority.

ಜಾಡಾ ತೆಗಿಯು, ಜಾಡಾ ನೋಡು **jâḍâ tegiyu, jâḍâ nôḍu.** To trace a thief (My.); from ಜಾಡು (jâḍu) a foot-step.

ಜಾಮಿನ್ **jâmin.** Bail, security (S. C.); –ಫಿತ್ವೆ (-phitve) security for good behaviour, or to keep the peace (S. C.).

ಜುರುಮಾನೆ, ಜುಲಮಾನೆ **jurumâne, julamâne.** Fine; –ಫಿತ್ವೆ (-phitve) a sentence of fine.

ಜುಲುಂ **julum.** Violence, oppression; –ಜಾಸ್ತಿ (-jâsti) aggression, violent measures; –ನಡಿಸು (-naḍisu) to assault (S. C.).

ಝುಡ್ತಿ **jhaḍti.** Search; –ಪಟ್ಟಿ (-paṭṭi) a search-list; –ವಾರಾಂಟ (-vârâṇṭ) a search-warrant.

ಟಕಾಯಿಸು **ṭakâyisu.** To cheat or deceive; *also* ಠಕಾಯಿಸು.

ಟಾಪು **ṭâpu.** Transportation (S. C.); ಜನ್ಮ– (janma-) transportation for life (S. C.).

ಠಕ್ಕ **ṭhakka.** A knave, a cheat.

ಠಾಣಾ **ṭhâṇâ.** A Police station.

ಡಕಾಯಿತಿ **ḍakâyiti.** Dacoity.

ತಕ್ಸೀರು **takširu.** A crime, an offence; —ನಾಮೆ (-nâme) the 'charge'.

ತಂಟೆ **tanṭe.** Mischief, row, dispute; —ತಕರಾರು (-takarâru) strife, contest.

ತನಖಿ **tanakhi.** Enquiry; ಸ್ಥಳ— (sthaḷa-) local enquiry; ಮೇಲ್— (mêl-) further enquiry (S. C.); 2, superintendance, bandobast (S. C.).

ತರದೂದು **taradûdu.** Adoption of prompt measures, promptitude (My.).

ತಲಾಶಿ **talâši.** Detection (S. C.); —ಮಾಡು (-mâḍu) to detect, to trace (S. C.).

ತುಫಾನಿ **tuphâni.** False accusation, blame.

ತುರಂಗ **turaṅga.** The jail; —ವಾರಾಂಟು (-vârâṇṭu) a jail-warrant.

ತೊಹಮತು **tohamatu.** False accusation, imputation.

ದಗೆ **dage.** Cheating, fraud.

ದರೋಡೆ **darôḍe.** Robbery (My.); 2, dacoity (S. C.).

ದಸ್ತಗಿರಿ **dastagiri.** Arrest, apprehension.

ದುರ್ಬೋಧನೆ **durbôdhane.** Instigation, abetment.

ದೊಂಬಿ **dombi.** Riot, *also* ಡೊಂಬಿ.

ದೋಚು **dôču.** To plunder.

ಧೋರಣೆ **dhôraṇe.** Negligence (My.); 2, reputation, prestige.

ನಿರ್ಬಂಧನೆ **nirbandhane.** Restraint.

ನೆಂಗಿ **neṅgi** Counterfeit, *also* ಇಂಗಿ; —ನಾಣ್ಯ (-nâṇya) a counterfeit coin.

ನೆಮ್ಮದಿ **nemmadi.** Peace; —ಭಂಗ (-bhaṅga) breach of the peace.

ನೇಣು, ನೇಣಿ **nêṇu, nêṇi.** *Lit.* A noose or rope; —ಹಾಕು (-hâku) to hang (S. C.)

ಪಂಜೆಕಳ್ಳರು **pañjekaḷḷaru.** Torch-light thieves.

ಪತ್ತೆ **patte.** A clue, a trace; —ಸಿಕ್ಕು (-šikku) to find a clue; —ಮಾಡು (-mâḍu) to apprehend, to track out (My.); —ಗಾರ (-gâra) an informer (My.).

ಪರಮಾರ್ಥಿಕತೆ **paramârthikate.** Good faith.

ಪಹರೆ **pahare.** Custody, guard (S. C.); 2, the lock-up (S. C.); ಬಿಚ್ಚುಕತ್ತಿ— (biččukatti-) a guard with drawn swords.

ಪುಸಲಾಯಿಸು **pusalâyisu.** To entice (S. C.).

ಪೈಗಸ್ತಿ **paigasti.** A detective.

ಪ್ರೇರೇಪಣೆ **prêrêpaṇe.** Instigation.

ಫರಾಮೋಶಿ **pharâmôši.** Negligence, oversight (S.C.); 2, accident (S.C.).

ಫರಾರಿ **pharâri.** A run-away; —ಆಗು (-âgu) to abscond.

ಫಾಶಿ **phâši.** Hanging, execution (S. C.); —ಹುಕುಂ (-hukum) a death-warrant.

ಫಿತೂರಿ **phitûri.** A complot, a conspiracy; —ಮಾಡು (-mâḍu) to intrigue; —ಕೊಡು (-koḍu) to instigate.

ಫಿತ್ವೆ **phitve.** Sentence (S. C.); ಟಾಪು— (ṭâpu-) sentence of transportation (S. C.); ಫಾಶಿ— (phâši-) death-sentence (S. C.); ಜಾಮೀನ್— (jâmîn-) a sentence in the shape of security for good behaviour or for keeping the peace (S. C.).

ಫಿರ್ಯಾದಿ **phiryâdi.** A complaint, *also* ಫಿರ್ಯಾದು (S. C.); 2, the complainant (My., Cg.).

ಫೌಜ್‌ದಾರಿ **phauzdâri.** Magisterial, criminal; —ಖಟ್ಲೆ (-khaṭle) a criminal proceeding (N. C.).

ಬಂದಿ **bandi.** Confinement; —ಖಾನೆ (-khâne) a jail (S. C.); —ವಾನ (-vâna) a prisoner (S. C.); ಬಲೋದ್— (balôd-) force, oppression (S. C.); ನಜರ್— (nazar-) *lit.* confinement under sight, a temporary confinement.

ಬಂದೋಬಸ್ತು **bandôbast.** Secure, safe; 2, precaution.

ಬಗೆಯು **bageyu.** To scratch.

ಬಚಾವು **baĉâvu.** Defence; 2, escape (S. C.).

ಬಚ್ಚಾಲ, ಬದ್ಧಚಾಲ **baĉâla, baddhaĉâla.** A known depredator, a 'K. D.', a bad character, a badmâsh.

ಬದನಾಮಿ, ಬದಲಾಮಿ **badanâmi, badalâmi.** A false accusation.

ಬನಾಯಿಸು **banâyisu.** To fabricate; ಬನಾವಣೆ (banâvaṇe) fabrication.

ಬರೆಹಾಕು **barehâku.** To brand.

ಬಾಂದಿತನ **bânditana.** Slavery.

ಬಾಯಿ ಬಿಡಿಸು **bâyi biḍisu.** *Lit.* To cause the mouth to open; to cause the confession of a crime under cajolery or torture (S. C.).

ಬೆದರಿಸು **bedarisu.** To intimidate; —ವಿಕೆ (-vike) intimidation.

ಬೆಲೆಯುಳ್ಳ ಸಾಧನ **beleyuḷḷa sâdhana.** A valuable security.

ಬೇಡಿ **bêḍi.** Fetters; —ಹಾಕು (-hâku) to hand-cuff, or to put in chains.

ಮಖಬಿ **makhabi.** Confidential; —ವರ್ತಮಾನ (-vartamâna) confidential information.

ಮದ್ದತು **maddatu.** Abetment (S. C.); —ಕೊಡು (-koḍu) to abet.

ಮಸಲತು **masalatu.** A conspiracy.

ಮಹಾಜರು **mahâjaru.** An inquest-report.

ಮಾನನಷ್ಟ **mânanashṭa.** Defamation.

ಮಾಫಿ **mâphi.** Pardon (S. C.); —ವಾಗ್ದಾನ (-vâgdâna) a tender of pardon to an accomplice (S. C.); —ಸಾಕ್ಷಿ (-sâkshi) an approver, 'queen's evidence' (S. C.).

ಮಾರಾಮಾರಿ **mârâmâri.** An affray, a riot, fighting (S. C.).

ಮುಚ್ಚಳಿಕೆ **muččaḷike.** A recognizance, a penalty-bond (S. C.).

ಮುದ್ದಯಿ **muddayi.** The complainant (C.); —ಅಲೆ, —ಆಲೆ (-ale, -âle) the accused (C.).

ಮೊಕ್ತೇಸರರು **moktêsararu.** The chief or leading men of a village.

ರುಜು ಮಾಡು **ruju mâḍu.** To prove, to bring home a charge.

ರುಜುವಾತು **rujuvâtu.** Evidence; different varieties of which are: 1, ಕೇಳಿಕೆ—, ಕೇಳಾಕೇಳಿ— (kêḷike-, kêḷâkêḷi-) hearsay evidence (S.C.); 2, ಪರೋಕ್ಷ— (parôksha-) indirect evidence; 3, ಪ್ರತ್ಯಕ್ಷ— (pratyaksha-) direct evidence; 4, ಸಂಗತ್ಯಾನುಸಾರ— (sangatyânusâra-) circumstantial evidence.

ರೊಷ್ಟು ಪಡಿಸು **roshṭu paḍisu.** To annoy.

ರೋಂದು **rôndu.** *Anglice:* rounds, patrolling.

ಲಂಚ **lanča.** Bribe, bribery, unlawful gratification; —ತಿನ್ನು (-tinnu) to receive bribe; —ಖೋರ —ಗುಳಿ (-khôra -guḷi) a habitual receiver of bribes.

ಲಾಭಿಸ್ತು ಮಾಡು **lâbhistu mâḍu.** To bring home a charge.

ಲೂಟಿ **lûṭi.** Plunder, pillage, loot.

ವಿಚಾರಣೆ **vičâraṇe.** Investigation; 2, enquiry; ಸ್ಥಳ— (sthaḷa-) local enquiry (My.).

ವಿಶ್ವಾಸಘಾತಕ **viśvâsaghâtaka.** Breach of trust.

ಶರಗಸ್ತು **šaragastu.** Patrolling.

ಶರಾರತು **šarâratu.** Criminal force, assault, violence.

ಶರೀಕ ಮಾಡು **šarika mâḍu.** To implicate (S. C.).

ಶಾಮಿಲ ಮಾಡು **šâmila mâḍu.** To join, to implicate (My.).

ಸಜಾ **sazâ.** Imprisonment; 2, punishment.

ಸಹಕರಿಸು **sahakarisu.** To abet; ಸಹಕಾರಿ (sahakâri) an abettor.

ಸಾಬೀತು, ಸಾಬೂತು **sâbitu, sâbûtu.** Proved or established, as an offence or a charge.

ಸುಲಿಗೆ **sulige.** Extortion.

ಸೃಷ್ಟನೆ **sṛishṭane.** Forgery.

ಹಂಗಾಂ **haṅgâm.** Violence, assault (My.); ಕಳ್ಳ– (kaḷḷa-) a felonious assault; –ನಡಿಸು (-naḍisu) to assault, to use violence.

ಹಾಜರ್ **hâzar.** Present; –ಜಾಮಿನ್ (-jâmîn) a bail for attendance.

ಹಾನಿ **hâni.** Harm, injury.

ಹಿಂಸೆ **himse.** Hurt; ಸಂಕಟಕರವಾದ– (saṅkaṭakaravâda-) grievous hurt.

ಹಿಸಕು **hisaku.** To squeeze, to press; to throttle.

ಹುಜ್ಜತು ಮಾಡು **hujjatu mâḍu.** To deter; ಹುಜ್ಜತುಗಾರ (hujjatugâra) one who deters an officer from doing his duty.

ಹೇಳಿಕೆ **hêḷike.** A statement, generally of an accused (S. C.).

ಹೊಡೆಯು **hoḍeyu.** To beat; ಪೆಟ್ಟು– (peṭṭu-) to slap; ಗುದ್ದು– (guddu-) to give blows; ಕೊರಡೆ– (koraḍe-) to whip, to lash; ತಲೆ– (tale-) to decapitate, to behead.

Departmental and Official.

ಅಧಿಕಾರ **adhikâra.** Power, authority; ಅಧಿಕಾರಿ (adhikâri) an officer; ಮೇಲಧಿಕಾರಿ (mêladhikâri) a superior officer.

ಅಮಾನತ್ **amânat.** Suspension; —ಮಾಡು (-mâḍu) to place under suspension, suspend (S. C.).

ಆವಕ್ **âvak.** A register of papers received, an 'inward register' (S. C.).

ಉಂಡಿಗೆಚೀಟು **uṇḍigeċiṭu.** A formal written order for the dismissal of a servant for misconduct.

ಉದ್ಯೋಗಸ್ಥ **udyôgasta.** An officer; ಮೇಲ್— (mêl-) a superior officer; ಒಳ—, ಕೀಳ್— (oḷa-, kîḷ-) a subordinate officer, a 'sub.'

ಉಮೇದ್ವಾರ **umêdvâra.** A candidate, a volunteer.

ಉಳುಮೆ **uḷume.** Salary in kind paid to government servants.

ಇಜಾಫೆ **ijâphe.** Increase of pay, promotion (My.).

ಇತ್ತಿಲ್ಲಾ, ಇತ್ತಿಲ್ಲೆ **ittillâ, ittille.** *Lit.* making known, a memorandum from a subordinate officer, as opposed to a ಟಾಕೀದು (tâkîdu) which is an *order* from a superior, and to ಯಾದಿ (yâdi) or ಯಾದಾಸ್ತು (yâdâstu) a memo. between equals.

ಇಸಂ **isam.** *Lit.* an individual, an individual's post, a 'berth' (S.C.).

ಇಸ್ತ್ಯಾರು **istyâru.** A notice, a notification (S. C.); 2, a circular order (My.); *also* —ನಾಮೆ (-nâme).

ಐವಜಿ **aivaji.** A substitute.

ಕಟ್ಟು **kaṭṭu.** The records or proceedings of a suit; *also* ನಂಬರದ— (nambarada-); ಕಟ್ಟಿನ ಷರಾ ಅಮಲ್ (kaṭṭina sharâ amal) the *precis* of a record (My.).

ಕದೀಮ **kadima.** A senior, an old servant; ಕದೀಮಿ (kadîmi) service (S.C.).

ಕಾಯಂ **kâyam.** Permanent; —ಮಾಡು (-mâḍu) to confirm.

ಕಾಯಿದೆ **kâyide.** Laws; —ಕಾನೂನ್ (-kânûn) laws and regulations; —ಶಿರ್ (-śir) formally (My.).

ಕಿರಕುಳ, ಕಿರುಕೊಳ **kirakuḷa, kirukoḷa.** Sundry expenses, expenses for sundries.

ಕುಮ್ಮಕಿ, ಕುಮ್ಕಿ **kummaki, kumki.** An assistant (S. C.).

ಗವಾಹಿ **gavâhi.** A witness (My.).

ಗೋಶ್ವಾರೆ **gôšvâre.** An abstract.

ಚಲ್ಲನ್ **čallan.** A voucher, challan, a memo. sent with things.

ಚಾಲ್ತಿ **čâlti.** Current.

ಜವಾಬು **javâbu.** An answer, a reply.

ಜಲಾಯಿಸು **jalâyisu.** To burn, as old records (S. C.).

ಜಾಗ, ದರ– **jâga, dara-.** 'Camp', a halting place (My.).

ಜಾಬಿತೆ **jâbite.** A schedule.

ಜಾರಿ **jâri.** Execution of the order of a court, as a summons, warrant, etc. (S. C.).

ಜಾವಕ್ **jâvak.** A register of papers despatched, an 'outward register' (S. C.).

ಜಾಹೀರ ಮಾಡು **jâhira mâḍu.** To represent, to 'beg to state'; ಜಾಹೀರ ನಾಮಾ (jâhîranâmâ) a notice or summons; 2, a written statement.

ತಖ್ತೆ **takhte.** A tabular statement.

ತಗೈರು **tagairu.** Dismissal from service.

ತರಬೇತ ಮಾಡು **tarabêta mâḍu.** To train up, as a novice (S. C.).

ತಲಬು **talabu.** Pay, salary; –ಬಟವಾಡೆ (-baṭavâḍe) disbursement of pay.

ತಳ್ಳಿ ಹಾಕು, –ಬಿಡು **taḷḷi hâku, -biḍu.** To dismiss, as a petition (S. C.).

ತಾಕೀದು **tâkidu.** An order to a subordinate officer.

ತೇರ್ಗಡೆ **têrgaḍe.** *Lit.* conclusion, acquittal, successful conclusion; –ಪಡು (-paḍu) to pass an examination (S. C.).

ತೈನಾತಿ **tainâti.** Being supported by one and employed by another; 2, a menial servant placed under an officer (S. C.).

ದಫ್ತರು **daphtaru.** A bundle of papers tied up in a cloth.

ದರ್ಯಾಫ್ತಿ **daryâphti.** A trial; 2, examination of witnesses; ಶಿರ– (sir-) second examination, or examination for a second time (My.).

ದಾಖಲೆ **dâkhale.** An entry; 2, exhibits, documents, etc. filed in a suit: ದಾಖಲು ಮಾಡು (dâkhalu mâḍu) to present, to file (S. C.).

ದೇರಿ **dêri.** Delay (S. C.).

ನಂಬ್ರ **nambra.** Number; 2, a case or a suit (S. C.); ಜಂಜರಾ— (jañjarâ-) serial number (S. C.); ಮೂಲ— (mûla-) an original suit.

ನಾನಾಪರವರ್ಷಿ **nânâparavarshi.** Pension or gratuity.

ನೌಕರ **naukara.** A servant; ನೌಕರಿ (naukari) service (C.).

ಪಗಾರು **pagâru.** Pay, salary (N. C.).

ಪತ್ತುವಳಿ **pattuvaḷi.** The amount of embezzlement chargeable against a public functionary; 2, bribery.

ಪರ್ವಾನಾ **parvânâ.** An order, a firman.

ಪೈವಸ್ತೆ **paivaste.** A year or month before the last (My.); 2, endorsement (S. C.); 3, initials (S. C.).

ಫಡಿಚಾ **phaḍičâ.** Disposal, settlement.

ಫೇರಿಸ್ತು **phêristu.** An index, a list.

ಬರ್ಖಾಸ್ತ **barkhâsta.** The close or breaking up of a court or office.

ಬರ್ತರಫು **bartaraphu.** Suspension or dismissal of a servant.

ಭತ್ತೆ **bhatte.** Allowance, batta.

ಭರಾವಣಿ **bharâvaṇi.** Filling in, as of a tabular form.

ಮಂಗಾಯಿ **mañgâyi.** Allowance, batta (N. C.).

ಮಂಜೂರು ಮಾಡು **mañjûru mâḍu.** To approve, to confirm; ನಾ— (nâ-) to disallow, disapprove.

ಮನ್ನಾ ಮಾಡು **mannâ mâḍu.** To prohibit.

ಮಜಕೂರು **majakûru.** The said, aforesaid; 2, contents.

ಮನವಿ **manavi.** A petition.

ಮರಕುಂ **marakum.** Dated (My.).

ಮಲಫೂಪ್ **malaphûp.** An enclosure (S. C.).

ಮವಖೂಫು, ಮೋಖೂಬು **mavakhûpu, môkhûbu.** Suspension; 2, adjournment or recess, as of a court (S. C.).

ಮರ್ಸೂಲ್ ಮಾಡು **marsûl mâḍu.** To enclose (S. C.).

ಮಾಜಿ, ಮಾಹೀರ್ **mâji, mâhir.** 'Late', old.

ಮಾರೂಜ **mârûza.** Representation (My.).

ಮಿನಾಹಿ, ಮಿನಾಯಿ **minâhi, minâyi.** Abolished (S. C.); 2, discharged, struck off.

ಮೊಕ್ಕಾಂ **mokkâm.** 'Camp', a halting place (S. C.).

ಮೊಕಫರ್ದೆ **mokapharde.** A wrapper (S. C.).

ಮೊಕರೂರಿ **mokarûri.** Appointment, deputation.

ರಜಾ, ರಜೆ **rajâ, raje.** Leave of absence; ಖಾಹಿಲೆ– (kâhile-) sick-leave; –ರಫ್ತ್ (-rapht) absence on leave; ಸ್ವತಂತ್ರ– (svatantra-) privilege leave (S. C.).

ರದ್ದು ಮಾಡು **raddu mâḍu.** To repeal, to annul or cancel; ರದ್ದಿಯಾತಿ (raddiyâti) repealment, cancellation; 2, refutation.

ರಹದಾರಿ **rahadâri.** A permit, a passport; 2, an intimation given by the Revenue officials—a Tahasildar or Deputy Collector—to a village-officer, at the instance of a traveller, for the purpose of providing the traveller with the necessary supplies on payment (S. C.).

ರಾಜಿ **râji.** Resignation (S. C.); –ಕೊಡು (-koḍu) to resign an office or a post (S. C.); –ಸ್ವೀಕರಿಸು, –ಮಂಜೂರು ಮಾಡು (-svîkarisu, -mañjûru mâḍu) to accept a resignation.

ರಿಖಾನೆ **rikhâne.** A column in a 'form'; –ಭರಾಯಿಸು (-bharâyisu) to fill in the columns of a form.

ರುಬಾಕರಿ **rubâkari.** An official memo.

ರುಸುಂ **rusum.** Fees.

ಲಗಾವ್ ಮಾಡು **lagâv mâḍu.** To make applicable to, to apply, as the provisions of law.

ಲಗ್ತ್ ಮಾಡು **lagt mâḍu.** To append, to enclose, to attach to (S. C.).

ಲವಾಜ್ಮೆ **lavâjme.** The establishment of a department drawing pay; 2, records or proceedings.

ಲಾಯಖ್ **lâyakh.** Fit, eligible; ನಾ– (nâ-) unfit, ineligible. ಲಾಯಖಿ (lâyakhi) qualification, merit; ನಾ– (-nâ) disqualification, demerit.

ವಂದರೆ **vandare.** Certain (S. C.).

ವಖೀಲ್ **vakhil.** A vakil, a pleader; ಒಳ– (oḷa-) an unlicensed vakil, a person pleading without license, also termed ಕರಾವತಿ– (?) (karâvati-) (S. C.).

ವಜಾ ಮಾಡು **vajâ mâḍu.** To dismiss, as an application (My.); 2, to cease or put a stop to (My.).

ವಿನಾಯಿತಿ **vinâyiti.** Exemption, as from passing an examination (S. C.).

ವಿಲೆ **vile.** Arrangement, sorting, as records; —ಇಡು (-iḍu) to arrange the papers of a case, to restore any case in its place, to record; ಗೈರ— (gaira-) mislaid; —ವಾರಿ (-vâri) arrangement.

ಶರಾ, ಷರಾ **šarâ, sharâ.** Remarks; —ಅಮಲ್ (-amal) precis (My.); ಕಮ್ಮ— (kammm-) reduction, degradation.

ಶ್ಯಾಪುಸ್ತಕ, ಶಾಹಾ—, ಶಿಯಾ— **šyâpustaka, šâhâ-, šiyâ-.** A day-book of receipts and disbursements of a village or estate (W.); 2, a book in which official correspondence is copied (S. C.).

ಶಿಫಾರಸ **šiphârasa.** Recommendation; —ಕಾಗದ (-kâgada) a letter of recommendation; —ಪತ್ರ (-patra) a testimonial, a certificate; —ಮಾಡು (-mâḍu) to recommend.

ಶಿಲಶಿಲೆ **šilašile.** Order of succession (S. C.).

ಸಂಬಳ **sambaḷa.** Pay, salary; ಕಸರಿ— (kasari-) a feigned salary, a diminished salary from increasing the length of the periods of payment, as 36 days for a month, 10 months for a year (R.); 2, stopping a portion out of the monthly stipend (R.).

ಸವಾಲು **savâlu.** Question; ಅಡ್ಡ— (aḍḍa-) cross-questions (C.); ಫಾಟಿ— (phâṭi-) cross-questions (N. C.); ಮರು— (maru-) re-examination (S. C.); ಕಾಯಲ್— (kâyal-) questioning the accused point-blank if he is guilty or not (My.); —ಜವಾಬು (-javâbu) questions and answers.

ಸಾದರು **sâdaru.** Reached, received;—this word is generally used by a subordinate officer addressing the 'head'.

ಸಾದಿಲ್‌ವಾರ್ ಖರ್ಚು **sâdilvâr kharču.** The sundry expenses of an office, contingencies of an office for stationery etc.; 2, the expenses of a ceremony called ರಸ್ತುಮುಹೂರ್ತ, *see* 'Revenue'.

ಸಾಲ್ **sâl.** A year, *also* ಸಾಲೆ; ಸಾಲಿಯಾನ್ (sâliyân) annual, yearly; —ಅಯಿಂದಾ (-ayindâ) next year; —ಗುಜಸ್ತಾ (-gujastâ) last year; —ಮಜ್ಕೂರ (-majkûra) current year; —ಝಾಡಾ (-jhâḍâ) an annual return (My.); —ಬಸಾಲ್ (-basâl) every year, annually (My.).

ಸಿಬಂದಿ, ಶಿಬ್ಬಂದಿ **sibandi, šibbandi.** An establishment; ಕಾಯಂ— (kâyam-) a permanent establishment; ಹಂಗಾಮಿ— (hangâmi-) a temporary establishment.

ಸುನಾವಣಿ, ಸುಲಾವಣಿ **sunâvaṇi, sulâvaṇi.** The 'hearing' of a case; 2, interpretation (S. C.).

ವರ್ಗ, ವರ್ಗಾವರ್ಗಿ **varga, vargâvargi.** Transfers (S. C.).

ಹಂಗಾಮಿ **haṅgâmi.** Temporary, for the time being; —ಸಿಬ್ಬಂದಿ (-sibbandi) a temporary establishment; —ಚಾಕರಿ (-câkari) a temporary service.

ಹರವಂಚು **haravańcu.** Defalcation, embezzlement.

ಹಾಜರ್, ಹಾಜ್ರ್ **hâzar, hâzr.** Present; ಗೈರ್— (gair-) absent; —ಮಾಡು (-mâḍu) to produce; —ಜವಾಬು (-javâbu) a ready answer, a prompt reply.

ಹಾಜರಿ **hazari.** Presence; —ಪಟ್ಟಿ (-paṭṭi) an attendance roll; —ಸಮ್ಮನ್ (-samman) a summons for attendance.

ಹಾಲಿ **hâli.** At present, now.

ಹುಕುಂ **hukum.** An order; —ಜಾರಿ ಮಾಡು (-jâri mâḍu) to execute the orders of a court; 2, to serve a notice or summons (S. C.).

ಹುದ್ದೆ **hudde.** Rank; —ದಾರ (-dâra) an officer, an office-holder.

A House and Compound.

ಅಂಗಣ **aṅgaṇa.** A yard, a courtyard, *also* ಅಂಗಳ; ರಾಜ– (râja-) a big courtyard in front of a house (s. c.); ತೊಟ್ಟಿ– (toṭṭi-) the open court in the center of a native dwelling.

ಅಂತಃಪುರ **antahpura.** An inner apartment for ladies, a zenana.

ಅಂಬಲ **ambala.** A veranda erected around or near a temple as a resting place for pilgrims.

ಅಟ್ಟ **aṭṭa.** A loft, a false ceiling of boards and planks (s. c.); 2, an upper room serving as a dormitory; 3, a manger for cattle; ಕುತ್ತಟ್ಟ (kuttaṭṭa) an upper loft for storing rice (s. c.); ಮೇಲಟ್ಟ (mêlaṭṭa) upper shelves.

ಅಡಿಗಲ್ಲು **adigallu.** The foundation stone of a building.

ಅಡಿಸ್ಥಳ **aḍisthaḷa.** The site of a building (s. c.).

ಅರಗುಗಲ್ಲು **aragugallu.** A door-step.

ಅಸ್ತಿವಾರ **astivâra.** A ground-plot, a foundation; *also* ಅಸ್ತಿಭಾರ.

ಆವರಣ **âvaraṇa.** A fence, an enclosure, also that round a well (s. c.).

ಉಪ್ಪರಿಗೆ **upparige.** The upper story of a house.

ಕಂಡಿ **kaṇḍi.** A window, a gap, *also* ಗಂಡಿ; ಕಳ್ಳ– (kaḷḷa-) a private door of escape.

ಕಡಗಟ್ಟು, ಕಡೆಗಟ್ಟು **kaḍagaṭṭu, kaḍegaṭṭu.** A balcony (s. c.).

ಕದ **kada.** A door; –ಚಾಟು (-čâṭu) a door-way; –ಪರಿ (-pari) venetians; ಯಲೆ– (yale-) a venetian door (My.); ಸಾದಾ– (sâdâ-) a battened door (My.).

ಕಿಟಕಿ **kiṭaki.** A window (s. c.); for –ಗೂಡು *see* p. 27.

ಕುಂಬೆ **kumbe.** A balustrade (s. c.).

ಕೆಸರ್ಗಲ್ಲು **kesargallu.** The foundation stone (s. c.).

ಕೊಗಳು **kogaḷu.** The ridge of the roof, the pinnacle (s. c.).

ಕೊಟ್ಟಿಗೆ **koṭṭige.** An out-house (s. c.); 2, a veranda.

ಕೊಠಡಿ **koṭhaḍi.** A room.

ಕೊಠಾರ **koṭhâra.** A veranda.

ಕೋಠಿ **kôṭhi.** A godown, a lumber-room.

ಕೋಣೆ **kôṇe.** A room; 2, a kitchen (My.); ಅಡಿಗೆ– (adige-) the kitchen (C.); ಅರೆ (are) a cell, a closet; ಉಗ್ರಾಣ (ugrâṇa) a store-room, a store-house; ದಳಿ– (daḷi-) a room having on one side of it wooden railings instead of a wall, a railed-room (S. C.); ನಿರಪು–, ನೆರಪು– (nirapu-, nerapu-) a room having a frame of boards fitted with planks easily removable (S. C.).

ಕೋಮು **kôma.** 'Quarters', street, *e.g.* ಮಾಪಿಳೆ– (mâpiḷe-) the Mopla quarters (S. C.).

ಗಡಮಂಚಿಕೆ **gaḍamaṅcike.** A stand about a cubit high on which beds etc. are placed.

ಗರೋಡಿ **garôḍi.** A veranda (S. C.).

ಗುಡಿಕಟ್ಟು **guḍikaṭṭu.** A row of buildings (S. C.).

ಗೋಡೆ **gôḍe.** A wall; ಅಡ್ಡ– (aḍḍa-) a partition-wall; ಇಡಿ– (iḍi-) a cross-wall; –ಕುಂಬೆ (-kumbe) the coping of a wall; ಜಿಡ್ಡಿ–, ದಿಡ್ಡಿ– (jiḍḍi-, diḍḍi-) a parapet wall; –ಪಾಯ (-pâya) the foundation of a wall; ತಡಿಗೆ– (taḍige-) a lath and plaster wall; ಹುಡಿ– (huḍi-) a wall built of loose mud (S. C.); ಮುಟ್ಟು– (muṭṭu-) a buttress, *also called* ಆನೆಕಂಭ (ânekambha); ಅಡ್ಡಲೋವೆ, ಪರಟೆ (aḍḍalôve, paraṭe) the tile coping of a wall; ಪಕ್ಕೆ– (pakke-) a wing-wall; ಪೌಳಿ– (pauḷi-) a wall of a compound.

ಚಾವಡಿ **čâvaḍi.** A veranda.

ಛಾವಣಿ **čhâvaṇi.** Repairing a roof, thatching; ಬರ್ಸಾತಿ– (barsât-) monsoon repairs (S. C.); ಹಂಚು– (hanču-) tiled thatching; ಹುಲ್ಲು– (hullu-) grass-thatching (S. C.).

ಜಗತಿ **jagati.** A garden-seat round a tree.

ಜಗಲಿ **jagali.** A pyal, a raised open veranda (S. C.).

ಜನಲು **janalu.** A window (My.); ತಿರಗಣಿ– (tiragaṇi-) a swing-window (My.).

ಜಾಲು **jâlu.** A yard, a compound (S. C.).

ಝೋಪಡಿ **jhôpaḍi.** A hut or shed.

ತಡಮೆ **taḍame.** A stile (S. C.).

ತರವು ಹಾಕು **taravu hâku.** To lay a foundation.

ತಳ, -ಹದಿ **taḷa, -hadi.** The foundation of a building; —ತೋಡು (-tôḍu) to dig a foundation.

ತಿಣೆ **tiṇe.** A raised seat on the veranda of Hindu houses, and used often as a rest for the head (s. c.).

ದಾಗದೂಜಿ **dâgadûji.** Thatch-repairs.

ದಿಡ್ಡಿ **diḍḍi.** A back-door; 2, a wicket-gate, *also* —ಬಾಗಲು (-bâgalu); —ದಾರಿ (-dâri) a bye-road.

ನಡವೆ **naḍave.** The first passage leading from the street to the inner part of a house, *also* ನಡೆ (s. c.); 2, the yard of a house (My.).

ನಾಗವಂದಿಗೆ, ನಾಗೊಂದಿಗೆ **nâgavandige, nâgondige.** A shelf made by placing a plank on two pegs or brackets—called ಮುಜಣ್ಣೈಗಳು—into a wall (s. c.).

ನೆಟ್ಟಳಿಗೆ **neṭṭaḷige.** The ground-floor of a storied house.

ನೆಲವಾಡ **nelavâḍa.** A doorway or opening for a door where there is no door-frame.

ಪಂಚಾಂಗ **pañĉâṅga.** The basement of a building (s. c.).

ಪಡಸಾಲೆ **paḍasâle.** A veranda; a reception-hall.

ಪಡಿಪುರೆ, ಪಡ್ಪುರೆ **paḍipure, paḍpure.** A porter's lodge, a building near a gateway (s. c.).

ಪಣತ **paṇata.** A room for storing paddy in.

ಪತ್ತಾಯಿ **pattâyi.** A wooden box; —ಪೊರೆ (-pore) a building where grain is stored up in a ಪತ್ತಾಯಿ, a granary (s. c.).

ಪಾಯ **pâya.** The foundation of a building.

ಪಾವಟಿಗೆ **pâvaṭige.** A step or stair.

ಪೌಳಿ **pauḷi.** An enclosure, a wall round premises.

ಬಗಾರ **bagâra.** A large hole in a roof for the egress of smoke.

ಬಚ್ಚಲು **baĉĉalu.** A bath-room; —ಕುಣಿ (-kuṇi) the reservoir in a bath-room.

ಬಾಕಿಮಾರು **bâkimâru.** A field in front of a house (s. c.).

ಬಾಗಲು **bâgalu.** *see p.* 31; ಆನೆ—, ತಲ— (âne-, tala-) the front gate or entrance; ಹೆಬ್ಬಾಗಲು (bebbâgalu) the front door of a house; ದಿಡ್ಡಿ—(diḍḍi-), *see* ದಿಡ್ಡಿ; ಹುಸಿ (husi) a doorway.

ಬಾಯಿಕಲ್ಲು, ಬೈಕಲ್ಲು **bâyikallu, baikallu.** A stone at the mouth of a well.

ಬಾಯಿದಂಡೆ, ಬೈದಂಡೆ **bâidaṇḍe, baidaṇḍe.** A beam of wood placed at the mouth of a well to facilitate the drawing of water (S. C.).

ಬಿಡಾರ **biḍâra.** A lodging-house (S. C.).

ಬುನಾದಿ **bunâdi.** The foundation of a building.

ಮಂಕಡಿ **maṅkaḍi.** A wooden pĕg or bracket driven into a wall and on which a plank is placed; *cf.* ನಾಗೊಂದಿಗೆ.

ಮಂಟಮೆ **maṇṭame.** An out-house (S. C.).

ಮದನಕೈ **madanakai.** A bracket (S. C.).

ಮದಲು **madalu.** The coping of a wall (S. C.).

ಮನೆ **mane.** A house; ಕವಳಿಗೆ– (kavaḷige-) a cupolaed house; ಚೌಕಿ– (čauki-) an open square court in the centre of a house; a house having a square court in front of it; ನಡು– (naḍu-) dining room; ಕಿರೆ– (kire-) a closet; ತಖ್ತಪೋಷಿ– (takhtapôshi-) a storied house, or a house with wooden ceiling (S. C.); ಬೋಳು– (bôḷu-) a house without a story, a flat-roofed or terraced house (S. C.); ಪಾರು– (pâru-) a gable-roofed house; ಮಾಳಿಗೆ– (mâḷige-) a storied house; –ಮುಟ್ಟು (-muṭṭu) the furniture and utensils of a house; –ಮಾರು (-mâru) property consisting of buildings.

ಮಹಡಿ **mahaḍi.** The second floor, a story.

ಮಾಳಿಗೆ **mâḷige.** A story; ನೆಲ– (nela-) a cellar; ಬಿಸಲು– (bisalu-) : terraced roof; ಬೆಕ್ಕು– (bekku-) a chimney or flue for the egress of smoke; ಬೋಳು– (bôḷu-) a terrace (S.C.); ಮುಂಡು– (muṇḍu-) a garret; ಒಳ– (oḷa-) a ceiling.

ಮಿದ್ದೆ **midde.** A flat-roofed house, *also* –ಮನೆ.

ಮುಖಮಂಟಪ **mukhamaṇṭapa.** A portico, the front porch of a temple.

ಮೆಟ್ಟು **meṭṭu.** Steps.

ಮೆಟ್ಲು **meṭlu.** A threshold (S. C.).

ಮೆತ್ತು **mettu.** A plastered loft, which an ಅಟ್ಟ is not (S. C.).

ಮೇಲ್ಪುರೆ **mêlpure.** The roof, ceiling and things appertaining thereto

ಮೊಗಟೆ **mogaṭe.** A front veranda, *also* ಮೊಗಸಾಲೆ.

ಲಾಡು **lâḍu.** A block of buildings, a row of buildings (S. C.).

ಲಾಯ **lâya.** A stable, *also* ತಬೇಲಿ (tabêli).

ವಠಾರ **vaṭhâra.** The enclosure of a house, a compound; 2, neighbourhood, vicinity (S. C.).

ವಯ್ಯಾಪುರೆ **vayyâpure.** A temporary shed (S. C.).

ವಸರೆ, ವಸ್ರೆ **vasare, vasre.** A dining hall (S. C.).

ವಸಾರಾ **vasârâ.** A veranda.

ಶಾಲೆ, ಚಾಲು **šâle, čâlu.** A row of buildings.

ಹಟ್ಟಿ **haṭṭi.** A cow-pen; ಗೋದಲಿ, ಚರಣಿ (gôdali, čaraṇi) a manger.

ಹವೇಲಿ **havêli.** A large house or edifice.

ಹೊಸ್ತಲು **hostalu.** A threshold.

ಹೋಗೋಲೆ **hôgôle.** A flue or chimney.

Implements, Instruments, etc.

ಅಗುಳಿ **aguḷi.** A latch; 2, a bolt.

ಅಚ್ಚು **ačču.** A mould; 2, a block; 3, a form; 4, an axle-tree.

ಅಡವು **aḍavu.** The fulcrum of a lever.

ಅಡಿಗಲ್ಲು **aḍigallu.** An anvil; *cf* ಅಡ್ಗಣಿ.

ಅಣಗು **aṇagu.** A ferrule; 2, an iron ring used by goldsmiths.

ಅಡ್ಗಣಿ **aḍgaṇi.** An anvil.

ಅರ **ara.** A file; ಗುಂಡರ (guṇḍara) a round file.

ಅಸಿಗಲ್ಲು **asigallu.** A stone for grinding condiments.

ಆಣಿಕೆ **âṇike.** The fulcrum of a lever.

ಆಲೆ **âle.** A sugar-cane press; —ಕಣೆ (-kaṇe) a roller of the press; —ಆಡಿಸು (-âḍisu) to work a mill; —ಗುಣಿ (-guṇi) a reservoir for the pressed juice.

ಆಸಂಗಿ **âsaṅgi.** An instrument used by goldsmiths to beat out bruises.

ಇಕ್ಕಳ **ikkaḷa.** Tongs, pincers.

ಇಸ್ತ್ರಿ **istri.** A smoothing iron (S. C.).

ಈಳಿಗೆ **iḷige.** A kitchen knife.

ಉದ್ದುಕೊರಡು **uddukoraḍu.** A carpenter's plane; *also* ಉಜ್ಜುಕೊರಡು.

ಉಳಿ **uḷi.** A chisel, an awl, a burin; ಉಗುರು— (uguru-) a gouge; ಕಲ್ಲು— (kallu-) a mason's chisel; ಕೀಸು— (kîsu-) a plane, a jack-plane (S. C.): a chisel for making lines or holes (My.); ತರಣಿ— (taraṇi-) the bit of a drill; ಗಾಡಿ— (gâḍi-) a gouge for making a groove.

ಒನಿಕೆ **onike.** A pestle; 2, a rice-pounder (S. C.).

ಒರಲು **oralu.** A mortar; 2, a rice-pounding mortar (S. C.).

ಕಂಠಾಣಿ **kaṇṭhâṇi.** A cobbler's awl.

ಕಂಬಚ್ಚಿ **kambačči.** A draw-plate; *also* ಕಂಬಿಯಚ್ಚು.

ಕಡ್ಚಿಲ **kaḍčila.** A turning lathe, a lathe (S. C.); *cf.* ಕಡೆಚಲು (My.).

ಕತ್ತಿ **katti.** A knife: 2, a bill-hook (S. C.); 3, a sword; —ಧಾರೆ. —ಬಾಯಿ, —ಮೊರೆ (-dhâre, -bâyi, -more) the edge of a knife; —ಒರೆ (-ore) the sheath of a knife; –ಹಿಡಿ, –ದಸ್ತು (-hiḍi, -dastu) the hilt of a sword or knife; ಅಲಗು (alagu) the blade of a knife; ಅಡ– (aḍa-) a nut-cracker; ಕಶಿ– (kaśi-) a grafting knife; ಕೋಳಿ– (kôḷi-) a cockspur; ತರ– (tara-) a toddy-knife (s. c.); ಮಚ್ಚು– (maččn-) a pruning knife; ಮೆಟ್ಟು– (meṭṭu-) a kitchen knife for mincing vegetables; ಮೇಜ– (mêja-) a table-knife; *also* ಮೇಷಾಕತ್ತಿ (s. c.).

ಕಪಿಲೆ kapile. A water-lift, a 'pecotta'; –ಮೋಕು (-môku) the large rope used in a water-lift; –ಬಾನೆ (-bâne) the bucket; –ಬಾಣಿ (-bâṇi) the head of the channel receiving the contents of the bucket.

ಕರಗಸ, ಗರ್ಗಸ karagasa, gargasa. A saw; ಚಪರಾಸ ಹಾಕು (čaparâsa hâku) to set a saw.

ಕರಣಿ karaṇi. A trowel.

ಕಲ್ಬತ್ತು kalbattu. A stone-mortar.

ಕುದುರು kuduru. A spindle; –ಚೀಲ (-čîla) a spindle-holder.

ಕುಲುಮೆ kulume. A forge, a furnace; –ಸರ (-sara) the wind-hole of a forge.

ಕೈಬಾಜಿ kaibâji. An adze.

ಕೈವಾರ kaivâra. A pair of compasses.

ಕೊಂಡಿ koṇḍi. A buckle; 2, the staple hasp of a padlock.

ಕೊಡತಿ koḍati. A sledge-hammer, a mallet.

ಕೊಡಲಿ koḍali. An axe; –ಕಾವು (-kâvu) the helve of an axe; ಕೈ– (kai-) a hatchet.

ಕೋವೆ kôve. A crucible.

ಖರಾರ್ kharâr. A curry-comb.

ಗಾಣ gâṇa. An oil-mill; ನುಲಿಗೆಯ ಗುಣಿ (nuligeya guṇi) the twisting pin of an oil-mill.

ಗಿರಣಿ, ಗಿರ್ಣಿ giraṇi, girṇi. A spinning mill, generally worked by steam.

ಗುದ್ದಲಿ guddali. A pickaxe; –ಕಾವು (-kâvu) the haft of a pickaxe; –ತೂಬು (-tûbu) the eye of a pickaxe; ಎಲೆ– (ele-) a broad pointed spade; ಕೋಲು– (kôlu-) a narrow pointed spade; ಮೊನೆ– (mone-) a pointed pickaxe; ಬಾಯಿ– (bâyi-) a hoe.

ಗುದ್ದುಕಲ್ಲು guddukallu. A stone used for tapping trees (s. c.).

ಚಂಚ **čańča.** A goldbeater's skin.

ಚಮಟಿಗೆ **čamaṭige.** A sledge-hammer.

ಚಾಣ **čâṇa.** A chisel, a burin; ಮಟ್ಟ– (maṭṭa-) an engraving chisel; ರ್ಯಾಕ– (ryâka-) a beading and carving firmer.

ಚಿಂತಾಲ **čintâla.** Large scales for weighing cotton, &c.

ಚಿಮಟೆ **čimaṭe.** A tweezer, pincers.

ಚಿಲಕ **čilaka.** The hasp of a lock, a door-staple; ಹೆಣ್ಣು– (heṇṇu-) the hasp of a padlock.

ಚೀಪು **čipu.** A bolt (S. C.).

ತಂಡಸ **taṇḍasa.** Tongs; *also* ದಂಡಸ.

ತಕ್ಕಡಿ **takkaḍi.** A pair of scales; –ಕಟ್ಲೆ (-kaṭle) scale-weights; –ಕಾಣಿ (-kâṇi) the unevenness of scales; –ಟಾಣೆ (-ṭâṇe) the evenness of scales; ಬಾರದಾನ್ (bâradân) the difference of weight in the two scales of a balance, suttle weight (S. C.); –ಬಿಲ್ಲೆ (-bille) a scale-pan; ಪೇರು (pêru) the unevenness of scales; ದಾಳ (dâḷa) the counterpoise for any vessel put in the scales.

ತಾಪೆ **tâpe.** A trowel.

ತಿಗಡಿ, ತಿಗಟೆ **tigaḍi, tigaṭe.** A bricklayer's level.

ತಿದಿ **tidi.** Bellows; –ಕೊಳವಿ (-koḷavi) the tewel.

ತಿರುಗಣಿ **tirugaṇi.** A pivot, a hinge or swivel; –ಕೊಳವಿ (-koḷavi) the socket of a swivel.

ತಿರುಗುಳಿ **tiruguḷi.** A carpenter's compasses: a turn-screw; a file to bore cadjan leaves.

ತ್ರಾಸು **trâsu.** A balance; ಗೂಡು (gûḍu) the opening through which the needle of a balance vibrates; ತಟ್ಟುವಾಸ (taṭṭuvâsa) the inequality of a balance, which is remedied by ಕಾಣಿಪೆಚ್ಚು or ಉಳುಪಡಿ (kâṇipeččau, uḷupaḍi) a thing put to even the balance; ಬಟ್ಲು (baṭlu) a scale-pan; ಮುಳ್ಳು (muḷḷu) the cock of a balance; ಕಂಬಿ (kambi) the beam of a balance; ಧಡಾ, ಧಡೆ (dhaḍâ, dhaḍe) an accumulation of weights in a balance (S. C.); ಪಡಿ, ಪಡಿಕಟ್ಟು (paḍi, paḍikaṭṭu) the weights; ಬಸಿ (basi) the centre of a balance.

ತುಪಾಕಿ **tupâki.** A gun; —ಕಟ್ಟಿಗೆ, —ಕುಂದೆ (-kaṭṭige, -kunde) a gun-stock; —ಚಾಪು, —ಕುದುರೆ (-čâpu, -kudure) the cock of a gun; ಚಾಪಿನ ಕೀಲು (čâpina kîlu) the trigger; —ಕಿವಿ (-kivi) the touch-hole; —ಕೀಲು (-kîlu) the lock of a gun; —ತೂಬು (-tûbu) the bore; —ಗಜ (-gaja) the ramrod; —ಜಾವಿಗೆ (-jâvige) the match of a matchlock; —ದಸ್ತು (-dastu) a cartridge box; —ನಳಿಗೆ, —ಕೊಳವಿ (-naḷige, -koḷavi) the barrel of a gun; ಕಿವಿ ಮಾಡು (kivi mâḍu) to prime a gun; ಕಂಚೂಟಿ, ನೋಟ (kañčûṭi, nôṭa) the aim taken when firing a gun; —ಜಡಿಯು (-jaḍiyu) to load a gun (S. C.); —ಹಾರಿಸು, —ಉಡಾಯಿಸು (-hârisu, -uḍâyisu) to fire a gun (S. C.).

ದಮಾಸು **damâsu.** A wooden leveller.

ಪಟಕಾರು **paṭakâru.** Nippers.

ಪಟ್ಟಡೆ **paṭṭaḍe.** An anvil.

ಪಾತಾಳಗರುಡ **pâtâḷagaruḍa.** A drag to catch things under water.

ಪಿಕಾಸು **pikâsu.** A pickaxe.

ಬಡಿಕಲ್ಲು **baḍikallu.** An anvil.

ಬಮ್ಮರಿ **bammari.** A potter's wheel.

ಬರಾಸ್ **barâs.** An instrument for making grooves or rabbets.

ಬಾಚಿ, ಬಾಜಿ **bâči, bâji.** An adze.

ಬಾರಿ **bâri.** A water-lift.

ಬಾಲು **bâlu.** A razor.

ಬಿಲ್ಮುರಿ, ಬಲ್ಮುರಿ **bilmuri, balmuri.** A wrench (S. C.).

ಬಿಲ್ಲೆ **bille.** The nut of a screw.

ಬೀಗ **bîga.** A lock; —ದ ಕೈ (-da kai) a key; ಪೊತ್ತ (potta) the shell of a lock; ಅಣಿಕೀಲು (aṇikîlu) the spring of a secret lock; ನಾಗವಾಸ, ನಾಗೋಸ (nâgavâsa, nâgôsa) the staple; ವತ್ತೆ— (vatte-) a single lock; ಜೋಡು—, ಅಚ್ಚಿನ— (jôḍu-, aččina-) a double lock; ಉಕ್ಕಡ— (ukkaḍa-) a secret-lock; ಕತ್ತರಿ— (kattari-) a cross-lock; ಉಂಗುರದ— (uṅgurada-) a pad-lock.

ಬೀಸುಗಲ್ಲು **bîsugallu.** A hand-mill, a quern.

ಬುರ್ಮ **burma.** A gimlet (S. C.).

ಬೆಸೆಕೋಲು **besekôlu.** A lever.

ಬೈರಿಗೆ **bairige.** An instrument for boring.

ಬೋಂಬು **bômbu.** A fire-engine; 2, a metallic instrument for tapping bales of rice, a rice-tapper (S. C.).

ಮಗ್ಗ **magga.** A loom; –ದ ಕುಂಟೆ (-da kunṭe) the web-beam; ಕುಣಿ (kuṇi) a hole for the weaver to put his feet in; –ದ ಹಲಿಗೆ, ಕುಂಚೆ (-da halige, kuñce) a weaver's lay or batten; ಉಂಕಿ, ಹಾಸು (uṅki, hâsu) the warp; ಹೊಕ್ಕು, ನೆಯಿಗೆ (hokku, neyige) the woof; ಅಕ್ಕಣಿ (akkaṇi) the close adhesion of the warp and the woof in the web of a loom; ಅಚ್ಚಿನ ಗುದಿ (accina gudi) a cord securing the lower side of the lugs in a loom (R.); ಅಡ್ಡಕೋಲು (aḍḍakôlu) a bar to which the rope holding up the warp is secured; ಅಣಿಗೆ (aṇige) the comb or reed in a loom; ಅಣಿಗೆ ಕೆಚ್ಚು (aṇige keccu) to fasten the warp to the reed; ಕೆಚ್ಚಣ ಲಾಳಿ (keccaṇa lâḷi) a weaver's shuttle; ಕೆಚ್ಚು, ಪಡಗು (keccu, paḍagu) the warp of a loom; ಎಕ್ಕು (ekku) to card wool or dress cotton; ಒರಕೋಲು (orakôlu) the extreme warp-beam; ಗಣಿಕೆ (gaṇike) the quill in a shuttle; ದಂಡುಸಲಿಗೆ (daṇḍusalige) the middle stay of a warp; ಬಟ್ಟೆ ಸುತ್ತುವ ಕುಂಟೆ (baṭṭe suttuva kunṭe) a knee-roll or web-beam; ಹಾವಿಗೇ ಪಾದ (hâvigê pâda) the treadle; ಹೊಕ್ಕಳುಗೂಟ (hokkaḷugûṭa) the weaver's shank on the left-hand side.

ಮಟದೋಲು **maṭadôlu.** A screw-driver.

ಮಟ್ಟ **maṭṭa.** A carpenter's square; ಜಲ– (jala-) a water-level; -ಹಲಿಗೆ (-halige) a ruler, a level, *also* ಮಟ್ಲಗೆ.

ಮಸಗಲ್ಲು **masagallu.** A whet-stone; ಮಸದೊಗಲು, ಮಸೆಯುವ ಚರ್ಮ (masadogalu, maseyuva carma) a whetting leather, a strap.

ಮುಡಿನಾಳಿ, ಮೂರ್ನಾಳಿ **muḍinâḷi, mûrnâḷi.** A metallic spike to tap bales of rices etc. when examining the quality (S. C.).

ಮೂಸೆ **mûse.** A crucible.

ಮೊಮ್ಮಟಿ **mommaṭi.** A spade, a mammoty, *also* ಮಮ್ಮುಟಿ.

ಯಾತ **yâta.** A water-lift, a 'pecotta'; –ದ ಕೀಲು (-da kîlu) the lever of a 'pecotta'; ಖಂಬ (khamba) the fulcrum of a water-lift; –ಬಾಣೆ (-bâṇe) the bucket.

ರಾಟೆ, ರಾಟ್ನ **râṭi, râṭna.** A spinning wheel, a windlass.

ರಾವುಕೋಲು **râvukôlu.** A poker.

ವೊಪ್ಪೆಕಡ್ಡಿ **voppekaḍḍi.** A burnisher used by goldsmiths; ವೊಪ್ಪೆಹೊಯಿಗೆ (voppehoyige) burnishing sand.

ಸನ್ನೆಕೋಲು **sannekôlu.** A lever.

ಸಬ್ಬಳ **sabbaḷa.** A crow-bar.

ಸವಣ **savaṇa.** Small pincers.

ಸಾಣೆಕಲ್ಲು **sâṇekaḷḷu.** A whet-stone, a hone; a stone for preparing sandal.

ಸುತ್ತಿ **sutti.** A hammer, *also* -ಗೆ (-ge); ಒಡ್ಡು- (oḍḍu-) a goldsmith's hammer with a round face; ಜುಟ್ಟು- (juṭṭu-) a goldsmith's hammer with a face and claw.

ಸೂಜಿ **sûji.** A needle; ದಬ್ಬಣ (dabbaṇa) a bodkin, a packing needle; ಅಂಗುಸ್ತಾನು (aṅgustânu) a thimble; ಅಸ್ತರು (astaru) lining; ತಿಬ್ಬಿ (tibbi) a hem, a seam (S. C.); ಅಪ್ಪಡೆ (appaḍe) a seam; ಒಳವಸ್ತ್ರ (oḷavastra) lining; ಟಾಕಾ (ṭâkâ) basting or pinning down; ನೂಲು, ದಾರ (nûlu, dâra) a thread; ರಪ್ಪೆ (rappe) darning; ಲಾಡಿ (lâḍi) a tape; ಸಂದು (sandu) a patch (S. C.); ಶಿಸ್ತು (śistu) the cut; ಹೊಲಿಗೆ (holige) a stitch; ಪಟ್ಟೆ (patte) a patch (S. C.); ಅಲ್ಲು (allu) to knit or braid; ಅಲ್ಲಣ (allaṇa) plaiting or knitting; ಕಸೂದಿ (kasûdi) embroidery; ಜಂಟೆ (jaṇṭe) a seam (My.); ಹೆಣಿ (heṇi) to braid or plait.

ಸೈಂಗೋಲು **saiṅgôlu.** A crow-bar (S. C.).

ಹಡಪ **haḍapa.** A barber's dressing case.

ಹದಕಲ್ಲು **hadakallu.** A hone.

ಹಮಾಮದಸ್ತು **hamâmadastu.** A mortar (with pestle).

ಹಿಡಿಕೆ **hiḍike.** A bit-stock.

ಹೆರಮಣೆ **heramaṇe.** A cocoanut grater (S. C.).

Land Tenures.

ಅರ್ಧೇಲಿ **ardhêli.** A leasehold tenure under which half the gross produce goes to the landlord's share, *see* ವಡಿಗೆಗೇಣಿ (N. C.).

ಅಮಾನಿ **amâni.** Lands held directly under the government, as opposed to those rented out.

ಇನಾಮ್ **inâm.** Lands held on favorable terms, such as grants subject to a light assessment. The following are some of the Inâm tenures:—1, ಅರ್ಧಮಾನ್ಯ, ಅರ್ಧಸ್ವಾಸ್ತಿ (ardhamânya, ardhasvâsti) lands assessed at half the usual rate, although the proportion is not strictly maintained, the share of government varying from $\frac{1}{10}$ to $\frac{3}{4}$ (My.); 2, ಉಂಬಳಿ, ಉತ್ತಾರ (umbaḷi, uttâra) *a,* lands held by village servants on condition of services and subject generally to the payment of the jôḍi (*see infra*) (Nagar, My.); *b,* rent-free land given for eminent services; 3, ಕೆರೆಬಂದಿ, ಕೆರೆಕುಳಗ (kerebandi, kerekuḷaga) inâms granted for the annual petty repairs of tanks; these inâms are confined to the present holders on $\frac{1}{2}$ assessment for life, and on their death are being brought under full assessment (My.); 4, ಕೊಡಗಿ (koḍagi) *a,* lands having an invariably fixed rent, not liable to any change on account of the seasons etc., and saleable (Manjarabad); *b,* lands granted for service in connection with the restoration or construction of tanks, or of their maintenance in good order (My.); ರಕ್ತಕೊಡಗಿ (raktakoḍagi) being lands given to the family of a man wounded or killed in a battle (My.); 5, ಜೋಡಿ (jôḍi) a tenure under which a person reclaims a certain portion of waste-land, settles on it, pays a half or a quarter of the gross value of the produce to government; this tenure differs from ಕಾಯಂ ಗುತ್ತಿ (q. v.) in the latter being a *permanent* contract for a government village on the annual payment of a fixed sum (My.); ಜೋಡಿ ಅಗ್ರಹಾರ (jôḍi agrahâra) are villages given to Brâhmins and held on favorable terms; 6, ಪಟ್ಟಗದ್ದೆ (paṭṭagadde) patches of lands held by the ryots of one village in another, not as foreign cultivators but as a part and parcel of their own village; the origin of this tenure may be traced to an exchange of lands or to mutual agreements between cultivators of adjoining villages, to allow those of one to cultivate the wet-lands under the tank of another, constructed by the joint labor of all (My); 7, ದೇವಾದಾಯ, ಧರ್ಮಾದಾಯ (dêvâdâya, dharmâdâya) grants made for the support of charitable or religious institutions; 8, ಬಾವಡಿದಸವಂದ (bâvaḍidasavanda) grants for the digging and up-keep of wells (Kolar, My.); 9, ಭಟ್ಟಮಾನ್ಯ (bhaṭṭamânya) personal grants and endowments of land to Brâhmins irrespective of the rendering of services (My.); 10, ಸರ್ವಮಾನ್ಯ (sarvamânya) lands held free of all demands, such as sâyar, mohatarphâ (My.).

ಕಂದಾಯ kandâya. Lands held in perpetuity on the payment of a fixed *money rent* (My.); ಅರೆ–, ಚತುರ್ಭಾಗ (are-, čaturbhâga) a tenure under which the landlord gets a fourth of the produce, pays only half the assessment, the remainder being discharged by the cultivator who enjoys ¾ as his share of the produce (My.); ಒಳ–, ವಳ– (oḷa-, vaḷa-) a tenure under which the tenant pays a fixed money, a sum that may be equal to, or more than, the assessment, to the landlord (My.).

ಕಟ್ಲೆ kaṭle. Tax, rent; ಚಿಗರ–, ಬ್ಲಹ– (čigara-, blaha-) these tenures, restricted only to the Hassan district, may be explained as follows: Each čigara or blaha (see pp. 12 and 16) is usually held by several ryots under a principal ryot who annually rents the whole village, composed of between 16 to 18 čigaras and becomes responsible to the government for the dues. In case of the death of, or desertion by, a ryot, a proportionate remission is granted by the government and the land given to others (My.).

ಗುತ್ತೆ gutte. A contract, a monopoly, a tenure. Under this head may be placed the various tenures of Mysore, some of which are obsolescent; 1, ಕಾಯಂ– (kâyam-) lands held permanently on a fixed money rent; these consisted of depopulated, waste villages whose revenue was decreasing, and were in consequence granted by the late Maharaja; this tenure obtains largely in the Bangalore Division; 2, ಭೂಮೂಲ–, ಕೊಳ– (bhûmûla-, koḷa-) waste lands let to strangers, under the Vijayanagara dynasty, originally for small sums and for a fixed period, after which they were annexed to the cultivated tracts; 3, ಒಂಟಿ— (vonṭi-) the tenure of a whole village by 2 or 3 individuals who rented it from the government for a settled amount; no remissions were made, the renters being held responsible for the amount; the lands could be sub-let to other ryots, whose death, desertion, or poverty did not affect the liability of the renters; 4, ಪ್ರಜಾ— (prajâ-) under this, the villagers themselves rented the whole village and made up among themselves any dues to government—owing to the death, desertion etc. of a villager; this tenure differs from the last mentioned in the tenure being held by the villagers themselves and in the loss being borne by *all* the villagers; the last two are confined to the Ashtagram Division; 5, ಕುಲಗಾರ— (kula-gâra-) a tenure under which one kulagâr of a village—and during his absence, the Shanbhag (and he was then called ಪಟ್ಟಗಾರ)—rented the whole village, sub-let it to others, who in their turn parcelled out the land to the ryots; the chief kulagâr, as the ostensible renter, was responsible to the government for the rent which was not remitted; in case of death or desertion, the villager's portion was parcelled out among the surviving members.

ಗೇಣಿ gêṇi. Rent, tenure on the payment of rent; 1, ಅರ್ಥಮೂಲ— (arthamûla-) a permanent lease obtained on payment to the landlord of a consideration-amount, called ಅರ್ಥ (S. C.); 2, ಅಳವಿ— (aḷavi-) a progressive rental for improvement of land; rent commencing at a low rate and increasing year by year with the increasing amount of cultivation or produce, till the maximum is obtained; 3, ಕಾಯಂ— (kâyam-) a perpetual tenancy on the payment of a fixed invariable rent (C.); 4, ಕ್ರಯ— (kraya-) purchase of the property and rights of an original proprietor (W.); 5, ಕ್ರಯಮೂಲ— (krayamûla-) tenure of permanent occupancy obtained originally by purchase, at a sale or otherwise (C.); 6, ಚಾಲ— (čâla-) tenancy at will, tenancy from year to year (C.); is the word derived from Sanskrit ಚಲ (to move, hence movable), or from Hindustani ಸಾಲ್ (a year, hence annual)? 7, ನಡಿ

ಗೆ— (naḍige-) a tenure applicable to garden lands and prevalent only in Honavar and Kumta; the occupant bears the expenses of planting the trees, the tenant bearing those of rearing them; the landlord, as in ಸುಳ್ಳಿ (q. v.), pays the assessment; the lease is terminable at the will of the tenant, but he cannot be ousted by the over-holder unless it is proved that the property has suffered neglect; the tenure is declining as it gives rise to numerous disputes (N. C.); 8, ನಿಗದಿ— (nigadi-) a perpetual lease, the same as ಮೂಲಗೇಣಿ (S. C.); 9, ಪಾಲು— (pâlu-) a tenancy for a fixed term under which an equal division of the crop is made between the proprietor and the cultivator or the lessee; in some parts of Honavar (N. C.) the occupant provides the seed, sometimes the oxen and the tools, and after deducting the seed with some interest on the loan, the remainder is divided according to the original agreement; 10, ಫಲ— (phala-) a lease for the produce of areca plantations in an estate (My.); 11, ಮೂಲ— (mûla-) a permanent tenancy, a perpetual lease; under this the owner virtually parts with the property on the condition of receiving a fixed invariable annual rent, generally payable on the 30th Bahuḷa of Phâlguṇa; the tenure is alienable notwithstanding the penal clauses generally inserted in the leases; there were two varieties of mûlagêṇi; *a*, ನಾಯರಮೂಲ— (nâyaramûla-) the derivation of the word ನಾಯರ, like the following word ಮೂಲ, is a matter of controversy; some would derive it from ನಾಯರ, or the Nairs, who are said to have been in South Canara prior to their expulsion by the Pâṇḍyan princes in 1252 A.D., and the expression to mean "tenure under the Nair landlords"; while others would have it from ನಾಯರು a plough, (see p. 13) and the expression to meaṇ "agricultural services including the right to use a plough", thus making the tenure correspond in some degree to the tenure known as 'socage tenure'; despite the ingenious derivations, this tenure seems to have been more secure and ancient than *b,* ಶುದ್ಧಮೂಲ— (śuddhamûla-) which means a purely permanent lease (S. C.); 12, ವಾಯಿದೆ— (vâyide-) čâlagêṇi for a specified period, a tenancy at will to terminate after a stipulated number of years (S. C.); 13, ಸ್ಥಳ— (sthala-) rent for the mere site of a building over which the owner has no right, but which may be bought by the landlord after expiry of the lease or on the tenant giving up the building; site-rent (S. C.).

ಗೊಂಚಿಪಟ್ಟ goñčipaṭṭa. A lease of lands held jointly by several co-occupants; *see* ಗೊಂಚಿ (p. 12) (My.).

ಚಿಗರವಂತಿಗೆ čigaravantige. A tenure by shares, in which the whole village is parcelled out in lots of equal value, each containing a proportion of wet, dry and garden land (My.); *see* ಚಿಗರಗಟ್ಟ p. 92.

ಜಮ್ಮಾ jammâ. The feudal tenure of Coorg; the holders pay an assessment of Rs. 5 per 100 bhaṭṭies (q. v.) and are liable to be called out for military or police duties, when called upon. Jamma lands cannot in any way be alienated by the holders, except by resignation.

ನಟ್ಟಿಕೃತ naṭṭikṛita. A temporary tenure under which tenants or usufructuary mortgagees agree to plant cocoanut or arecanut palms on the lands in their possession, rear the plants, and when about to bear re-lease the trees to themselves, after obtaining from the landlord a sum for the improvments effected—*cf.* kuḷi-kâṇam of Malabar—or a set-off in the annual rent; the amount to be paid or set-off varies on the proximity or otherwise of water to the trees—a cocoanut palm fetching as much as 1 to 4 Rupees, and an areca palm from 8 Annas to Re. 1 (S. C.).

ನಟ್ಟಿಮೂಲ naṭṭimûla. A permanent tenure under which the holder can plant trees and enjoy the property as he pleases; a different name for mûlagêṇi (S. C.).

ನಾಲ್ಗೋರು nâlgôru. Untilled land let to farmers on condition of the payment of one part of the produce, the three others being for the farmers themselves (My.).

ಪಣ್ಯ paṇya. Lands formerly held by the Rajas and now leased out on the condition of their being surrendered when government makes a demand; crown-lands (Cg.).

ಮುಕ್ಕುಪ್ಪೆ **mukkuppe.** *Lit.* Three heaps; a tenure under which two-thirds of the produce go to the cultivator, (a third for labor, a third for seeds and implements), and the remainder to the landlord (as rent for the ground) who pays the assessment (My.).

ವಾರಂ **vâram.** A tenure under which an equal division of the produce is made between the landlord and the tenant, the former paying the assessment to the government, (*see* ಬಟಾಯಿ, p. 15) (My., Cg.); this tenure is better than ಕಂದಾಯ or ಕಾಯಂ ಗುತ್ತೆ, because of the payment being dependent on the *actual* produce.

ಶ್ರಯ **śraya.** A tenure on progressive rental; in this waste lands are granted originally at a *nominal* assessment, the full assessment being charged when the waste land is brought to a good condition.

ಸಾಗು **sâgu.** The ordinary tenure of lands in Coorg; the assessment is higher than that of Jamma lands—quite the double—; Jamma lands when alienated or when passed into the hands of unprivileged classes (for Jamma lands are held only by the privileged classes), become liable to assessment at Sâgu rates; unlike Jamma lands, Sâgu lands can be alienated, by absolute sale or mortgage, subject to the right of pre-emption by the ryot who has held any portion of the farm for the longest period; the tenants are not bound to render feudal service, and can claim remission of assessment when unable to cultivate any portion of their vargs (Cg.).

ಸಾಗುಚೀಟು **sâgučiṭu.** A lease for a stipulated time conditioning relinquishment at the end of it.

ಸುಲ್ಗಿ **sulgi.** A tenure under which full-grown trees are made over to a tenant who receives a third of the produce for his labor (N.C.).

ಹೊಲಕುಲ **holakula.** A tenure of Nanjarajpatna in which 3 or 4 families unite together to cultivate pieces of dry-land, each ryot contributing his share of labor and agricultural stock according to his means and receiving a corresponding proportion of the farm produce, the manager being responsible for the assessment (Cg.).

ಹೊಲೆಯ **holeya.** A Pariah. Under this head come the predial slaves—*glebæ ascriptus*—who till recently formed part and parcel of a holding. The ಮೂಲಿಹೊಲೆಯರು (mûliholeyaru) of South-Canara, the ಜಮೆದಾಳು (jamedâḷu) of Coorg, the ಮಣ್ಣಾಳು (maṇṇâḷu) of the Malnad (My.), were slaves who could be transferred with the land itself. Certain limits, ಮೆಟ್ಟು (meṭṭu), were fixed beyond which they could not go. ಹೊನ್ನಾಳು (honnâḷu) of the Malnad was a slave who could be transferred at will.

Letters and Penmanship.

ಅಂಕವಾತು **aṅkavâtu.** Cipher writing.

ಅಡಿವತ್ತಳಿ **aḍivattaḷi.** (ಅಡಿ + ಪತ್ರಿಕೆ) A writing pad (S. C.).

ಅಸಲ್ **asal.** An original.

ಉತ್ರಾಯಿಸು **utrâyisu.** To copy out an original, *e. g.* ನಕಲು– (nakalu-) to make a copy of the original (S. C.).

ಒಕ್ಕಣೆ, ವಕ್ಕಣೆ **okkaṇe, vakkaṇe.** The heading or address of a letter; 2, style or composition (S. C.); ಚಮತ್ಕಾರದ– (ċamatkârada-) a subtle or ambiguous style.

ಒಪ್ಪ **oppu.** Signature; –ಹಾಕು (-hâku) to sign.

ಕಲಂ **kalam.** A pen; 2, a paragraph; –ದಾನಿ (-dâni) an inkstand; ತಾಜಾ– (tâjâ-) *lit.* a new para, a post-script; ಹಾಸಲ್– (hâsal-) writing to the point.

ಕಾಗದ **kâgada.** A letter; 2, a paper; ಬಾಶಿ– (bâsi-) a plain paper, as opposed to ಠಸೆ– (ṭhase-) a stamp-paper; ಖರಡು– (kharaḍu-) waste-paper; –ಪತ್ರ (-patra) correspondence.

ಕಿತ್ತೆ **kitte.** Leaves, pages (S. C.).

ಕೈ **kai.** Hand; –ಬರಹ, –ಅಕ್ಷರ (-baraha, -akshara) hand-writing; ತಿದ್ದಿದ– (tiddida-) a settled hand; –ತಪ್ಪು (-tappu) a slip of the pen.

ಕೈವಾಡ **kaivâḍa.** *Lit.* Handicraft, penmanship (S. C.).

ಗೀಚು **giču.** To scribble; 2, to scratch out, erase.

ಗುರ್ತು **gurtu.** A mark, generally put by illiterate people instead of, and serving for, a signature; different varieties of which are 1, one or more straight lines called ಗೆರೆ (gere); 2, a cross, used by the Christians; 3, ಶ್ರೀಕಾರ (srîkâra) only used by Hindus that can do so; 4, a circle called ಬಳೆ (baḷe), used by Mahomedan females, and 5, a dagger ಕಠಾರಿ (kaṭhâri) used by Mahomedan males (S. C.).

ಗೋಂದು **gôndu.** Gum; –ದಾನಿ (-dâni) a gum-pot.

ಚಿತ್ತು, ಚಿತ್ತ **ċittu, ċitta.** A blot, an erasure; a correction of a letter, word or sentence; –ನಕಲು (-nakalu) a rough copy, a draft; –ಶರಾ (-śarâ) a note of errors, an erratum (S. C.).

ಟಾಂಕು, ಟಾಕು **ṭâṅku, ṭâku.** The nib of a pen; —ಹೊಡಿಯು (-hoḍiyu) to nib a pen.

ಡಜೆ ಹೊಡಿಯು **ḍaje hoḍiyu.** To score out a word (S. C.).

ತಹಲ್ **tahal.** Up to date; *correctly* ತಾಹಾಲ್ (My.).

ದಸ್ಕತು **daskatu.** Signature; ಗೆರೆ— (gere-) signature by marks, *see* ಗುರುತು p. 98.

ನಕಲು **nakalu.** A copy; ಯಥಾ— (yathâ-) a true copy; ಮಂಜೂರ— (manzûra-) a certified copy; ಸಹಿ— (sahi-) a facsimile.

ಪಂಗ್ತಿ **paṅgti.** A line; ಕುಂಟ— (kunṭa-) an interlineation (S. C.); ಮೇಲ್— (mêl-) the first line in a copy book, the "head-line" (S. C.).

ಪತ್ರ **patra.** A letter; —ವ್ಯವಹಾರ (-vyavahâra) correspondence; *also* ಲೇಖನ—.

ಪಾನು **pânu.** A page, leaf.

ಪುಟ **puṭa.** A page; ಗರು— (garu-) the first or rough side of a cadjan, easy to write on, as opposed to ನಯ—, ಮರು— (naya-, maru-) the smooth or the other side and difficult to write on (S. C.).

ಪುಸ್ತಿ **pusti.** A portfolio (S. C.).

ಪೂರ್ವಣಿ **pûrvaṇi.** A page, generally after the first (S. C.); 2, a supplement.

ಪ್ರತಿ **prati.** A copy; ತಾಜಾ— (tâzâ-) a fair copy; ಯಥಾ— (yathâ-) a true copy; ನೋಣ— (noṇa-) a word-for-word copy, a copy made without any judgment regarding clerical errors (S. C.).

ಬಕ್ಕಲಂ **bakkalam.** Written by (My.).

ಬರವಣಿಗೆ **baravaṇige.** Mode of writing; 2, style, composition (S. C.).

ಬರಹ **baraha.** Hand-writing, writing. Different materials used for writing are:—1, ಕಡತ (kaḍata) cloth thickened with charcoal and gum; 2, ಕಾಗದ (kâgada) paper; 3, ವಾಲೆ, ವೋಲೆ (vâle, vôle) cadjan leaf; 4, ಹಲಿಗೆ (halige) a piece of plank smeared with white glutinous clay; ಜೇಡಿ— used even now by Mopla boys; 5, ಹೊಯಿಗೆ (hoyige) sand, thrown in thin layers on the ground whereon beginners are made to scribble with their fingers. The instruments used are:— 1, ಕಂಠ (kanṭha) or ಮುಳ್ಳು (muḷḷu) an iron style for writing on cadjan leaves; 2, ಲೇಖನಿ

(lêkhaṇi) a pen made of either a goose quill or the Chinese bamboo or the galuka reed (*Saccharum fuscum*, Roxb.); 3, ಬಳಪ (baḷapa) a pot-stone pencil to write on kaḍata. Different kinds of writing are: 1, ತಿದ್ದಿದ– (tiddida-) a settled hand; 2, ತಿದ್ದದ– (tiddada-) a scrawling hand; 3, ನೀಟ– (nîṭa-) a straight hand; 4, ಮೋಡಿ– (môḍi-) a running hand; 5, ಸುರ್ಟಿ– (surṭi-) a round hand; 6, ಮೊರಡುಕರಡು– (moraḍu-karaḍu) a coarse and blotted writing; 7, ವಾರೆ– (vâre-) leaning towards the right or left; 8, ಖತ್ತಿನ– (khattina-) a writing in which the letters run into one another; 9, ಗೊಡಸು– (goḍasu-) an illegible hand; ವತ್ತಿ ಬರೆಯು (vatti bareyu) to press the pen in writing, to write heavily (S. C.).

ಮತಲಬು, ಮತ್ಲಬು **matalabu, matlabu.** The contents or purport of a letter or document.

ಮಶಿ **maśi.** Ink; –ಬುರುಡೆ (-buruḍe) an inkpot.

ಮಸೂದೆ **masûde.** A draft.

ಮುಖಾಬಿಲೆ, ಮೊಖಾಬಿಲೆ **mukhâbile, mokhâbile.** Collation, comparison.

ಯಾದಿ, ಯಾದಾಸ್ತು **yâdi, yâdâstu.** A memorandum.

ರವಾನೆ **ravâne.** Despatch; ಮುದ್ದಾಮ್– (muddâm-) despatch by express or one's messenger (S. C.).

ರುಜು **ruju.** A signature; –ಹಾಕು (-hâku) to sign.

ರೇತಿ **rêti.** Sand employed to dry writing.

ರೋಖ, ರೋಖಾ **rôkha, rôkhâ.** A note, a chit, a memo.

ಲಕೋಟೆ, ಲಿಫಾಪೆ **lakôṭe, liphâpe.** An envelope, a cover (S. C.).

ಲೇಖನ **lêkhana.** A writing, a letter; –ಪದ್ಧತಿ (-paddhati) forms of letter-writing.

ಶಾಯಿ **śâyi.** Ink; –ದಾನಿ, –ದೌತಿ (-dâni, -dauti) an inkstand.

ಶಿಕಸ್ತು **śikastu.** Doubling or folding a paper before writing on it; ಫರದು (pharadu) ¼ part of a sheet; ಬಂದು, ಕಡಾಬಂದು (bandu, kaḍâbandu) ⅛ of a sheet lengthwise, when folded into octavo size (S. C.).

ಸಫೆ **saphe.** A page.

ಸಹಿ **sahi.** A signature; –ನಕಲು (-nakalu) a facsimile, a true copy.

ಹಂಸಪಾದ **haṁsapâda.** A caret mark.

ಹರಿ, ಹಲ **hari, hala.** A page of ಕಡತ (S. C.).

Medical and Veterinary

(Note Veterinary words are marked V

ಅಂಗಳಾಂತಿರೋಗ **añgaḷantiroga.** Inflammation of the lungs (V.).

ಅಂಟುರೋಗ **aṇṭurôga.** A contagious disease.

ಅಂಡವ್ಯಾಧಿ **aṇḍavyâdhi.** Hernia; 2, hydrocele.

ಅಂತರಾಯಾಮ **antarâyâma.** Chorea, St. Vitus's dance.

ಅಗ್ನಿ **agni.** Fire; –ಬಲ (-bala) digestive power; –ಮಾಂದ್ಯ (-mândya) want of digestion, dyspepsia; –ಸರ್ಪ (-sarpa) erysipelas (S. C.).

ಅಗ್ರ **agra.** A sore mouth, aphthæ, thrush; ಗಂಟ್ಲ– (gaṇṭla-) quinsy.

ಅಜೀರ್ಣ **ajirṇa.** Indigestion; ಅಜೀರ್ಣಾಂಶ (ajîrṇâṁśa) water-brash, pyrosis.

ಅತಿಸಾರ **atisâra.** Diarrhœa; ರಕ್ತ– (rakta-) dysentery, bloody-flux.

ಅಪಸ್ಮಾರ **apasmâra.** Epilepsy.

ಅರಸಿನಮುಂಡಿಗೆ **arasinamuṇḍige.** Jaundice.

ಅರ್ಬುದರೋಗ **arbudarôga.** Cancer.

ಅಶ್ಮರಿ **aśmari.** Stone in the bladder..

ಆಂದ್ರವೃದ್ಧಿ **ândravṛiddhi.** Hernia; ಜೇರ್ಕಟ್ಟಿಗೆ (jêrkaṭṭige) a truss for 'rupture' (R.).

ಆಕಳೇರು **âkaḷêru.** The biliary concretions.

ಆನೆಕಾಲು **ânekâlu.** Elephantiasis.

ಆನೆಗೊಬ್ಬರ **ânegobbara.** Scarlatina.

ಆಮಶಂಕೆ **âmaśaṅke.** Dysentery.

ಆಮ್ಲಪೈತ್ಯ **âmlapaitya.** Acidity of the stomach.

ಆಸನ **âsana.** The rectum, the anus; –ಕುರು, –ಬಾವು (-kuru, -bâvu) anal fistula; –ರೋಗ (-rôga) prolapsus of the anus.

ಆಸ್ಯಪಾಕ **âsyapâka.** Ulceration of the mouth.

ಇಂದ್ರಿಯ **indriya.** Semen; –ಸ್ಖಲನ, ಸ್ವಪ್ನೇಂದ್ರಿಯ (-skhalana, svapnêndriya) spermatorrhœa.

ಉಗುರುಸುತ್ತು ugurusuttu. Whitlow, gatherings under the nail.

ಉಗುಳುರೋಗ **uguḷurôga.** Salivation.

ಉತಾರು **utâru.** An antidote (S. C.).

ಉದರ **udara.** The stomach; ಜಲೋದರ (jalôdara) dropsy; ಮಹೋದರ (mahôdara) ascites; ಪ್ಲೀಹೋದರ (plîhôdara) enlargement of the spleen; ವಾತೋದರ (vâtôdara) tympanites, tympany.

ಉಬ್ಬರ **ubbara.** Tympanites, distention of the stomach: 2, hove, blown (V.).

ಉಬ್ಬಸ **ubbasa.** Asthma.

ಉರಿ **uri.** Inflammation, scalding sensation; —ಕಣ್ಣು (-kaṇṇu) opthalmia; —ಮೂತ್ರ (-mûtra) scalding urine; ಕಂಠ— (kaṇṭha-) inflammation of the throat; ಎದೆ— (ede-) heartburn; —ಶೀತ (-śîta) influenza

ಉಸುರು **usuru.** Breathing; —ಶಿಕ್ಕು (-śikku) difficult breathing: ನಿಟ್ಟು— (niṭṭu-) panting, sighing.

ಉಳುಕು, ವಳಕು **uḷuku, vaḷaku.** A sprain.

ಒತ್ತಡೆ, ಒತ್ತಟ್ಟೆ **ottaḍe, ottaṭṭe.** Nightmare.

ಕಂಚಿಟ್ನ **kañciṭna.** A cyst, stye.

ಕಟ್ರೆ **kaṭre.** Sickness arising from eating deleterious things (R.).

ಕಣ್ಣು **kaṇṇu.** The eye; —ಕುಟಿ, —ಬಿಟ್ಲೆ (-kuṭi, -biṭle) an imposthume on the eyelids, a stye; —ಕತ್ತಲೆ (-kattale) fainting; —ನಾತಿ (-nâti) a lachrymal fistula; —ಜುಟ್ಟು (-juṭṭu) a fungus, or protuberance of flesh, in the eye; —ನೋವು (-nôvu) sore-eye; —ಪರೆ (-pare) gutta serena, cataract.

ಕಪ್ಪೆ, -ನಾಲಿಗೆ, -ಬಾವು **kappe, -nâlige, -bâvu.** Epizootic aphthæ (V.).

ಕಲ್ಲು **kallu.** A stone, gravel; —ವ್ಯಾಧಿ (-vyâdhi) stone in the bladder; —ಒತ್ತು (-ottu) a heel-abscess.

ಕಸ **kasa.** Second-birth or the placenta.

ಕಾಮಲಿ, ಕಾಮಿಲಿ **kâmali, kâmili.** Malignant jaundice.

ಕಾಲುಕುಂಟ ರೋಗ **kâlukuṇṭa rôga.** Epizootic aphthæ, foot and mouth disease, also called ಜರಸಲು (jarasalu) (V.).

ಕೀಲುಮಂಡಿ **kilumaṇḍi.** Spavin (V.).

ಕುರಕುರಿ **kurakuri.** Paralysis (V.).

ಕುರು **kuru.** A boil; —ಹಣ್ಣಾಗು (-haṇṇâgu) a boil to suppurate or come to a head; ರಶಿಕಿ, ರಶಿ (raśiki, raśi) sanies; ಕಚ, ಕಲೆ (kača, kale) a cicatrix; ಕೋಚು, ಗೋಚು (kôču, gôču) slough, the bad flesh in a boil;

ಜಕ್ಕಳಿ, ಹಕ್ಕು, ಹಕ್ಕುಳೆ (jakkaḷi, hakku, hakkuḷe) the scab of a sore or boil; ಆಸನ– (âsana-) *see* ಆಸನ; ನೆತ್ತರು– (nettaru-) a boil from which blood flows on being opened (S. C.); ಕೀವು (kîvu) pus.

ಕುಷ್ಠ kushṭha. Leprosy; ಶ್ವೇತ–, ಔದುಂಬರ–, ತೊನ್ನು (svêta-, audumbara-, tonnu) white leprosy, leucoderma; ರಕ್ತ– (rakta-) St. Anthony's fire, ulcerous leprosy; ಗಿಣ್ಣಿ (giṇṇi) black leprosy.

ಕುಸುಮರೋಗ kusumarôga. Immoderate flow of lochia.

ಕೃಶರೋಗ kṛiśarôga. Atrophy.

ಕೆಂಪಿ kempi. Scarlatina.

ಕೆಚ್ಚಲುಹುಣ್ಣು keććaluhuṇṇu. Garget (V.).

ಕೆಪ್ಪಟೆ keppaṭe. Mumps; *also* ಕೆಪ್ಪಡೆ.

ಕೆಮ್ಮು kemmu. Cough; ನಾಯಿ–, ಕೋವೆ–, ಕಪ್ಪೆ– (nâyi-, kôve-, kappe-) whooping cough.

ಕೊಟ್ಲೆ koṭle. Chicken-pox, *also* ನೀರು– (S. C.).

ಕೋರ kôra. Measles (S. C.).

ಕ್ರಿಮಿ krimi. Worms.

ಖಜ್ಜಿ, ಗಜ್ಜಿ khajji, gajji. Itch; ಮಾರಿ– (mâri-) the scab (V.).

ಖಾಸ khâsa. Asthma (S. C.); –ಶ್ವಾಸ (-śvâsa) bronchitis.

ಗಂಟ್ಲು gaṇṭlu. The throat; –ಅಗ್ರ (-agra) quinsy; –ಒಡೆಯೋಣ (-oḍeyôṇa) hoarseness; –ನೋವು (-nôvu) angina; –ಉಬ್ಬು, –ವಾಳ (-ubbu, -vâḷa) goitre.

ಗಂಡಮಾಲೆ gaṇḍamâle. Scrofula.

ಗಜಕರ್ಣ gajakarṇa. Ringworm.

ಗಬ gaba. The throbbing of an inflammation.

ಗಟ್ಟು gaṭṭu. The crisis of a disease.

ಗರ್ಭ garbha. The womb, fœtus; –ಪಾತ, –ಸ್ರಾವ (-pâta, -srâva) abortion; –ವಾಯು (-vâyu) hysteria; –ಶೂಲೆ (-śûle) painful affections of the uterus, dysmenorrhœa; ಗರ್ಭಿಣಿ (garbhiṇi) an *enceinte,* a pregnant woman.

ಗುಣ guṇa. Improvement; 2, the property of a drug; ಕೈ– (kai-) the quality of effecting a cure, personal skill or practice. According to the Hindu science, properties of drugs are 1, ಪಿತ್ತ (pitta) bilious;

2, ಕಫ (kapha) phlegmatic; 3, ವಾತ (vâta) rheumatic; 4, ಉಷ್ಣ, ಗರ್ಮಿ (ushṇa, garmi) heat producing or calorific; 5, ನಂಜು (nañju) psoric or stimulating scabbiness; 6, ಥಂಡಿ, ತಂಪು, ಸಂಪು (thaṇḍi, tampu. sampu) cooling.

ಗುಲ್ಮವ್ಯಾಧಿ gulmavyâdhi. Enlargement of the spleen, 'the spleen'.

ಗುಳ್ಳೆ guḷḷe. Blisters, *also* ಚಳ್ಳೆ (čaḷḷe).

ಗೂದೆ gûde. Prolapsus of the anus.

ಗೂರಲು gûralu. Asthma, *also* ಗೂರು; —ತೆಮಡೆ (-temaḍe) asthmatic phlegm.

ಗ್ರಹಣಿ, ಗ್ರಾಣಿ grahaṇi, grâṇi. Rickets, wasting disease of children (S. C.).

ಚಳುಕು čaḷuku. Acute rheumatism.

ಚಿಕ್ಕಮ್ಮ čikkamma. Measles.

ಚಿಕಿತ್ಸೆ čikitse. Medical treatment.

ಚಿಟಿಕೆ čiṭike. A cautery; ಬರೆ (bare) a cautery by heated iron, an 'actual' cautery.

ಚಿತುಕು čituku. To suppurate.

ಜಡ್ಡು jaḍḍu. A slight indisposition, *also* ಜಾಡ್ಯ; 2, callosity of the skin from friction.

ಜರಗಡ್ಡೆ, ಜರಗೆಂಡೆ jaragaḍḍe, jarageṇḍe. Ague-cake, enlargement of the spleen.

ಜರಸಲು jarasalu. Foot and mouth disease (V.).

ಜುಂಡು juṇḍu. Dandriff.

ಜುಲಾಬು julâbu. An aperient; 2, diarrhœa; ಉಖಾಲ್— (ukhâl-) cholera (S. C.).

ಜ್ವರ jvara. Fever; ಮಲೆ— (male-) jungle fever, malarial fever; ಛಳಿ— (čhaḷi-) ague; ವಿಷಮ— (vishama-) remittant fever; ಪಿತ್ತ— (pitta-) bilious fever; ಸಿಡುಬು— (siḍubu-) eruptive fever; ಅಸ್ತಿ— (asti-) *lit.* fever which has gone into the bones, a low fever, hectic fever; ಕೆಂ— (keṅ-) scarlatina; ಕಠಿಣ— (kaṭhiṇa-) ardent fever; ವರಿಚೆ— (variče-) ague; ನಂಜು— (nañju-) puerperal fever (S. C.).

ಜ್ವಾಲೆ jvâle. Burning sensation, scalding, irritation.

ತಲೆ tale. *see p.* 22; —ಖಜ್ಜಿ (-khajji) eczema, scald head; —ಚುಂಡು (-čuṇḍu) scurfy head; —ಪಟ್ಟು (-paṭṭu) an application against headache; —ಶಿಡಿತ, —ನೋವು (-śiḍita, -nôvu) headache; —ತಿರುಗುವಿಕೆ (-tiruguvike) vertigo, giddiness.

ತಾಮರೆ tâmare. A peculiar disease attended with languor and debility, marasmus (S. C.); 2, green-sickness (S. C.).

ತೀಟೆ tiṭe. Itch.

ತುರಿದಡಿಕೆ turidaḍike. Nettle-rash, urticaria.

ತೆವಲು tevalu. The rot (V.).

ತೊಡೆವಾಳ toḍevâḷa. Bubo; ಕೊಳಕು— (koḷaku-) phagedenic bubo.

ದಡಿಕೆ daḍike. Rash (S. C.).

ದಡ್ಡು daḍḍu. Corns.

ದದ್ದು daddu. Ringworm.

ದೇಹಪ್ರಕೃತಿ dêhaprakṛiti. Constitution.

ನಂಜು nañju. Puerperal poison; 2, anything stimulating the formation of pus or itch; —ಏರು (-êru) the puerperal poison to take effect; 2, any poison to circulate.

ನರಡಿ naraḍi. Sore-throat (V.); ಒಣ— (oṇa-) dry sore-throat (V.).

ನರೋಲಿ, ನರಹುಲಿ narôli, narahuli. Wart.

ನಳ naḷa. Colic; —ವಾಯು (-vâyu) hernial colic (S. C.).

ನಾಗರು nâgaru. A sore below the tongue (V.).

ನಾಡಿ nâḍi. The pulse; —ಬಡಿಯುವದು (-baḍiyuvadu) pulsation; —ಪರೀಕ್ಷೆ (-parîkshe) examination of the pulse; —ವ್ರಣ (-vṛiṇa) anal fistula.

ನಾಳಿಸ್ತಂಭ nâḷistambha. Asphyxia.

ನಿಚ್ಚು ničču. Heart-burn.

ನೀರುಕೊಟ್ಲೆ nirukoṭle. Chicken-pox (S. C.).

ನೂತಿ (vlg. ಲೂತಿ) nûti. A cancer; ಕಣ್ಣು— (kaṇṇu-) lachrymal fistula.

ನೆಗಡಿ negaḍi. Catarrh.

ನೆತ್ತರಗಡ್ಡೆ nettaragaḍḍe. Boils.

ನೇವಸ nêvasa. Asthma.

ನೋವು nôvu. Any pain, ache; ಎದೆ— (ede-) pleurisy; ತಲೆ— (tale-)

headache; ಹೊಟ್ಟೆ— (hoṭṭe-) colic, stomach-ache; ಕಣ್ಣು— (kaṇṇu-) ophthalmia; ಕಿವಿ— (kivi-) ear-ache; ಗಂಟ್ಲು— (gaṇṭlu-) sore-throat; ಬಾಯಿ— (bâyi-) sore-mouth; ಅಳ್ಳೆ— (aḷḷe-) pain in the groins. Pain may be divided into 1, ಸುಡುವ (suḍuva) burning; 2, ಒತ್ತುವ (ottuva) pressing; 3, ಎಳೆಯುವ (eḷeyuva) spasmodic; 4, ಸೀಳುವ (sîḷuva) lacerating; 5, ಚುಚ್ಚುವ (čuččuva) lancinating; 6, ತಿವಿಯುವ (tiviyuva) pricking; 7, ಕುತ್ತುವ (kuttuva) throbbing.

ಪಥ್ಯ pathya. Regimen, diet; ಅ— (a-) violation of diet-rules; ಮರು— (maru-) a secondary light diẹt (S. C.).

ಪಾಂಡು pâṇḍu. White leprosy, leucoderma; ವಿಷ— (visha-) anasarca.

ಪಾಶಿ pâši. Hæmorrhage from the nose (S. C.); 2, foul-mouth (S. C.).

ಪಿತ್ತ pitta. Bile; —ದ ಕಲ್ಲು (-da kallu) gall-stone; —ಗಾದರಿ (-gâdari) nettle-rash (S. C.).

ಪಿನಾಶಿ pinâši. Polypus (S. C.).

ಪುರಿ puri. Warts.

ಪ್ರಮೇಹ pramêha. Gonorrhea, *also* ಮೇಹ.

ಬಟ್ಟಿ baṭṭi. Dysentery; 2, a rupture, hernia; —ಕಟ್ಟು (-kaṭṭu) to truss.

ಬಯಕೆ bayake. A generic term for a longing by *enceintes* and includes 'pica'; 2, morning-sickness (S. C.).

ಬವಳಿ bavaḷi. Fainting.

ಬಸಾರ basâra. Looseness of the bowels.

ಬಾಣಂತಿ bâṇanti. A woman in confinement, a lying-in-woman; —ರೋಗ (-rôga) puerperal fever.

ಬಾಲ bâla. An infant; —ಗ್ರಹ (-graha) infantile convulsions; —ಪೀಡೆ (-pîḍe) rickets.

ಬಾವು bâvu. An abscess; ಕಳ್ಳ—, ಮಂಗ—, (kaḷḷa-, maṅga-) mumps; ಹರಿ— (hari-) an axillary abscess; ಗದ್ದ— (gadda-) quinsy.

ಬೀಗು bîgu. Inflammation; 2, dropsy; ಕುತ್ತಿಗೆ— (kuttige-) stiff-neck; ಕೆನ್ನೆ— (kenne-) mumps.

ಬೀಟು, ಬೀಟೆ bîṭu, bîṭe. Chilblain.

ಬುಗು bugu. A tumour.

ಬೆವರು **bevaru.** Perspiration; —ಸಾಲೆ (-sâle) prickly-heat.

ಬೆಸಲು **besalu.** Travail.

ಬೊಕ್ಕಿ, ಬೊಕ್ಕೆ **bokki, bokke.** A pimple, a pustule.

ಬೋಧ **bôdha.** Consciousness; —ತಪ್ಪುವದು (-tappuvadu) unconsciousness. delirium.

ಭಗಂದರ **bhagandara.** Carbuncle, *also* ಭಗಂದಳ.

ಭ್ರಮಣೆ **bhramaṇe.** A wandering of the senses, confusion of the mind; ಅದಲ— (aḍala-) delirium tremens.

ಭ್ರಾಂತಿ **bhrânti.** Madness, insanity; ಮುದಿ— (mudi-) dotage.

ಮದಕರಿ **madakari.** Leprosy (S. C.).

ಮದ್ದು **maddu.** Medicine; —ಕೊಡು (koḍu-) to treat or prescribe; ಕಟ್ಟು— (kaṭṭu-) an antidote (S. C.). Different forms in which medicine is given are: 1, ಕಷಾಯ (kashâya) decoction; 2, ಕಲ್ಕ (kalka) infusion; 3, ಧೃತಿ (dhṛiti) tincture; 4, ಚೂರ್ಣ (čûrṇa) trituration; 5, ಮಾತ್ರೆ, ಗುಳಿಗೆ (mâtre, guḷige) pills, globules; 6, ಮುಲಾಮು (mulâmu) cerate, ointment; 7, ಲೇಹ (lêha) electuary; 8, ಲೇಪ (lêpa) plaster; 9, ಭಸ್ಮ (bhasma) oxides of metals; 10, ತೈಲ್ಯ (tailya) medicated oil; 11, ಸತ್ವ (satva) essence; 12, ಅಂಜನ (añjana) salves; 13, ಮುಕ್ಕುಳಿ (mukkuḷi) gargle.

ಮರಕಳಿಕೆ **marakaḷike.** A relapse.

ಮಲ **mala.** Excrement, fæces; —ಬದ್ಧತೆ (-baddhate) constipation; —ಮೂತ್ರ (-mûtra) fæces and urine; —ಶೋಧನ (-śôdhane) opening of the bowels.

ಮಸುಳು **masuḷu.** Scurf in the head.

ಮಾರಿರೋಗ **mârirôga.** Epidemic disease; 2, rinderpest (V.).

ಮುಟ್ಟಸ **muṭṭasa.** A nostrum (S. C.).

ಮುಡುಬು **muḍubu.** Pimples.

ಮುರತ **murata.** An antidote; *also* ಉತಾರು.

ಮೂತ್ರ **mûtra.** Urine; ಬಹು— (bahu-) diabetes; ಉರಿ— (uri-) scalding urine; —ಕೃಛ್ರ (kṛičhra-) stricture, strangury.

ಮೂರ್ಛೆ **mûrčhe.** Fainting.

ಮೂಲವ್ಯಾಧಿ **mûlavyâdhi.** Piles, hæmorrhoids.

ಮೇಲ್ಪುಡಿ **mêlpuḍi.** A corrigent, an adjuvant (S. C.).

ಮೈ **mai.** The body; —ಗರೆವಿಕೆ (-garevike) atrophy; —ಗಾಡು (-gâḍu) swelling; —ಇಳಿಯೋಣ (-iḷiyôṇa) abortion; —ಸೊಕ್ಕು (-sokku) fainting.

ಮೈಲಿಗೆ **mailige.** Small-pox, *also* ಮೈಲಗಜ್ಜಿ.

ಮೊಡವೆ **moḍave.** Painful nodes.

ಮೊರಡಿ **moraḍi.** Swelling.

ಮೊಳೆರೋಗ **moḷerôga.** Piles, hæmorrhoids.

ರಕ್ತ **rakta.** Blood; –ಕೊರತೆ (-korate) anæmia; –ಕಾರುವದು (-kâruvadu) hemoptysis; –ಪಿತ್ತ (-pitta) hæmorrhage from the internal organs; scurvy; –ಮೂತ್ರ (-mûtra) hæmaturia; ರಕ್ತಾತಿಶಯ (raktâtiśaya) plethora; –ಸ್ರಾವ (-srâva) flooding; 2, anthrax (V.); ರಕ್ತಾತಿಸಾರ (raktâtisâra) dysentery.

ರಾಜ **râja.** A king; –ಕುರು (-kuru) carbuncle; –ಹುಣ್ಣು (-huṇṇu) scrofula, king's-evil; –ಕ್ಷಯ (-kshaya) pulmonary consumption, phthisis.

ರುಚಿ **ruči.** Appetite; 2, taste, divided into: ತೀ (tî) sweet; ಹುಳಿ (huḷi) sour; ಉಪ್ಪು (uppu) saline; ಕಹಿ (kahi) bitter; ಖಾರ (khâra) pungent, acrid; ಒಗರು (ogaru) astringent; ಸಪ್ಪೆ (sappe) insipid.

ರೋಗ **rôga.** A disease; –ಪ್ರಕೃತಿ (-prakṛiti) the abnormal state, morbid condition; ಕ್ಷುದ್ರ– (kshudra) a trifing disease; ಅಂಟು– (anṭu-) a contagious disease; ಲಾಗ್– (lâg-) foot and mouth disease (V., N. C.); ದೊಡ್ಡ– (doḍḍa-) rinderpest (V.); ಚಂದು–, ಛಾಂದಣಿ (čandu-, čhândaṇi-) throat-disease (V., N. C.); ಅಳ್ಳೆ– (aḷḷe-) rickets; ಪುರುಷ– (purusha-) Hunterian cancer (S. C.); ಸೋಕು– (sôku-) a contagious disease.

ವಟ್ಟಿ **vaṭṭi.** Convulsion in adults.

ವಾಂತಿ **vânti.** Vomiting; –ಭೇದಿ (-bhêdi) cholera; –ಮದ್ದು (-maddu) an emitic.

ವಾತ **vâta.** Rheumatism; –ಕಾಲು (-kâlu) elephantiasis; ಕುಟಿಲ– (kuṭila-) rickets; ಹರಿ– (hari-) neuralgia, *tic-douloureux;* ಸೊಂಟ– (sonṭa-) lumbago; ಕಳ್ಳ– (kaḷḷa-) false pleurisy; ಪಕ್ಷ– (paksha-) partial paralysis; ಧನುರ್- (dhanur-) tetanus; ಕಂಪ– (kampa-) paralysis agitans; ಕೃಶ– (kṛiśa-) palsy; ಶ್ರೋಣಿತ– (śrôṇita-) rheumatic gout.

ವಾಯು **vâyu.** Flatulence; ಗರ್ಭ– (garbha-) hysteria; ನಡು– (naḍu-) lumbago; ನಳ– (naḷa-) colic; ರುದ್ರ– (rudra-) apoplexy; ಅದರು– (adaru-) palsy.

ವಾಳುಕ **vâḷuka.** Nodosities (S. C.).

ವ್ರಣ **vṛiṇa.** An ulcer; ನಾಡಿ– (nâḍi-) anal fistula; ಮೇಹ– (mêha-) syphilitic ulcer.

ವ್ಯಥೆ **vyathe.** Labor, travail (s. c.).

ಶಿಬ್ಬಿ, ಶಿಬ್ಬ **šibbi, šibba.** Leucodermic patches on the skin (s. c.).

ಶಿರೋಭ್ರಮಣೆ **širôbhramaṇe.** Vertigo, giddiness.

ಶೀತ **šita.** Cold: ಉರಿ- (uri-) influenza.

ಶೂಲೆ **šûle.** Pain, spasmodic pain; ಉದರ- (udara-) colic: ಕಟಿ- (kaṭi-) lumbago; ಪಾರ್ಶ್ವ- (pâršva-) affection of the liver, 'the liver'.

ಶೋಫ **šôpha.** Dropsy.

ಶ್ಲೇಷ್ಮ **šlêshma.** Phlegm, mucus.

ಸನ್ನಿ **sanni.** Raving; 2, brain-fever; -ಪಾತ (-pâta) typhus fever; ಪ್ರಲಾಪ- (pralâpa-) epilepsy; ಬಗಳು- (bagaḷu-) delirium; ಕ್ಷಿಪ್ರ- (kshipra-) apoplexy; ಗಳುಗು- (gaḷugu-) insanity.

ಸಬ್ಬಲು **sabbalu.** Dandruff.

ಸರದಿ **saradi.** Glanders (v.).

ಸೀತಾಳ **sitâḷa.** Chicken-pox.

ಸ್ರಾವ **srâva.** A discharge or falling off; ಅಸ್ಥಿ- (asti-) leucorrhœa; ಗರ್ಭ- (garbha-) abortion; ಇಂದ್ರಿಯ- (indriya-) spermatorrhœa.

ಸ್ವಪ್ನೇಂದ್ರಿಯ **svapnêndriya.** Spermatorrhœa, 'wet-dreams'.

ಹಲವಿಳಿಯು **halaviḷiyu.** To miscarry.

ಹಲ್ಲರ್ಸಿ **hallarsi.** A dental fistula; a cancer of the mouth (s. c.).

ಹಲ್ಲು **hallu.** Tooth; -ನೋವು (-nôvu) toothache; ಹಳುಕು- (haḷuku-) a carious tooth; -ಬರುವದು (-baruvadu) teething.

ಹುಣ್ಣು **huṇṇu.** A sore; ಜರಡಿ- (jaraḍi-) an ulcer breaking in holes; ಸೋರುವ- (sôruva-) a fistula, a phagedenous ulcer; ಫರಂಗಿ- (pharaṅgi-) syphilis.

ಹುಳ **huḷa.** Worms; ಲಾಡಿ- (lâḍi-) tape-worm; ಕಿಲಿಬೆ- (kilibe-) ascarides; ತೀರೆ, ಮಲ- (tîre, mala-) teres.

ಹೊಕ್ಕಳುವ್ಯಾಧಿ **hokkaḷuvyâdhi.** Navel ill (v.).

ಕ್ಷಯ **kshaya.** Consumption, phthisis; ರಾಜ- (râja-) pulmonary consumption.

Metals.

ಅಂಜನಕಲ್ಲು **añjanakallu.** Antimony.

ಅದುರು **aduru.** Ore.

ಉಕ್ಕು **ukku.** Steel.

ಕಂಚು **kañču.** Bell-metal.

ಕಪ್ರುಸುತ್ತು **kaprusuttu.** Pewter, platina, tin (s. c.).

ಕಬ್ಬಿಣ **kabbiṇa.** Iron; ಕಂಬು, ಶಳ್ಳ (kambu, śaḷḷa) a bar of iron; ಕಿಟ್ಟ (kiṭṭa) scoria, dross of iron.

ಘಟ್ಟಿ **ghaṭṭi.** An ingot, a nugget.

ತಂಬಾಕು **tambâku.** Pinch-beck, tambac.

ತವರ **tavara.** Tin; 2, white oxide of lead.

ತಾಂಡವಾಳ **tâṇḍavâḷa.** Gun-metal.

ತಾಂಬ್ರ, ತಾಮ್ರ **tâmbra, tâmra.** Copper.

ತೂಕ ಬಣ್ಣ **tûka baṇṇa.** Weight and touch of metals; quality and quantity of metals.

ತೇಮಾನು **têmânu.** Loss in assaying gold; 2, an allowance in gold made to goldsmiths when gold is wrought into ornaments (s. c.).

ಪಂಚಲೋಹ **pañčalôha.** A compound of five metals copper, brass, tin, lead and iron.

ಪತ್ತೆ **patte.** Soldering.

ಪಾದರಸ **pâdarasa.** Mercury, quicksilver; *also* ರಸ.

ಪಾಳ **pâḷa.** An ingot.

ಪುಟ **puṭa.** Calcination of metals by fire.

ಬಣ್ಣ **baṇṇa.** 'Touch' or quality of gold; ಅಪರಂಜಿ (aparañji) supposed to be 18 'touches'; ಪವನು (pavanu) or a sovereign, 10 touches; ಕುರ್ಜಾತ್ (kurjât) a moidore 11 touches; ಪುತ್ತಳಿ (puttaḷi) 12 touches; ಇಸ್ತಾಂಬೂಲ್ (istâmbûl) 9 touches; ವರಹಾ (varahâ) 8 touches; ಸಂತಮಿ (santami) 6 touches (s. c.).

ಬಿಡುತ್ತದೆ **biḍuttade.** The word is used when testing gold, and means inferiority in touch to the test-piece or sample (s. c.).

ಬಿರುಸು **birusu.** Refractory, not malleable.

ಬೀಡು **biḍu.** Cast iron.

ಬೆಟ್ಟೆ **beṭṭe.** Excessive hardness of bad metals, brittleness.

ಬೆಸಗೆ, ಬೆಸಿಗೆ **besage, besige.** Soldering; –ಬೆಚ್ಚು, –ಹತ್ತಿಸು (-beččū, -hattisu) to solder.

ಬೆಳ್ಳಿ **beḷḷi.** Silver; ಕಂದು– (kandu-) impure silver; ಚೀನಿ–, ಚೊಕ್ಕ– (čīni-, čokka-) pure silver; ಮಕ್ಕರಿ– (makkari-) silver containing a larger quantity of alloy than is usual.

ಭಂಗಾರ **bhaṅgâra.** Gold; ರೇಕು– (rêku-) gold leaf; –ತಗಡು (-tagaḍu) godl foil, termed *also* ವರ್ಣತಗಡು; ಅಪರಂಜಿ– (aparañji-) pure gold; ಕೊಟ್ಟೆ– (koṭṭe-) inferior gold; ಕಡುಪು– (kaḍupu-) gold containing a larger quantity of alloy than is usual; ಅಸುರು–, ಅಸ್ರು–, ಹಸ್ರು– (asuru-, asru-, hasru-) pure, unalloyed gold (S. C.); –ವರಕು (-varaku) gilt.

ಭಸ್ಮ **bhasma.** Calx, an oxide of a metal.

ಮಚ್ಚತುಂಡು **maččatuṇḍu.** A test-piece, a piece of gold or silver kept as a sample to test with (S. C.); –ವರೆಸು (-varesu) to rub a test-piece for testing.

ಮುಲಾಮು **mulâmu.** Gilding, electroplating, enamel.

ಮೂಸೆ **mûse.** A cupel, crucible.

ಲೋಹ **lôha.** A metal; –ಭಸ್ಮ (-bhasma) zinc; 2, reduced iron; –ಮಂಡೂರ (-maṇḍûra) manganese.

ವಂಗ **vaṅga.** Tin; –ಭಸ್ಮ (-bhasma) an oxide of tin.

ವಪ್ಪೆ **vappe.** The burnish or polish of an ornament; –ಕಡ್ಡಿ (-kaḍḍi) a burnisher; –ಹೊಯಿಗೆ (-hoyige) a peculiar kind of reddish sand used in burnishing.

ಶಿರ **śira.** The vein of a metal.

ಶೀಸ **śīsa.** Lead; ಕಪ್ಪು– (kappu-) plumbago or black lead.

ಹತ್ತಕಾಸು **hattakâsu.** To weld.

ಹದ ಮಾಡು **hadamâḍu.** To temper.

ಹಿತ್ತಾಳಿ **hittâḷi.** Brass.

Military.

ಅಗಳು **agaḷu.** A moat or fort ditch, a trench; —ಬಾಗಲು (-bâgalu) a draw-bridge over a moat; —ಗಡ್ಡೆ (-gaḍḍe) the mound thrown up from a moat.

ಅಲಂಗ **alanga.** A rampart.

ಅಳಂಡೆ **aḷaṇḍe.** An ambuscade, a place of ambush.

ಆಳಿವೇರಿ **âḷivêri.** A barricade.

ಈಟಿ **iṭi.** A lance, a spear.

ಉಪಾಯ **upâya.** A trick, a strategy. Four means of bringing about an object are: ಸಾಮ (sâma) conciliation, ದಾನ (dâna) presents, or bribery, ಭೇದ (bhêda) creating dissension, ದಂಡ (daṇḍa) punishment.

ಊಜಿ **ûji.** A balustrade.

ಏಟು **êṭa.** A shot; ಅಡ್ಡ— (aḍḍ-) a random shot; ಗುಡ್ಡ— (guḍḍ-) a good shot.

ಕವಾತು **kavâtu.** Drill, parade.

ಕಾಟಕಾಯಿ **kâṭakâyi.** Mutiny, insurrection (S. C.).

ಕಾವಲು **kâvalu.** A guard; —ಆಗಿ ನಿಲ್ಲು (-âgi nillu) to mount guard.

ಕಿಲ್ಲೆ **kille.** A fort; —ಸಾಧಿಸು (-sâdhisu) to take a fort.

ಕೂಚು **kûču.** The march of a regiment.

ಕೊತ್ತಳ **kottaḷa.** The bastion of a fort.

ಕೊಲೆ **kole.** A massacre.

ಕೋಟೆ **kôṭe.** A fort; —ತೆನೆ, —ಕೊಂಬೆ (-tene, -kombe) battlements; ಬುರುಜು (buruju) the bastion of a fort; ಕೋವರ (kôvara) the watch-tower; ಜಿಡ್ಡಿ (jiḍḍi) a sally-port; ಖಣಿ (khaṇi) a trench.

ಕೋಹಾಟ **kôhâṭa.** A challenge.

ಖಂದಕ **khandaka.** A moat, a trench.

ಗಂಡಿ **gaṇḍi.** Embrasure.

ಗಾಟು, ಗಾಡು **gâṭu, gâḍu.** *Anglice* guard; ಮೇ— (mê-) main guard (My.); ಬಾರಿ— (bâri-) body-guard (My.), *also* ಮೈಗಾವಲು.

ಗುಣ **guṇa.** A means of defence, of which 6 are enumerated, viz:—

ಸಂಧಿ (sandhi) mediation; ವಿಗ್ರಹ (vigraha) war; ಯಾನ (yâna) a march; ಆಸನ (âsana) a halt; ದ್ವೈತೀಭಾವ (dvaitîbhâva) stratagem; ಸಮಾಶ್ರಯ (samâśraya) protection.

ಗೋಲಂದಾಜಿ **gôlandâji.** Gunnery, artillery.

ಚಾವಣಿ **čâvaṇi.** A camp.

ಜಾಂಡೆ **jâṇḍe.** An ensign, a flag; —ಹಾಕು (-hâku) to set up a flag.

ಜೇರುಗಂಡಿ **jêrugaṇḍi.** Battlements.

ಜೋಡಣೆಗಾರ **jôḍaṇegâra.** A quarter-master.

ಠಾಣ್ಯ **ṭhâṇya.** A garrison; —ಹಾಕು (-hâku) to garrison.

ತೆನೆಕಂಡಿ **tenekaṇḍi.** Embrasures for cannon.

ತೋಪುಖಾನೆ **tôphukhâne.** An ordnance store, a magazine.

ದಂಗೆ **daṅge.** An insurrection, rebellion.

ದಂಡು **daṇḍu.** An army; —ಎತ್ತು (-ettu) to raise an army.

ದಸಿ **dasi.** A palisade.

ದಳ **daḷa.** An army; ಮುಂ— (mun-) a vanguard; ಹಿಂ— (hin-) rear guard; —ವಾಯಿ (-vâyi) the general of an army; —ಮುಖ (-mukha) the van of an army; ಪಾಯಿ— (pâyi-) infantry.

ದಾಳಿ **dâḷi.** Maraud; —ಜನ (-jana) moss-troopers.

ದೌಡು **dauḍu.** An expedition, a campaign; —ಗೊಳ್ಳು (-gollu) to be invaded.

ನಿಗಾದಸ್ತು **nigâdastu.** The review of an army.

ನಿಶಾನಿ **niśâni.** A banner; —ಏರಿಸು (-êrisu) to set up a flag.

ಪಟಾಲ **paṭâla.** *Anglice* battalion, a regiment; *also* ಪಟ್ಟಾಲಾಂ.

ಪಡೆ **paḍe.** An army; —ಮಾಡು (-mâḍu) to draw up an army.

ಪತಾಕೆ **patâke.** A flag, a banner.

ಪಾಳತಿ **pâḷati.** Espionage, reconnoitring; —ನೋಡು (-nôḍu) to reconnoitre.

ಪಾಳೆಯ **pâḷeya.** A halting place, a camp; —ಮಾಡು (-mâḍu) to bivouac, to encamp.

ಪಾಳ್ಯ **pâḷya.** An army.

ಫರಾರಿ **pharâri.** A run-away, a deserter.

ಫೌಜು **phauzu.** An army; ಛಡೆ— (čhaḍe-) light troops.

ಬತ್ತೇರಿ **battêri.** *Anglice* battery.

ಬಲಗಾಯಿಸು **balagâyisu.** To secure, as a fort, from invasion.

ಬಾರ್ **bâr.** Infantry.

ಬಾರೂದು **bârûdu.** Ammunition (S. C.); —ಖಾನೆ (-khâne) an arsenal, a powder-magazine.

ಬಾವಟೆ **bâvaṭe.** A flag, a standard.

ಬೇಗು, ಬೇಹು **bêgu, bêhu.** A spy; —ಜನ (-jana) a reconnoitring party.

ಮಟ್ಟಡಿ **maṭṭaḍi.** A siege.

ಮಸ್ತೀಬು ಮಾಡು **mastîbu mâḍu.** To accoutre.

ಮಿಸಲು **misalu.** The review of an army (R.).

ಮುತ್ತಿಗೆ **muttige.** A siege; —ಹಾಕು (-hâku) to besiege; —ತೆಗಿಯು (-tegiyu) to raise a siege.

ಮುಸ್ತೈದೆ **mustaide.** Accoutrements; ಕವಚ, ಚಿಲಖತ್ತು (kavača, čilakhattu) an armour; ಪದಕ (padaka) a cuirass, a breast-plate; ಮುಖರಕ್ಷೆ (mukharakshe) a beaver; ಕಂಠಕವಚ (kanṭhakavača) a gorget; ಭಕ್ತರು (bhaktaru) a gauntlet; ಶಿರಸ್ತ್ರಾಣ (širastrâṇa) a casque.

ಮೇರುವೆ **mêruve.** A stockade.

ಮೋರ್ಚ, ಮೋರ್ಚಾ **môrča, môrčâ.** A battery; a platform.

ಮೋದಿಖಾನೆ **môdikhâne.** A commissariat store.

ಯುದ್ಧ **yuddha.** War; —ಸನ್ನಾಹ (-sannâha) armament; ಫಿರಂಗಿ— (phirangi-) cannonade.

ರಸ್ತು, ರಸದು **rastu, rasadu.** Provisions laid for an army; 2, ammunition.

ರಿಸಾಲ್ **risâl.** A battalion of cavalry.

ಲಗ್ಗೆ **lagge.** Escalade, scaling a wall. —ಹತ್ತು (-hattu) to scale.

ಲಡಾಯಿ **laḍâyi.** War; 2, a fight.

ವ್ಯೂಹ **vyûha.** Military array; ದಂಡ— (danḍa-) array in lines; ಭೋಗ— (bhôga-) array in columns.

ಶಾಗೀರ್ದಪೇಷಾ **šâgirdpêshâ.** A quarter-master.

ಶೆರೆ **šere.** Capturing; ಸುಖ— (sukha-) a patrole of honor.

ಸಂಚು **sanču.** Finesse, stratagem; —ನಡಿಸು (-naḍisu) to cabal; —ಗಾರ (-gâra) a spy.

ಸಂಧಾನ **sandhâna.** Truce.

ಸಲ್ಲಾ **sallâ.** Peace; 2, treaty.

ಸುರುಟು, ಸುಟುರ್ **suruṭu, surṭu.** *Anglice* "salute" (S. C.).

ಹತ್ಯಾರ **hatyâra.** Arms; ಚಾಪುಕೊಡಲಿ (câpukoḍali) a battle-axe; ಸನೀನು, ಸನಿಲು (sanînu, sanilu) a bayonet; ಕಠಾರಿ (kaṭhâri) a dagger, a poniard ಖಡ್ಗ (khaḍga) a scimiter, a sword; ಚಂದ್ರಾಯುಧ (candrâyudha) a cutlass; ಬರ್ಚಿ, ಈಟಿ (barči, iṭi) a javelin, a spear; ಭಲ್ಲೆ (bhalle) a lance; ಚಿಲ್ಲಣ (čillaṇa) a rapier; *see also* ತುಪಾಕಿ; ಗುಪ್ತಿ (gupti) a sword-stick; ನಾಯರ ಕತ್ತಿ (nâyarakatti) the sword used by a Nâyar.

ಹಲ್ಲಾ **hallâ.** An escalade, scaling a fort; 2, an onset.

ಹುಡೆ **huḍe.** A bastion.

Mineralogy.

ಅನ್ನಭೇದಿ **annabhêdi.** Ferrous sulphate or sulphate of iron.

ಅಭ್ರಕ **abhraka.** Mica, talc.

ಆವೆಮಣ್ಣು **âvemaṇṇu.** Clay.

ಉಪ್ಪು **uppu.** Salt; ಇಂದುಪ್ಪು (induppu) Indus salt; ಪೆಟ್ಲುಪ್ಪು, ಸೋರುಪ್ಪು (peṭluppu, sôruppu) nitrate of potash, nitre; ಕಲ್ಲುಪ್ಪು (kalluppu) rock-salt.

ಕಲ್ಲು **kallu.** Stone; ಕಲ್ನಾರು (kalnâru) asbestos; —ಅರಗು (-aragu) asphalt; —ಉಪ್ಪು (-uppu) rock-salt; ಕರಿ— (kari-) granite, *also* ಕಗ್ಗಲ್ಲು; ಕಾಟ— (kâṭa-) gravel; ಕಾವಿ— (kâvi-) ochre-stone; —ಇದ್ದಲು (-iddalu) coal; ಗಡಿಗೆ— (gaḍige-) soap-stone; —ಪಡಿ, —ಪಣೆ (-paḍi, -paṇe) a quarry; ಪದದಾರು— (pada-dâru-) sand-stone; ಬೆಣಚು— (beṇaču-) quartz; ಮುರ— (mura-) laterite (S. C.); ಸೋಮನಾಥ— (sômanâtha-) soft black granite; ಸುಣ್ಣದ— (suṇṇada-) lime-stone.

ಖಡು **khaḍu.** Chalk.

ಗಂಧಕ **gandhaka.** Sulphur; —ಧೃತಿ (-dhṛiti) sulphuric acid.

ಗುರುಸು **gurusu.** Gravel.

ಚಂದ್ರಕಾಂತ **čandrakânta.** Alabaster, white marble.

ಚಕ್ಕಮುಕ್ಕಿ **čakkamukki.** Flint-stone.

ಚೌಳು **čauḷu.** Muriate of lime, *also* ಸೌಳು.

ಜೇಡಿ **jêḍi.** Marl, potter's earth.

ತುತ್ತು **tuttu.** A sulphate; ಪಾಲ್— (pâl-) sulphate of zinc; ನೀಲ—, ಮೈಲ್— (nîla-, mail-) sulphate of copper, verdigris.

ನವಸಾಗರ **navasâgara.** Sal ammoniac.

ಪನ್ನಂಬರ **pannambara.** Ambergris.

ಪದರು **padaru.** A stratum, layer.

ಪಾಷಾಣ, ಶಂಖ— **pâshâṇa, šaṅkha-.** Arsenic; ದೊಡ್ಡಿ— (doḍḍi-) red arsenic; ಇಲಿ— (ili-) ratsbane.

ಬಿಳಿಗಾರ **biḷigâra.** Borax; ಎಣ್ಣೆ— (eṇṇe-) tinkal.

ಮುರದಾರಸಿಂಗಿ, ಮುಡದಾರಸಿಂಗಿ **muradârasiṅgi, muḍadârasiṅgi.** Litharge, vitrified oxide of lead.

ರಕ್ತಧಾತು **raktadhâtu.** Realgar.

ರಸಕರ್ಪೂರ **rasakarpûra.** Calomel, white sublimate of mercury.

ಶಿಲಾ, ಶಿಲೆ **śilâ, śile.** Granite; ಅಮೃತ— (amṛita-) porphyry; ಕೃಷ್ಣ— (kṛishṇa-) black granite, basalt; ಮಣಿ— (maṇi-) red arsenic, realgar, *also* ಮನಶ್ಶಿಲ; —ಧಾತು, —ಜಿತ (-dhâtu, -jita) bitumen; —ರಾಳ (-râḷa) amber.

ಸಂಗಮಿರ **saṅgamira.** Marble, *also* ಸಂಗಮರ್ಮರ್.

ಸುಂಬಳಕಾರ **sumbaḷakâra.** Arsenic.

ಸುರಮಾವು **suramâvu.** Antimony oxide, *surmao.*

ಸುವರ್ಣಮುಖಿ **suvarṇamukhi.** Pyrites

ಹರಿದಳ **haridaḷa.** Yellow orpiment, yellow arsenic; *also* ಅರಿದಳ.

ಹಿರಾಕಸು **hirâkasu.** Sulphate of iron.

Miscellaneous Words.

ಅಂದಾಜು **andâju.** An estimate; –ಕಟ್ಟು, –ಮಾಡು (-kaṭṭu, -mâḍu) to estimate.

ಅಂದಾದುಂದಿ **andâdundi.** Mismanaged, despotic.

ಅಡಾಣಿ **aḍâṇi.** Compulsory labour, unrequited labour.

ಅದದು **adadu.** Number (S. C.).

ಅದನಾ **adanâ.** Mean, low; –ಮನುಷ್ಯ (-manushya) a mean person.

ಅದಬು **adabu.** Politeness, civility; ಬೇ– (bê-) insult, incivility, *also* ಬೇದಬು.

ಅದಲಾಬದಲಿ **adalâbadali.** Exchange of persons or things.

ಅಪ್ಪಂತ **appanta.** An honest man, a reputable person.

ಅಯಿಜನ್ **ayijan.** The said, above-mentioned, *also* ಐಜನ್ (My.).

ಅಯಿಬು **ayibu.** Flaw or defect, *also* ಐಬು.

ಅಲಾಹಿದಾ **alâhidâ.** Separate, *also* ಅಲ್ಯಾದಾ.

ಅಹವಾಲ್ **ahavâl.** Representation, circumstances; ಹಾಲ್– (hâl-) state of circumstances.

ಆಖೈರ್ **âkhair.** The end; 2, final; –ಮಾಡು (-mâḍu) to close or finish.

ಆಬ್ರು **âbru.** Honour, reputation; ಬೇ– (bê-) dishonour, defamation; *also* ಬೆಬರು. ಬ್ಯಾಬ್ರು.

ಆಜುಬಾಜು **âjubâju.** Neighbouring (My.); *cf.* ಆಸ್ಪಾಸ್ (âspâs) (S. C.).

ಆದ್ಮಿ **âdmi.** A person, an individual; ಭಲೇ– (bhalê-) a great man.

ಇತಬಾರ **itabâra.** Confidence; –ಸ್ಥ (-stha) a trustworthy man.

ಉಡಾಫೆ **uḍâphe.** Evasion, shuffling.

ಉಡಾಯಿಸು **uḍâyisu.** To execute; 2, to blow up.

ಉಮೇದಿ **umêdi.** *Lit.* Expectation; zeal, zest (S. C.).

ಉರಠಾ **uraṭhâ.** Against the grain, contrarywise; *also* ಉಲಟಾ.

ಉಲುಪೆ **ulupe.** Supplies given to officials on tour; 2, supplies sent by the bride's party to the bridegroom's (S. C.).

ಉಸ್ತುವಾರಿ **ustuvâri.** Precaution, 'bandobast' (My.).

ಎಡವಟ್ಟು **eḍavaṭṭu.** Mediocre, indifferent, passable.

ಏಕಸಾ **êkasâ.** Incessently, uninterruptedly.

ಐಂದಾ **aindâ.** Hereafter, in future.

ಕಸಬು **kasabu.** Profession. ಅಡ್ಡ– (aḍḍa-) a trade not hereditary.

ಕಾರಣ **kâraṇa.** Marriage (S. C.); *see p.* 51.

ಕಿರುಕೋಳ, ಕಿರಕುಳ **kirukôḷa, kirakuḷa.** *Lit.* Unnecessary trouble given to ryots by inferior officers, unnecessary trouble in minute things; 2, miscellaneous, sundry.

ಕೂಟ **kûṭa.** A strike, conspiracy (S. C.).

ಕೂಡುಗಟ್ಟು **kûḍugaṭṭu.** An association, an assembly (S. C.).

ಖಂಡತುಂಡು, ಖಡಾಖಡಿ **khaṇḍatuṇḍu, khaḍâkhaḍi.** Point-blank, decisive.

ಖಲಲ್ **khalal.** Disturbance, confusion, injury; –ಮಾಡು (-mâḍu) to disturb, to injure, to waste.

ಖುಷಾಲು **khushâlu.** Merriment (S. C.); –ಗಾರ (-gâra) a 'jolly fellow.'

ಖಾಮಖಾ **khâmakhâ.** Assuredly, positively.

ಖುಲ್ಲಾ **khullâ.** Open.

ಗರಜು **garazu.** Want, necessity.

ಗರೀಬ **gariba.** Poor; a pauper; –ತನ (-tana) poverty.

ಗುಲಾಮ **gulâma.** A slave, a menial servant.

ಗೂಳೆ **gûḷe.** Leaving a place *en masse* during war or famine.

ಗೈವಾಳ **gaivâḷa.** *Lit.* A man of Gayâ where priestly extortion is said to be common, a rapacious man, an extortioner.

ಗೌಡಬಂಗಾಳಿ **gauḍabaṅgâḷi.** *Lit.* Gour Bengal, trickery, imposture, cheating (S. C.).

ಘಾಬರಿ, ಘಾಬ್ರಿ **ghâbari, ghâbri.** Flutter, flurry, confusion of mind (S. C.).

ಚಹರೆ, ಚಾರೆ **ĉahare, ĉâre.** Features, complexion; 2, green fodder.

ಚಡಾಯಿಸು **ĉaḍâyisu.** To execute, *also* ಚಿಪಾಯಿಸು.

ಜಯಿಲ್ **jayil.** Sequel, following; 2, endorsed (S. C.).

ಜುಜಿವಿ **jujivi.** A little, in a small quantity.

ತಜವೀಜು **tazavizu.** Endeavour, effort; —ಮಾಡು (-mâḍu) to arrange, to plan (S. C.).

ತಫಾವತ್ **taphâvat.** Difference (S. C.); 2, cheating, defrauding.

ತಬಲಕು **tabalaku.** A bundle of loose papers tied with a string.

ತರತೀಬ **taratiba.** Method, arrangement (My.).

ತರದೂದು **taradûdu.** An attempt (*see p.* 70); ಹರ- (har-) all means, every effort (My.).

ತವಾಯಿ **tavâyi.** Delay (S. C.).

ತಾಕುಬಡಿ **tâkubaḍi.** Extra expenses.

ತಾಜಾ **tâzâ.** New, bran-new, fresh.

ತಾರಿಫ **târifa.** Recommendation of a thing; 2, *ironically* to make a jest of (S. C.).

ತೀಂತೇರಾ **tintêrâ.** Dispersed or scattered.

ತೇದಾತು **têdâtu.** Quantity.

ದಗಲ್‌ಬಾಜಿ **dagalbâji.** Deceit, fraud.

ದಫಾ **daphâ.** A time, a turn (S. C.).

ದರದೂದ್ **daradûd.** Repairs.

ದರೋಬಸ್ತ್ **darôbast.** All, entire.

ದಸ್ತೂರಿ **dastûri.** Custom, usage.

ದಾಂಡಗಾಯಿ **dânḍagâyi.** Impudent conduct, overbearing behaviour.

ದಾಗ್‌ದಾಗನಿ **dâgdâgani.** A thing or article.

ದಾಗಿನಾ **dâginâ.** Jewels, ornaments.

ದಾಸ್ತಾನು **dâstânu.** Storing up.

ದಿಲ್‌ದಾರ **dildâra.** A generous or noble-minded man (S. C.).

ಧೊಂದಲೆ **dhondale.** Disorder, confusion.

ನಾದಾರ್ **nâdâr.** Insolvent, poor.

ನಿಗಾ **nigâ.** Superintendence, taking care; ನಿಗೆವಾನಿ (nigevâni) taking care of, looking after.

ನಿಮಿತ್ಯ **nimitya.** Concern, business (My.); 2, augury.

ನಿಶಿ **niśi.** With, together with.

ಪಕ್ಕಾ **pakkâ.** Fit, 'first-class', A 1.

ಪಸಂದು **pasandu.** Nice; —ಮಾಡು (-mâḍu) to approve.

ಪೀಡಿ, ಪೀಳಿಗೆ **piḍi, piḷige.** Generation; ಪೀಳಿಪೀಳಿಗೆಯಾಗಿ (pîḷipîḷigeyâgi) in lineal descent (S. C.); ಪೀಡಿದರ್ ಪೀಡಿ (pîḍidar pîḍi) head after head, lineally (My.).

ಪುಂಡ **punḍa.** A mischievous man; —ತನ (-tana) mischievousness.

ಪುಕಾರ, ಪುಕಾರೆ **pukâra, pukâre.** Rumour, report; 2, an alarm.

ಪುಸ್ತಿ **pusti.** A second or help; —ಕೊಡು (-koḍu) to support or assist; —ಬಂದಿ (-bandi) support.

ಪೈಕಿ **paiki.** Out of, respecting.

ಪೋಕ್ರಿ **pôkri.** Mischievous, dissolute; —ತನ (-tana) mischievousness.

ಫಜೀತಿ **phajiti.** *Lit.* Ignominy, disgrace; 2, dilemma, difficulty.

ಫಟಿಂಗ **phaṭiṅga.** A rake, a liar.

ಫಡಪೋಸಿ **phaḍapôsi.** Evasive, shuffling, neglectful; —ಮನುಷ್ಯ (-manushya) a careless man; —ಕೆಲಸ (-kelasa) work done 'anyhow'.

ಫಲಾನಿ **phalâni.** Certain, such and such.

ಫಾಯ್ಸ್ **phâys.** Public; —ಮಾಡು (-mâḍu) to publish, to notify, to proclaim.

ಫುಕ್ಕಟೆ **phukkaṭe.** Gratis; *also* ಫುಕಸಾಟೆ.

ಫುರ್ಸತ್ **phursat.** Time, leisure, recess.

ಬಖೇಡಿ **bakhêḍi.** One who has become poor from debts, an insolvent.

ಬರಾಬರ್ **barâbar.** Correct, 'all right'.

ಬೇಖೂಬ್ **bêkhûb.** Stupid, senseless.

ಬೇಜಾ **bêjâ.** Bad, indifferent.

ಬೇಷ್ **bêsh.** Excellent.

ಬೇಷಕ್ **bêshak.** Without doubt, positively.

ಭರ್ **bhar.** Full, whole; —ಕೋರ್ಟು (-kôrṭu) 'open court' (S. C.).

ಮಜಬೂತ್ **mazabût.** Strong, substantial.

ಮರ್ಜಿ **marji.** Opinion; 2, humour, manner (S. C.).

ಮಟ್ಟು **maṭṭu.** Capacity, extent; 2, the secret of any thing (S. C.).

ಮಲಾಮತ್ **malâmat.** *Lit.* Blame, reproach; a cause of trouble, inconvenience (S. C).

ಮಾತಬರಿ, ಮಾತುಬರಿ **mâtabari, mâtubari.** Substantial, trustworthy respectable.

ಮಾಫಕ್ **mâphak.** Due, according to a thing's value.

ಮಾಫಿ **mâphi.** Excusing, overlooking; 2, remission, exemption.

ಮಾರಿಫತ್ **mâriphat.** By means of, through.

ಮಿಜಾತಿ, ಮಿಜಾದು **mizâti, mizâdu.** *Lit.* Ostentation, impudence or overbearing conduct (S. C.).

ಮುಗ್ತೆ **mugte.** Contract; –ಕೆಲಸ (-kelasa) work taken up on contract, as opposed to ದಿನಕೂಲಿ (dinakûli) or work paid by the day (S. C.).

ಮುಟ್ಟುವಳಿ **muṭṭuvaḷi.** Cost, outlay.

ಮುನಾಸಬು **munâsabu.** A person's worth or property; –ಮೇಲೆ (-mêle) having regard to one's circumstances, at one's discretion.

ಮುಲಾಜೆ **mulâje.** Respect, regard, obligation.

ಮೆಹನತ್ **mehanat.** Exertion, pains.

ಮೊಕ್ತಾ **moktâ.** Personally; –ಮಾಡು (-mâḍu) to confront (S. C.).

ಮೋಗುಮ್ **môgum.** Secret, implied (S. C.).

ರಿಯಾಯತಿ **riyâyati.** Protection; 2, lenience; –ಮಾಡು (-mâḍu) to make an exception of, to treat leniently or with indulgence.

ರೂಬರೂಬ್ **rûbarûb.** In one's presence; personally.

ಲಗ್‌ಬಗ್ **lagbag.** *Lit.* Haste, almost, approximately, nearly (S. C.).

ಲತಾಡೆ **latâḍe.** Pressure (S. C.).

ಲಾಗವಾಡು **lâgavâḍu.** Expenses, outlay.

ವಾಜಬಿ **vâjabi.** Reasonable, proper; ಗೈರ್– (gair-) improper.

ಶಿಕಸ್ತ್ **śikast.** Out of repairs.

ಸಬಬ್ **sabab.** Reason, cause; *also* ಸಬಬು.

ಸಮಜಾಯಿಸು **samajâyisu.** To comfort; 2, to satisfy.

ಸರಂಜಾಮ **sarañjâma.** Furniture; 2, paraphernalia.

ಸರಬರಾಯಿ **sarabarâyi.** Purveying, furnishing supplies.

ಸರಾಸರಿ **sarâsari.** Average.

ಸಲಾಕಿ **salâki.** *Lit.* Full-grown, 'first class, A 1 (S. C.); 2, a ramrod, a bar.

ಸಾದಾ **sâdâ.** Plain, simple.

ಸಾಧಕ ಬಾಧಕ **sâdhaka bâdhaka.** Offensive and defensive; good or bad consequences; *pros* and *cons*.

ಸಾಫು **sâphu.** Plain, clear.

ಸುಸ್ತಿ **susti.** Delay, procrastination.

ಸೋಡ್ತಿ **sôḍti.** A lottery, raffle (S. C.); *cf.* ಸೋಬಳಿ (sôbaḷi) (S. M.).

ಹಕೀಕತ್ತು **hakikattu.** An account of one's circumstances.

ಹದ್ದು **haddu.** A limit; –ಹಾಳಿತ (-hâḷita) a prudent limit, economy.

ಹಮಾಕೋಮು **hamâkômu.** All classes and castes, all sorts and conditions.

ಹಮೇಶಾ **hamêshâ.** Always, constantly.

ಹರಕತ್ತು **harakattu.** Obstacle, hindrance, opposition.

ಹಿಕ್ಮತ್ **hikmat.** Cunning, trickery.

ಹಿಷಾರೆ **hishâre.** A sign or token; *also* ಇಷಾರೆ.

ಹುಶಾರ್ **hušâr.** Smart, clever, apt; 2, vigilent.

ಹೈರಾನ್ **hairân.** Distressed, perturbed, exhausted.

ಹೋಲ್ವೆ **hôlve.** Likelihood, probability (S. C.).

Music.

Note:—The Italian words are merely *suggestive* rather than authoritative. Hn. and Kn. are abbreviations for Hindustâni and Karnâṭak, the two modes of Indian Music.

ಅಂತರಾ **antarâ.** The song, as distinguished from the chorus (Hn.).

ಅನುಪಲ್ಲವಿ **anupallavi.** The chorus; *also* ಪಲ್ಲವಿ (Kn.).

ಅಲಗು **alagu.** Quaver, trill, shake.

ಅವರೋಹಣ **avarôhaṇa.** Cadence, *diminuendo.*

ಅಸ್ತಾಯಿ **astâyi.** The chorus, the burden of a song, refrain (Hn.).

ಆಟಂದಿಕೊಳ್ಳು **âṭandikoḷḷu.** To sing or play alternately, as in a catch or antiphony.

ಆರೋಹಣ **ârôhaṇa.** Treble in an ascending scale, *crescendo.*

ಆಲಾಪನೆ **âlâpane.** Prelude, humming a tune before singing (Kn.); 2, modulation (Hn.).

ಉಸ್ತಾದ್ **ustâd.** A music-master, a *maestro, incorrectly* ವಸ್ತಾದ (S. C.).

ಕಂಪಿತ **kampita.** *Tremolo.*

ಕಾಕಳಿ **kâkaḷi.** A mild, charming voice.

ಕೃತಿ **kṛiti.** A musical composition.

ಗಮಕ **gamaka.** A general term for a rapid vibration of the voice; 2, one of the 22 quarter tones in music.

ಗಾನ **gâna.** Music; *also* ಗಾಯನ; ಅನು- (anu-) keeping tune with another.

ಗ್ರಾಮ **grâma.** An octave, the diatonic scale, *also* ಸ್ವರ-.

ತಂತಿ **tanti.** The string of a musical instrument; ಸಾರಿಣಿ (sâriṇi) the first string; ಅನುಸಾರಿಣಿ (anusâriṇi) the second string; ಮಂದ್ರ (mandra) the third string; ಅನುಮಂದ್ರ (anumandra) the fourth string; ಜೋಡಿ (jôḍi) two strings kept on one and the same pitch.

ತಾನ್ **tân.** Grace notes (Hn.); 2, pause or hold (Hn.): -ಕರ್ಮ (-karma) running over the notes to catch the key.

ತಾಳ **tâḷa.** Musical time, *tempo,* of which there are seven modes; -ರೇಖೆ (-rêkhe) bar; -ಗತಿ (-gati) the keeping of time to music; -ಲಕ್ಷಣ (-lakshaṇa) the art of beating time to music; ಏಕ- (êka-) harmony. The three terms ಆಡ್ or ದೇಡಿ (âḍ, dêḍi), ದುಗುಣ (duguṇa), ತಿಗುಣ (tiguṇa), respectively denote acceleration of the original time to 1½, 2 and 3 times (Hn.); ಠಾಯ (ṭhâya) denotes both slow time, and return to the original time, *a tempo* (Hn.).

ತಿಲ್ಲಾಣ, ತಿಲ್ಲಾನಾ tillâṇa, tillânâ. A mode of singing in which unmeaning sounds are uttered.

ತ್ರಿಸ್ಥಾಯಿ, ತ್ರಿಸ್ಥಾನ tristhâyi, tristhâna. The third octave.

ದಕ್ಷಿಣಾದಿ dakshiṇâdi. The Southern or Karnatic mode of music.

ಮುಕ್ತಾಯ muktâya. Cadence, the conclusion of a song; —ಪೆಟ್ಟು (-peṭṭu) the finishing stroke on the drum.

ಮುದ್ರಿಕೆ mudrike. Dedication of a poem to a person or deity

ಮೂರ್ಛನೆ mûrčhane. A tone or semi-tone placed in a scale; 2, modulation.

ಮೇಳ mêḷa. Harmony, counter-point; *also* ಸ್ವರ— (svara-); 2, a choir.

ರಾಗ râga. A tune; a principal tune (Hn.); *also* called ಘನ— (ghana-) (Kn.); ರಾಗಿಣಿ (râgiṇi) a secondary or derivative tune (Hn.); ರಕ್ತಿ— (rakti-) a secondary or derivative tune (Kn.); an agreeable tune.

ಲಯ laya. Musical time, *tempo*, divided into ದ್ರುತ (druta) quick, *presto*; ಮಧ್ಯ (madhya) mean or moderate, *moderato*; ವಿಲಂಬಿತ (vilambita) slow, *largo*, *incorrectly* ಬಿಲಂಪದ.

ವಾದ್ಯ vâdya. Music; 2, a musical instrument; ಘನ— (ghana-) music on vibrating surfaces *e. g.* ತಾಳ, ಚಕ್ರತಾಳ (tâla, čakratâla) cymbals, ಟಿಪ್ರಿ (ṭipri) a castanet, ಸ್ವರಮಂಡಲ (svaramaṇḍala) an Æolian harp, ಜಲತರಂಗ (jalataranga) seven metal cups of different sizes filled with water and beaten with thin sticks; ತತ— (tata-) music on stringed instruments, *e. g.* ವೀಣೆ (viṇe), ಸಾರಂಗ (sâranga), ತಂಬೂರ (tambûra), ಬಿನ್ (bin), ತೌಜೆ (tauze), ಸುರಸಿಂಗಾರ (surasingâra), ಸತಾರ್ (satâr), ಸರೋದ್ (sarôd)—all, different varieties of lutes or violins, ಕಿನ್ನರಿ or ಏಕತಾರ (kinnari, êkatâra) a monochord; ಮುಖ— (mukha-) music on wind-instruments, *e. g.* ಮುಖವೀಣೆ (mukhaviṇe) a fife, ಕೊಳಲು (koḷalu) a flute, ಮೋರ್ಚಂಗ್ (môrčang) a Jew's harp, ಶ್ರುತಿ (śruti) a drone, ಪಿಳಂಗೋವಿ (piḷangôvi) a bagpipe, ಸನಾದಿ (sanâdi) a hautboy, ತುತೂರಿ (tutûri) a trumpet; ಚರ್ಮ— (čarma-) music on drums, varieties of which are: ಭೇರಿ (bhêri) a large drum, ನಗಾರಿ (nagâri) a kettle-drum, ಡಕ್ಕೆ (ḍakke) a double drum, ಡಮ್ಮಿಡಿ (ḍammiḍi) a tambourine, ಸಮ್ಮೇಳ (sammêḷa), ತಬ್ಲ (table), ಪಕ್ವಾಜ್ (pakvâz), ಚಂದ್ರವಾದ್ಯ (čandravâdya), ಮದ್ದಳೆ (maddaḷe).

ಶ್ರುತಿ śruti. A quarter tone or interval; —ಮಾಡು (-mâḍu) to put an instrument into tune.

ಸಂಗ್ತಿ saṅgti. Grace notes (Kn.).

ಸರಳೆ saraḷe. The notes of a gamut.

ಸಾಜ್ sâz. Accompaniment, *obbligato* (Hn.), corresponding to ಸಾಹಿತ್ಯ (sâhitya) (Kn.).

ಸೂರ sûra. Pitch; —ಹಿಡಿ (-hiḍi) to pitch a tune.

ಸೊಲ್ಲು sollu. The chief part of a song, corresponding to ಅಂತರಾ (Kn.).

ಸ್ವರ svara. A note; ಸಪ್ತ— (sapta-) an octave consisting of 1, ಸ, ಷಡ್ಜ (sa, shaḍja) C, *do;* 2, ರಿ, ಋಷಭ (ri, ṛishabha) D, *re;* 3, ಗ, ಗಾಂಧಾರ (ga, gândhâra) E, *mi;* 4, ಮ, ಮಧ್ಯಮ (ma, madhyama) F, *fa;* 5, ಪ, ಪಂಚಮ (pa, pañcama) G, *sol;* 6, ಧ, ಧೈವತ (dha, dhaivata) A, *la;* 7, ನಿ, ನಿಷಾದ (ni, nishâda) B, *si;* ಅಪ— (apa-) a false note, a note not in the key; ಗಂಭೀರ, ಮಂದ್ರ (gambhîra, mandra) voice of the lowest pitch, bass or *contralto* (Kn.), corresponding to ಖರಜ್, ಖರ್ಜ್ (kharaz, kharz) (Hn.); ಶುದ್ಧ— (śuddha-) a correct note; ಉಠಾವ್— (uṭhâv-) the key-note, tonic (Hn.); ಅರ್ಧ—, —ಅಂಶ (ardha-, -aṁśa) a semi-tone; ತಾರ—, ತಾರಕ— (târa-, târaka-) a voice of the highest pitch, treble, *soprano*; ದೀರ್ಘ— (dîrgha-) a lengthened note; ಹ್ರಸ್ವ— (hrasva-) a short note; ವರ್ಜ— (varja-) a note to be omitted in a tune or passage; —ಜ್ಞಾನ (-jñâna) a musical ear; ತೀವ್ರ— (tîvra-) a sharp note; ಕೋಮಲ— (kômala-) a flat note; —ಬಿಡು (-biḍu) to bring in a false note; ಜಂಟೆ— (jaṇṭe-) a double note, as CC DD; —ಕಲ್ಪನೆ (-kalpane) grace-notes; —ಸಾಹಿತ್ಯ (-sâhitya) the words of a song denoted by symbols.

ಹಾಡು hâḍu. To sing.

ಹಿಂದುಸ್ತಾನಿ hindustâni. The Northern mode of music.

Natural and Artificial Divisions of Land and Water.

I. Land.

a) *Divisions of Land.*

ಅಗ್ರ **agra.** A cape.

ಊರು **ûru.** A town or village.

ಕಸಬಾ, ಕಸಬೆ **kasabâ, kasabe.** The chief station or head-quarters of a district or mâgaṇe.

ಕುದುರು **kuduru.** An island formed in a river by alluvial deposit, an islet (S.C.).

ಕೊಂಬು **kombu.** A district, so termed in the 16th century (Cg.).

ಕೊನೆ **kone.** A cape, a point.

ಕೊಪ್ಪಲು **koppalu.** Suburbs or outlying villages of a town.

ಗಡಿ **gaḍi.** A district composed of four to ten hôbaḷis (My.).

ಗ್ರಾಮ **grâma.** A village; ಅಸಲಿ– (asali-) a primary or original village, or that on which the revenue was originally assessed, as opposed to ದಾಖಲಿ– (dâkhali-) an included or secondary village (My.).

ಗೂಡ **gûḍa.** A small hamlet near a village.

ಜಿಲ್ಲಾ **zillâ.** A district made up of several sub-districts (ತಾಲೂಕ).

ತರ್ಫ **tarpha.** *Lit.* A side, a part of a tâluk, a mâgaṇe

ತಾಲೂಕು **tâlûku.** A group of mâgaṇes.

ತುಕಡಿ **tukaḍi.** A district, a division (My.).

ದ್ವೀಪ **dvipa.** An island; ಅರ್ಧ– (ardha-) a peninsula.

ನಾಡು **nâḍu.** A rural place (S. C.); 2, an ancient name for ಸೀಮೆ (My.); ಮಲೆ– (male-) a hill-tract; ನಡೆ– (nade-) a midland.

ಪಟ್ಟಣ **paṭṭaṇa.** A town, city; ಮುಖ್ಯ– (mukhya-) a capital.

ಫಿರ್ಕಿ **phirki.** A group of villages for which there is one Mâgaṇe Shânbhâg, the division of a Tahasildar.

ಭೂ **bhû.** Land; –ಖಂಡ (-khaṇḍa) a continent; –ಸಂಧಿ, –ಕಂಠ, (-sandhi, -kaṇṭha) an isthmus.

ಮಂದೆ **mande.** The sub-division of a hôbaḷi, corresponding to ಫಿರ್ಕ (Manjarabad).

ಮವುಜೆ **mavuze.** A hamlet.

ಮಾಗಣೆ **mâgaṇe.** A group of villages; ಫೂಟ- (phûṭ-) a mâgaṇe assessed and managed separately (My.).

ಮುಜರೆ, ಮುಜ್ರೆ **mujare, mujre.** A hamlet.

ಸೀಮೆ **sime.** A province; 2, a province of 10 to 20 gaḍis (My.).

ಸಮತು **samatu.** A division of a district (My.).

ಹಳ್ಳಿ **haḷḷi.** A village, a hamlet; *also* –ಗಾಡು (-gâḍu); 2, an ancient village (My.); ಕಲು– (kalu-) a new additional village (My.).

ಹೋಬಳಿ **hôbaḷi.** A sub-district composed of 10 to 40 villages (My.); in the Kanara province, there were three hôbaḷis—Mangalore, Barkur, Bhagwadi.

b) Distinction of land as to elevation.

ಅಗ್ಗಳ **aggaḷa.** A moat; *see p.* 112; –ಹಾಕು, –ಕಟ್ಟು (-hâku, -kaṭṭu) to dig a moat and raise a wall (S. C.).

ಅಡ್ಕ **aḍka.** A low waste-land, a low waste ground; *also* ಅಡಗ (aḍaga) (S. C.).

ಅಣೆ **aṇe.** Steepness, a steep footpath (S. C.).

ಇಳಕಲು **iḷakalu.** A precipice or declivity.

ಇಳಿಜಾರು **iḷijâru.** A slope, a descent or declivity (S. C.); *also* ಇಳಿವಾರು.

ಏರು **êru.** An acclivity, an ascent.

ಕಂದರ, ಕೊನ್ನಾರ **kandara, konnâra.** A valley.

ಕಣಿಮೆ **kaṇime.** A defile, a pass, a ravine; *also* ಕಣಿವೆ.

ಕರೆ, ಕರಾವಳಿ **kare, karâvaḷi.** A coast-line.

ಕಲ್ಬೀಣೆ **kalbiṇe.** A spur between two hills connecting them (S. C.).

ಕೈಪುಡಿ **kaipuḍi.** A parapet wall (My.).

ಕೋಡು **kôḍu.** The summit of a mountain; *also* –ಗಲ್ಲು.

ಗವಿ **gavi.** A cave, cavern; *also* ಗುಹೆ.

ಗುಡ್ಡ, ಗುಡ್ಡೆ **guḍḍa, guḍḍe.** A hill; –ಗಟ್ಟು (-gaṭṭu) a table-land on the top of a hill, a plateau; –ತಪ್ಪಲು (-tappalu) table-land round the foot of a hill; ಹುಬ್ಬು– (hubbu-) a hill range; –ನೆತ್ತಿ (-netti) the top or summit of a hill, the saddle of a hill. In S. Canara, this is sometimes the boundary-mark of lands; sometimes a stone exists or is placed at the top of a hill to mark the point from which rain-water commences to scatter in all directions and water adjacent lands, in which case the stone is called ನೀರುಯಾರಕಲ್ಲು or ಯರಕಲ್ಲು (nîruyara-kallu, yarakallu); sometimes there is no stone but an imaginary point on the apex of a hill from which water commences to flow in a certain direction, the point being called ನೀರುಮಗುಳ್ತೆ (nîrumagulte).

ಗಿರಿ **giri.** A mountain.

ಚಡಾವು **caḍâvu.** An ascent (S. C.).

ಚಿಟ್ಟೆ **ciṭṭe.** An elevated dry-land, *also* ಶಿಟ್ಟು; *cf.* ಶಿಟ್ಟ (N. C.).

ಟಾಕು **ṭâku.** A descent or valley under a hill.

ತಗ್ಗು **taggu.** A descent, declivity; –ಭೂಮಿ (-bhûmi) a low land, *also* ತಗ್ಗಡ (taggeḍa).

ತೆವರು **tevaru.** A rising ground, a hill; 2, a valley.

ದಿನ್ನೆ **dinne.** A hillock, a low-rising ground; –ತಗ್ಗು (-taggu) hill and dale.

ಡೊಂಗರ **doṅgara.** A hollow, a ravine.

ನೆತ್ತಿಕಟ್ಟು **nettikaṭṭu.** The crest of a hill adjoining cultivation; the water-shed of a hill (S. C.).

ಪಡಿ, ಪಡೆ **paḍi, paḍe.** A cliff.

ಪದವು **padavu.** A table-land, a plateau; an ascent (S. C.).

ಪರ್ವತ **parvata.** A mountain; –ಶಿಖರ (-śikhara) the peak.

ಪಳ್ಳ **paḷḷa.** A hollow (S. C.).

ಪಾಗಾರ **pâgâra.** An enclosure of earth.

ಬೆಂಗರೆ, ಬೆಂಗ್ರೆ **beṅgare, beṅgre.** A strip of land between the sea and the land or river, seashore (S. C.).

ಬೆಟ್ಟ **beṭṭa.** A hill; ಬಾಣ– (bâṇa-) a hill on a higher elevation.

ಬೈಲು **bailu.** A plain; 2, a wet land; ಬಟಾ–, ಬಟ್ಟ– (baṭâ-, baṭṭa-) an open plain; –ಸೀಮೆ (-sîme) a champaign.

ಮೈದಾನು **maidânu.** An open plain, a *maidan*.

ಸರಕು **saraku.** A ravine.

ಸಾನುಭೂಮಿ **sânubhûmi.** A table-land.

c) Land and Vegetation.

ಅಡವಿ **aḍavi.** A forest; ಅಟ್ಟ– (aṭṭa-) an impervious forest.

ಅರಣ್ಯ **araṇya.** A desert, wilderness.

ಉಡುವೆ **uḍuve.** A village jungle or forest, with an undergrowth of bamboos and thorns, sometimes entirely surrounded by rice-fields; jungly tract for coffee cultivation (Nagar and Hasan).

ಕಾಡು **kâḍu.** A jungle; ಕಣಿವೆ– (kaṇive-) forests on the lower hill ranges and passes (Cg.); ಕುಚ್ಚಿ– (kuċċi-) a brush-wood, scrub-jungle (from ಕುತ್ತಿ a stump ?), *also* ಕುಚ್ಚಿಸ್ಥಳ (S. C.); ಗೆರೆ– (gere-) a scrub-jungle near rice-fields (Cg.); ಮಲೆ– (male-) mountain-forests (Cg.); ಸುರಕ್ಷಿತ–, ಕಾಪಿನ– (surakshita-, kâpina-) a preserved or reserved forest; ದೇವರ– (dêvara-) a jungle attached to a village temple and dedicated to a deity, a sacred grove (Cg.).

ಕಾಣ **kâṇa.** Large tracts of forest, 8 or 9 miles in extent, in which pepper, cardamoms are cultivated.

ಕುಂಜಾರ್ **kuñjâr.** A small jungle (S. C.).

ಗಿಡ **giḍa.** Woods (My.).

ಗುಜ್ಜಿ **gujji.** An elevated piece of land overgrown with shrubs, a scrub-jungle (S. C.); *cf.* ಕುಚ್ಚಿಕಾಡು.

ಝಾಡಿ **jhâḍi.** A place overgrown with shrubs, a scrub-jungle (My.); *also* ಝಾನ್ (jhân).

ಪೊದೆ **pode.** A bush.

ಬನ **bana.** A grove (S. C.); ನಾಗರ– (nâgara-) a grove where 'snake-stones' are kept, a sacred grove (S. C.).

ಬಾಣೆ **bâṇe.** Land adjoining rice-fields, generally covered with jungle (Cg.); a glade.

ಮಲೆ **male.** A ghaut-forest, forest tracts situated close to the crest of hills or mountains.

ಲಚ್ಲು, ಲಚ್ಚಿಲು **laċlu, laċċilu.** An enclosed pasture-ground, brush-wood (S. C.).

ವಳಚಿಲು **valaċilu.** (from ಬಳ + ಅಚ್ಚಿಲು ?) Underwood, a fenced wood near a house (S. C.).

ಹಕ್ಲು **haklu.** An elevated piece of ground covered with brush-wood; a piece of dry-land irrigated by rain and used for raising vegetable on.

ಹಾಡಿ **hâḍi.** A copse, brush-wood; —ಹಕ್ಲು (-haklu) coppice attached to a farm.

ಹಾಡ್ಯ **hâḍya.** A tract of land covered with brush-wood (My.).

II. Water.

ಅಳವೆ, ಅಳುವೆ **aḷave, aḷuve.** An arm of the sea, an estuary (S. C.); —ದಂಡೆ (-daṇḍe) the "bar" (S. C.).

ಕೊಲ್ಲಿ **kolli.** A bay, *also* ಅಖಾತ (akhâta).

ಕೊಳ್ಳ **koḷḷa.** A rivulet; 2, a small tank; —ವಾಯಿ (-vâyi) head-sluice (My.).

ಖಾರಿ **khâri.** An arm of the sea, backwater; 2, a ferry (S. C.).

ಜಲಸಂದು **jalasandu.** A strait.

ನದಿ **nadi.** A river; ಉಪ— (upa-) an affluent. a tributary river.

ನೀರುನೆತ್ತಿ **nirunetti.** A watershed.

ಮಾನುಬಾಯಿ **mânubâyi.** A temporary sluice (My.).

ರೇವು **rêvu.** A harbour.

ಸಂಗಮ **saṅgama.** A junction of two rivers, confluence.

ಸಮುದ್ರ **samudra.** A sea; ಸಾಗರ (sâgara) an ocean.

ಹೊಳೆ **hoḷe.** A river; —ಒಡಲು (-oḍalu) the bed of a river.

b) Water and Land.

ಕೆರೆ **kere.** A tank; ಮಡಗ (madaga) a large lake, *also* ತಲಾವ (talâv).

ಕೊಂಡ **koṇḍa.** A small shallow tank (Cg.).

ಕೊಳ **koḷa.** A pond or tank.

ಚಿಲಿಮೆ **ċilime.** A small shallow tank (S. C.); 2, a hole in the sand for water.

ಜೋಗು **jôgu.** A cataract, 'falls' (C.).

ನಿರ್ತೆ **nirte.** A spring (s. c.).

ಬುಗ್ಗೆ **bugge.** A fountain.

ಬೆಂಚೆ **beñče.** A lake; 2, a rivulet.

ಭಾವಿ **bhâvi.** A well, *also* ಬಾವಿ; —ತಳ, —ದಳ (-taḷa, -daḷa) the bottom of a well; ಜಲೆ— (jale-) a spring well; ತಲಪಿರಿ (talapiri) a well made in sandy ground and requiring a wooden frame-work to prevent the sides falling in.

ಸರಸ್ಸು **sarassu.** A lake, *also* ಸರೋವರ (sarôvara).

ಹಳ್ಳ **haḷḷa.** A streamlet, *also* —ಪಳ್ಳ (-paḷḷa).

c) Rain, etc.

ಆನೆಕಲ್ಲು **ânekallu.** Hail.

ಇಬ್ಬನಿ **ibbani.** Dew.

ನೀರ್ಗಲ್ಲು **nirgallu.** Ice, hail-stone.

ಮಂಜು **mañju.** Fog; —ಧೂಳಿ (-dhûḷi) a thick fog.

ಮಳೆ **maḷe.** Rain, *for the periodicity of which see* ನಕ್ಷತ್ರ p. 36; ಅಡ್ಡ— (aḍḍa-) a heavy rain; ಕಲ್ಲ— (kall-) hail-storm; ಜಡಿ— (jaḍi-) a continued shower; ತುಂತುರು— (tunturu-) a drizzle; ಬೆದರ್— (bedar-) short and impetuous rain; ಸೋನೆ— (sône-) a gentle light rain; ಹೊಂಚು— (hoñču-) an unexpected shower; ಹದ— (hada-) a quantity of rain sufficient to render the earth fit for sowing.

ಹಿಮ **hima.** Snow; —ಗಡ್ಡೆ (-gaḍḍe) ice; ಹಿಮಕ (himaka) sleet; ಹಿಮಾನಿ (himâni) hoar-frost.

Nautical.

ಅಂತಸ್ತು **antastu.** The deck of a ship.

ಅಗ್ರಸಣಿ **agrasaṇi.** Lading one vessel from another, *also* ಹಗ್ರಸಣಿ (S. C.).

ಅಡಿತಟ್ಟೆ **aḍitaṭṭe.** The keel (S. C.).

ಅಡ್ಡಮರ **aḍḍamara.** The boom of a mast (S. C.).

ಅಣ್ಯ **aṇya.** The prow (S. C.).

ಅಬರ **abara.** The stern (S. C.).

ಅಲಾತು **alâtu.** The cables.

ಅಳವೆಸಾಯರ **aḷavesâyara.** The marine department.

ಆರ್ಕಾಟಿ **ârkâṭi.** A pilot (S. C.).

ಇಳಿತ **iḷita.** Low or neap tide, ebb.

ಈಜು **îju.** To swim; 2, to paddle a boa

ಉಡುಪ **uḍupa.** A float or raft.

ಉಳಂದಿ, ಉಲ್ಲಂದಿ **uḷandi, ullandi.** The balancing out-rigger of a boat (N. C.).

ಒಟ್ಟಿಕಣ್ಣಿ **oṭṭikaṇṇi.** The ring of an anchor (S. C.).

ಓಡ **ôḍa.** A boat; –ನಡಿಸು (-naḍisu) to steer a boat.

ಕಡವು **kaḍavu.** A ferry (S. C.).

ಕದಮ್ತುಂಡು **kadamtuṇḍu.** Shores, shoars (S. C.).

ಕಪಿ **kapi.** A pulley (S. C.).

ಕಮಾವಿಷಿದಾರ **kamâvishidâra.** A -custom superintendent.

ಕಳ್ಳಕುಣಿ **kaḷḷakuṇi.** Quicksand.

ಕಿಳಾಯ **kiḷâya.** The hull of a ship (S. C.).

ಕೂವೆಮರ **kûvemara.** The mast of a ship (S. C.)

ಕೊಂತಳ **kontaḷa.** A light boat (S. C.).

ಕೊಲ್ಲಾಯಿ **kollâyi.** An anchor (S. C.).

ಖಲಾಸಿ **khalâsi.** The crew of a ship.

ಖಾರಿ **khâri.** A back-water, an arm of the sea.

ಗಣೆ **gaṇe.** The mast of a ship, *also* ಅಡ್ಡ– (aḍḍa-).

ಗರಿ **gari.** A ferry.

ಗಾಳಿ **gâḷi.** Wind; ಅಡ್ಡ- (aḍḍa-) side-wind; ಎದುರು- (eduru-) opposite wind; ಕರೆ- (kare-) land-wind; ಬಿರು- (biru-) a stiff breeze; ಸುಳಿ- (suḷi-) whirl-wind, cyclone.

ಗೊಸಬು **gosabu.** Quicksand.

ಗೋಸ್, ಗೋಸು **gôs, gôsu.** Leeward; 2, sea-ward (S. C.).

ಚಪ್ರಕೊಗಳು **čaprakogaḷu.** A temporary shed or awning of cadjan leaves erected on a native vessel for the accommodation of passengers (S. C.).

ಚುಕ್ಕಾಣಿ **čukkâṇi.** A rudder, helm; *also* ಸುಂಕಾಣಿ; -ಚಕ್ರ (-čakra) a rudder-wheel; -ಹಿಡಿಕೆ (-hiḍike) the tiller.

ಚೋಪಟ್ಟ್ **čôpaṭṭ.** A kind of pitching or calking a boat or ship with a substance called ಬೊಳಕ್ (boḷak) fat of fish, or fish oil (S. C.).

ಜಂಗಾಲ್ **jaṅgâl.** A wooden platform placed on two boats tied together (ಸಂಗಡ saṅgaḍa) for the carriage of horses, carts, etc.; hence a boat so constructed (S. C.).

ಜಲ್ಲ **jalla.** An oar (S. C.).

ಜಾಲಿಗ **jâliga.** The captain of a ship.

ಜೀಬು **jibu.** *Anglice* Jib (S. C.).

ಟಾಂಕಿ **ṭâṅki.** A water-cistern, a tank (S. C.).

ತಂಡೇಲ **tanḍêla** The captain of a native craft, a "tindal".

ತಾರಿ **târi.** A ferry, ford (N. C.).

ತುಫಾನು **tuphânu.** Storm, typhoon.

ತೂತಾಕ **tûtâka.** The deck (S. C.); -ಮುಚ್ಚುಹಲಿಗೆ (-muččuhalige) hatchways (S. C.).

ತೆಪ್ಪ **teppa.** A raft or float.

ದವಾನ್ **damân.** The large sail of a boat (S. C.); 2, lee-ward (S. C.).

ದಂಡು **danḍu.** The oar of a boat (S. C.); -ಮೆಕ್ಕಳೆ (-mekkaḷe) rowlocks (S. C.).

ದಾಂಡಿ **dânḍi.** The stone-mark on a seashore.

ದಿಕ್‌ಚಕ್ರ **dikčakra.** A mariner's compass.

ಡೋಣಿ **dôṇi.** A boat.

ಧಕ್ಕೆ **dhakke.** The deck; 2, a quay, wharf; —ಯ ಜಕಾತಿ (-ya jakâti) wharfage.

ನಂಗರು **naṅgaru.** An anchor, *also* ಲಂಗರು (S. C.); —ಬಿಡು, —ಹಾಕು (-biḍu, -hâku) to cast anchor; —ಎತ್ತು (-ettu) to weigh anchor; —ವಾಡೆ (-vâḍe) anchorage (S. C.).

ನಕೋದಾ **nakôdâ.** A pilot; 2, a mate.

ನಗ **naga.** A sailing vessel (S. C.).

ನಾಟಿ **nâṭi.** An unwrought piece of wood (S. C.).

ನಾಳಿ **nâḷi.** The bow, stem or prow (S. C.); —ತುಂಡು (-tuṇḍu) the stern-post (S. C.).

ನಿಲಂ **nilam.** The ballast of a ship (S. C.).

ನೀರಳತೆ ಹಗ್ಗ **niraḷate hagga.** A plummet-line.

ನೋರು **nôru.** Freight (S. C.); 2, passage-money (S. C.).

ಪಟಾಣ **paṭâṇa.** The keel of a boat or ship (S. C.).

ಪಡಿ **paḍi.** The seats on a boat (S. C.).

ಪರಪು **parapu.** A sandbed (S. C.).

ಪರಬನ್ನ **parabanna.** The yard of a ship.

ಪರಮಾನ್ **paramân.** A sail-yard (S. C.).

ಪಾಂಡಿ **pâṇḍi.** The keel of a ship (S. C.).

ಪಾವಡ **pâvaḍa.** An anchor with two flukes (S. C.).

ಪೊಂಗಾಯಿ **poṅgâyi.** A light boat (S. C.).

ಬಂದರ **bandara.** A port (S. C.); —ಕಟ್ಟೆ (-kaṭṭe) a wharf; —ಮಾಡು (-mâḍu) to anchor (S. C.); —ಮಾಸ್ತರ (-mâstara) a sea-custom superintendent.

ಬಲಾವು **balâvu.** The ribs of a ship (S. C.).

ಬಾಣಿ **bâṇi.** The gunwale (S. C.).

ಬಿಜೆ **bije.** The bamboo matting of a native craft (S. C.).

ಬೆಳಗಂಡಿ **beḷagaṇḍi.** The sky-light or scuttle of a ship.

ಬೊಂಬ **bomba.** The bowsprit (S. C.).

ಭರ್ತ **bharta.** The spring or full tide (S. C.).

ಭರಾವಣಿ **bharâvaṇi.** The tonnage of a ship; —ಚೀಟು (-cîṭu) a bill of lading (S. C.).

ಭಾಟಿ **bhâṭi.** A shoal, sandbank (S. C.).

ಮಗ್ಗಲು **maggalu.** Larboard (S. C.).

ಮಣಿಕಾರ **maṇikâra.** The hull, ribs of a ship (S. C.).

ಮರಕಾಲ್ **marakâl.** A tindal (S. C.).

ಯೆರೆಹಲಿಗೆ **yerehalige.** The gunwale (S. C.).

ರೊಯಿಲಿ **royili.** A grapnel (S. C.).

ವಾಂಕಿ **vâṅki.** The ribs of a ship (S. C.); –ತುಂಡು (-tuṇḍu) the outer rim of a wheel; 2, the ribs of a ship (S. C.).

ವಾಸರ **vâsara.** The unevenness or unsteadiness of a ship.

ಸಂಗಡ **saṅgaḍa.** Two boats fastened together; *see* ಜಂಗಾಲ್ *p.* 134.

ಸಂತಮಿ **santami.** A manifest, *also* ಮಾನಿಫೆಸ್ತು (S. C.).

ಸುಳಿ **suḷi.** A whirlpool, an eddy.

ಸುಂಕದಕಟ್ಟೆ **suṅkadakaṭṭe.** A sea-custom office.

ಸೆಳತ **seḷata.** The current, the force of a stream, *also* ಸೆಳವು.

ಹರಗೋಲು **haragôlu.** A wicker boat covered with leather.

ಹುಟ್ಟು **huṭṭu.** A paddle; a rudder, *also* –ಹಲಿಗೆ (-halige); –ಹೂಡು (-hûḍu) to fix a paddle to a boat; –ಹೊಡೆಯು (-hoḍeyu) to paddle a boat, to use a paddle with a boat.

ಹಾಯಗಡ **hâyagaḍa.** A place where a stream can be forded.

ಹಾಯಿ **hâyi.** A sail; –ಇಳಿಸು (-iḷisu) to strike or take in sail; –ಏರಿಸು (-êrisu) to set sail; –ಪಟ್ಟೆ (-paṭṭe) canvass, sail-cloth.

ಹೊಯಿಲು, ಹೊಯ್ಲು **hoyilu, hoylu.** A strong current, a current.

ಹೊರಜಿ **horaji.** An hawser.

Precious Stones.

ಅಡಿಗೆಕಲ್ಲು **aḍigekallu.** An artificial gem.

ಕಟ್ಟು **kaṭṭu.** To set or mount a stone.

ಕಣಜ **kaṇaja.** A weight used for selling coral.

ಕಪ್ಪಚೋಕ್ **kappčôk.** A dark-red ruby (S. C.).

ಕೆಂಪು **kempu.** A ruby.

ಕೊಲ್ಲಂ **kollam.** Of Colombo, applied to an onyx (S. C.).

ಕೋಡಿ **kôḍi.** A score or lot of 20 loose rubies, emeralds or sapphires.

ಖಚಿಸು **khačisu.** To set a stone.

ಖನಿ **khani.** A mine; ಜುನಾ— (junâ-) a diamond from an old mine (S. C.); (ನವಾ— navâ-) a diamond from a new mine (S. C.).

ಖಾಷ್ಕಲ್ಲು **khâshkallu.** A jade.

ಖುರಂದದಕಲ್ಲು **khurandadakallu.** An emery.

ಗೂಡು **gûḍu.** The 'setting' of a ring.

ಗೋಮೇದಿಕ **gômêdika.** An onyx.

ಚಮಖು **čamakhu.** The lustre of a stone.

ಜವಾಹಿರ **javâhira.** Precious stones, *also* ornaments.

ಜಾಜುಕಲ್ಲು **jâjukallu.** Blood-stone.

ಜೀರಂ **jiram.** A crack in a precious stone (S. C.); *also* ಜೀರ (jîra).

ಠಕಾರಿ **ṭhakâri.** "Imitation", false; —ಮುತ್ತು (-muttu) an imitation pearl.

ತೆರಪು **terapu.** An inferior kind of precious stone, an imitation diamond (S. C.); *also* —ಕಲ್ಲು (-kallu).

ತಾಬ್ಲ **tâbla.** Table-cuts, facets (S. C.).

ತೇಪು—, ತೇಪೆ ಹಿಡಿಯು **têpu-, têpe hiḍiyu.** To polish a stone (S. C.).

ಧರ್ಮಕಂಟ **dharmakaṇṭa.** A place where the value of a gem can be definitely fixed and its quality ascertained.

ನೀರು **nîru.** The 'water' of a stone (S. C.).

ನೀಲ **nila.** A sapphire.

ಪಚ್ಛ **paččha.** An emerald, beryl; a chrysolite.

ಪದ್ಮರಾಗ **padmarâga.** A ruby, a ligure.

ಪುಷ್ಯರಾಗ **pushyarâga.** A topaz.

ಫಿರೋಜಾ—, ಪೇಡೇಜು ಕಲ್ಲು **phirojâ-, pêḍêju kallu.** A turquoise.

ಬಿಡಿ **biḍi.** *Lit.* Single, not set, loose as stones not set.

ಬಿಲಿಯಾನ್ **biliyân.** Brilliant (s. c.).

ಮರಕತ **marakata.** An emerald.

ಮಾಣಿಕ **mâṇika.** A ruby or carbuncle; *also* ಮಾಣಿಕ್ಯ.

ಮುತ್ತು **muttu.** A pearl; ಸಣ್ಣ— (saṇṇa-) seed-pearl; ಗುಳ್ಳೆ— (guḷḷe-) inferior pearl; ಚಿಪ್ಪಿನ— (čippina-) mother-of-pearl; ಚೊಕ್ಕಾಣಿ— (čokkâṇi-) a choice pearl.

ರತಿ **rati.** $1\frac{5}{16}$ of a grain, by which 'cut' stones are sold.

ರಾಮಿ **râmi.** A spurious ruby (s. c.).

ವಜ್ರ **vajra.** A diamond.

ವಡಕು **vaḍaku.** A crack, as in a gem.

ವಲ್ಲಂದಿ **vallandi.** Holland-cut.

ವೈಢೂರ್ಯ **vaiḍhûrya.** A cat's-eye or amethyst.

ಶಲ್ಯಾನಿ **šalyâni.** A Ceylon ruby (s. c.).

ಹವಳ **havaḷa.** Coral.

Revenue.

ಅಚ್ಚಕ, ಅಚ್ಚವಡಿ aččaka, aččavaḍi. Assessment; ಅಚ್ಚವಳಿಗ (aččavaḷiga) a tax-payer.

ಅಜಮಾಷಿ, ಅಜಮಾಯಿಷಿ ajamâshi, ajamâyishi. An estimate of the produce, or extent of land, made from mere inspection without actual measurement; 2, a standing-crop survey; —ಖರ್ಡಾ (-khardâ) an estimate-book; —ಪಟ್ಟಿ (-paṭṭi) a survey statement.

ಅಡಂಗಲ್ aḍaṅgal. Inspection of cultivated fields by village-officers, prior to the annual settlement (S. C.); examination of village-cultivation.

ಅತ್ರಾಫ್ atrâph. Surrounding (S. C.).

ಅಬಕಾರಿ abakâri. Revenue derived from taxes on the manufacture and sale of spirituous liquors.

ಅಮರಾಯಿ amarâyi. Tax on productive trees (My.).

ಅಮಲು amalu. Revenue (My.); —ದಾರ (-dâra) the chief revenue officer of a tâlûk (My.).

ಅರುಕಾಣಿಕೆ arukâṇike. A tax on ploughs.

ಅಸುವರಿ asuvari. Extra levy on a village (W.); ಕಟ್ಟು— (kaṭṭu-) a private fee formerly paid to Šânabhâgs (My.).

ಅವರ್ಜಾ avarjâ. A ledger-book showing a ryot's cultivation, assessment and payment; 2, a particular head of account abstracted from the day-book and containing a separate account of each cultivator's land, the revenue and charges thereon; 3, a record of entries of payments made by each individual ryot (Ch.); 4, an abstract in which entries are posted for the preparation of a statement.

ಆಗರ âgara. A salt-pan.

ಆಠವಣೆ âṭhavaṇe. Revenue (N. C.); —ಇಲಾಖೆ (-ilâkhe) the revenue department (N. C.).

ಆದಾಯ âdâya. Customs, toll (My.), ಮಾರ್ಗ— (mârga-) transit duties (My.); ಮಾಮೂಲ್— (mâmûl-) export duties (My.); ಸ್ಥಳ— (sthaḷa-) customs on goods imported to be sold at one place (My.).

ಆಮದ್ **âmad.** *Lit.* Imported, imports; —ಹಾಸಲ್ (-hâsal) import duties (My.).

ಆಯಂ **âyam.** Allowance of grain to village servants.

ಆಯಕಟ್ಟು, ಅಚ್ಚಕಾಟ **âyakaṭṭu, aĉĉakâṭa.** The measurement of land, determining the boundaries of a village; 2, the whole extent of taxable lands in a village; 3, the total area of land attached to a village, or the total extent of land capable of being watered by any particular irrigation-work (My.); —ಆಳುವೊಗಳು (-âḷuvogaḷu) an account of the lands of a village and of their distribution among the cultivators; the whole extent of taxable lands in a village.

ಆಯಸಾಯ, ಆಯಸಾಮ್ಯ **âyasâya, âyasâmya.** The share of the crop paid to village servants (My.).

ಆರಿನಿಪಟ್ಟಿ **â-inipaṭṭe.** An account of the number of ploughs belonging to each farmer.

ಇಜಾರ, ಇಜಾರಿಗೆ **ijâra, ijârige.** A monopoly, a contract.

ಇನಾಮತಿ, ಇನಾಮ್ತಿ **inâmati, inâmti.** Free of tax or rent (My.); *see also* ಉತ್ತಾರ *infra;* ಜಾರಿ- (jâri-) rent-free land (My.).

ಇರವಾರ **iravâra.** The total produce before division under the baṭâyi system (My.).

ಇಸಾಲು **irsâlu.** Remittance of Government money to the treasury; —ಕಟ್ಟು (-kaṭṭu) to do up a remittance, to send in the remittance.

ಇಸಂ **isam.** An individual; —ವಾರ್ (-vâr) according to individuals; —ವಾರ್ಪಟ್ಟಿ (-vârpaṭṭi) a list dealing with payments made by each individual (S. C.).

ಈಡಿಗುತ್ತಿಗೆ **iḍiguttige.** A duty on toddy (My.).

ಉಂಡಿಗೆಚೀಟು **uṇḍigeĉiṭu.** A custom-house permit.

ಉತ್ತಾರ, ಉದ್ಧಾರ **uttâra, uddhâra.** Remission of land-rent on account of imperfectly ripened crops from inclemency of season and failure of rain (My.); in Nagar the word is used for inâmati *(supra).*

ಉಪ್ಪಿನ ಮೊಲ್ಲ **uppina molla.** A tax, under the Vijayanagara dynasty, on people extracting salt from Sarkâr land (My.).

ಐನು **ainu.** Net, whole; —ಜಮಾ (-jamâ) the actual, regular or ordinary revenue, as distinguished from ಶಿವಾಯಿಜಮಾ or extras; —ಬಾಕಿ (-bâki) balance on account of tax in money.

ಕಂದಾಯ **kandâya.** Tax, cess; ನೀರು— (nîru-) water-tax; 2, water-tax paid by villagers in Mysore on account of water for irrigating fields, drawn from streams in North Coorg (Cg., My.).

ಕಂದೂಳಿ **kandûḷi.** A fixed rate of assessment.

ಕಚ್ಚಾ ಖಾಂ ವಸೂಲಿ **kaččâkhâm vasûli.** Gross receipts (My.).

ಕಟ್ಟಳೆ **kaṭṭaḷe.** Taxes under Kṛishṇarâja Voḍeyar (My.); ಹೆಚ್ಚು— (hečču-) extraordinary taxes (My.).

ಕಟ್ಟುತ್ತಾರ **kaṭṭuttâra.** Remission of revenue on account of the upkeep of dams and embankments.

ಕಟ್ಟುದಳೆ **kaṭṭudale.** Rate of assessment, settlement, agreement.

ಕಟ್ಟುಬಡಿ **kaṭṭubaḍi.** A fixed invariable quit-rent; 2, invariable quit-rent assessed on lands granted to public servants (W.).

ಕಬೂಲಾತಿ **kabûlâti.** An account showing the decrease of revenue on account of lands given up by the holders, the increase by new applications for lands, the estimated value of baṭâyi cultivation (*see* p. 15). The account is to be sent by the Amildars once in 10 or 12 days commencing from April till the end of July (My.).

ಕಲ್ಲು **kallu.** *Lit.* A stone, a boundary stone, *also* ಎಲ್ಲೆ— (elle-); under this may be classed the Liṅgamudre and Vâmanamudre stones of Udipi and Kundapore (S. C.); the ಜಂತಿಕಲ್ಲು (jantikallu) composed of three stones in a line (Cg.); ಮುಕ್ಕವಚ (mukkavača) a boundary or demarcation mark consisting of three stones put down so as to form an angle and mark a change in the line of the boundary (Cg.).

ಕಾಲಾವಧಿ **kâlâvadhi.** The end of a season (My.); ಜ್ಯೇಷ್ಠ— (jyêshṭha-) the month of June when all revenue accounts are settled (My.); —ಇಜಾರೆ (-ijâre) tenders made by people to Amildars from March to May, for renting villages, and at the end of which month the ryots are collected and the villages rented to the highest bidder; *otherwise called* ಶ್ರಯ ಇಜಾರೆ (śraya ijâre) (My.).

ಕಾರಕ **kâraka.** A tax, generally of the nature of mohatarphâ; 2, a tax paid by certain classes in Kṛishṇarâja Voḍeyar's time for relief from payment of sâyar duties (Nagar. My.).

ಕ್ಯಾಗಜ್ **kyâgaz.** *Lit.* Paper; "an individual paṭṭâ given annually to each ryot under the Collector's seal and signature, and specifying the proportion of the bêriz which may be fixed as his jamâbandi for the Fasli year" (S. C.).

ಕಿಸಂ **kisam.** Class, sort, kind, description of land; —ವಾರ್ (-vâr) classified according to sort or kind (S. C.). Lands in revenue accounts were classified into the following heads for the purpose of fixing the assessment:—ಅವಲ್ (aval) the best; ದುಯಂ (duyam) the second best or middling; ಶಿಯ್ಯಂ (siyyam) third class or inferior; ಚಹರಂ (čaharam) fourth class, and ಆಮೇಜಿ (âmêzi) miscellaneous (My. & C.). In S. Canara the present classification is as follows:—ಬೈಲು, ಬೆಟ್ಟು, ಮಜಲು, ಹಕ್ಲು, ಬಾಗಾಯತು—for definitions of which see "Agricultural and Rural". In Mysore lands were classified into: 1, Village settlements, comprising of ಕಾಯಂಗುತ್ತ, ಕ್ರಯ, ಕಾಲಾವಧಿ ಇಜಾರೆ, and ಜೋಡಿ, 2, Individual settlements into ಕಂದಾಯ, ಬಟಾಯಿ, ಅರ್ಧಮಾನ್ಯ, ಜೋಡಿ (Mysore Commission); but since 1863 there are only two *chief* classifications: 1, ಸರ್ಕಾರ comprising of either ಕಂದಾಯ (lands assessed in money) or ಬಟಾಯಿ (lands paying rent in kind), 2, ಇನಾಮ್.

ಕಿಸ್ತು, ಕಿಸ್ತ್ **kistu, kist.** An instalment of the payment of assessment; —ಬಂದಿ (-bandi) a settlement of instalments both as to time and money (S. C.); 2, a document given to a landholder showing the instalments payable by him; —ವಾಯಿದೆ (-vâyide) fixed periods for the payment of the instalments; ಕಾಣ— (kâṇa-) cess on a ಕಾಣ (*p.* 130).

ಕುಡ್ತಲೆ **kuḍtale.** The registered right of paying land-revenue, a revenue registry (S. C.); —ದಾರ (-dâra) a person in whose name the revenue registry stands, a paṭṭâdâr (S. C.); —ತಬ್ದೀಲಿ (-tabdîli) the change of the revenue registry from one's name to another's. Such changes take place in one of the following ways; ರಾಜಿಕಬೂಲಿ (râjikabûli) where two persons, the ರಾಜಿದಾರ್ (râjidâr) the vendor or transferrer, and the ಕಬೂಲಿದಾರ್ (kabûlidâr) the vendee or transferee agree to the change of the registry, the former consenting to the change, the latter to be held liable for payments of future assessment; ಮೃತ– (mrita-) where on account of the decease of the last kuḍtaledâr, the transferee, assignee, or heir applies for the change of the registry; ಬಲಾತ್ಕಾರ– (balâtkâra-) where the change is made arbitrarily by the Revenue Courts—*a,* in cases in which there is a dispute about the title, or *b,* in cases in which a confusion arises owing to the original kuḍtale having been left unchanged—leaving the parties to settle the matter in Civil Courts (S. C.).

ಕುತ್ತಿಕಾಣಿಕೆ **kuttikâṇike.** Seignorage on stumps, stump-fee (S. C.).

ಕುಮ್ಕಿ **kumki.** Government land within 100 yards of assessed cultivated land; unassessed land for the use of cultivation; auxiliary land granted to help the cultivator. Under kumki rights a cultivator can use fuel, leaves, etc. on the kumki land for his *private* use (S. C.).

ಕುಮ್ರಿ **kumri.** Dry cultivation carried on in the forests during the rainy season. Large tracts of forests are prepared by cutting down under-growth, which is burnt, and crops are raised. The Forest Act now forbids this cultivation, *otherwise called* wood-ash tillage. The word is also applied to forest tracts where such cultivation is carried on. Different kinds of kumri are: 1, ಮೂಲಪಟ್ಟೆ– (mûlapaṭṭe-) kumri rights under a mûlapaṭṭa granted by the Government or its recognized agent; 2, ವರ್ಗದಾರ– (vargadâra-) kumri rights enjoyed by a vargadâr (S. C.); when the vargadâr got the kumri worked by his tenants and paid a cash assessment of a rupee per acre, the kumri became ವರ್ಗದಾರ ಕುಮ್ರಿ (N. C.); 3, ಸರಕಾರ– (sarakâra-) kumri over which the Government alone has a right and which is allowed to be cultivated under licenses granted on payment (S. C.); when the *actual husbandman* paid assessment for the land he cultivated, he enjoyed the land on Sarakâr kumri rights (N. C.); 4, ಅರ್ಕಲ್– (arkal-) kumri on which ಅರ್ಕಲ್ cultivation (*p.* 7) is carried on (S. C.); 5, ಇಲಾಖೆ– (ilâkhe-) kumri cultivation carried on in vargs on which kumri shist has been fixed, *also* ವರ್ಗದಾರ್ ಇಲಾಖೆ— (vargadâr ilâkhe-) (S. C.); —ಕೊರ್ಲಾಯ (-korlâya) a tax on the cutting of kumris.

ಕುಳ **kuḷa.** An individual paying taxes to Government, a payer of Government dues; ಒಳ— (oḷa-) an individual paying taxes to Government under others (S. C.); —ಕಟ್ಟು (-kaṭṭu) to fix the amount of taxes; —ನಷ್ಟ (-nashṭa) lands, the identity of which cannot be ascertained, or of which the cultivator has died or deserted; hence lands without a holder; —ವಾರ್ಪಟ್ಟಿ (-vârpaṭṭi) a list of lands farmed, and assessment payable thereon, by each individual cultivator (S. C.); —ವಾರ ಲೆಖ್ಖ (-vâra lekhkha) individual accounts, in contradistinction to ಧರೆವಾರ ಲೆಖ್ಖ (q. v., S. C.); a detailed account of land cultivated by each holder (My.); —ವಾರ ತಖ್ತೆ (-vâra takhte) a rent-roll containing the rent paid by each ryot, the amount of ṭharâvu bêriz, whether the land is ಥರಿ or ಕಂಥರಿ (q. v.) etc.; and upon which the annual settlement of ಕಂಥರಿ vargas were fixed (Ch.); ಅರೆ— (are-) traders of the second class paying a mohatarphâ of Rs. 2¼ per annum (Cg.); ನಿಜ— (nija-) traders of the first class paying a mohatarphâ of Rs. 3½ per annum (Cg.); ಬಿಡು— (biḍu-) laborers and coolies not paying assessment (Cg.).

ಕೈಕಾಗದ **kaikâgada.** An agreement entered into by the Revenue officers stating that they will collect kists from the ryots and remit the amount to the Huzoor Cutcherry (Cg.).

ಕೈಕಾಮಿಲ್ **kaikâmil.** A term applied (under the later Government of Mysore) to denote a statement of the gross annual assessment of each district, without the deductions to which the assessment was subject (My.).

ಕೈವಳಿ **kaivaḷi.** A cess formerly levied on betel gardens and rice-fields (My.).

ಕೊಡಗಿ **koḍagi.** A grant of land; *see p.* 91.

ಕೊಂಡವಾಡ **koṇḍavâḍa.** A cattle-pound.

ಕೋರು **kôru.** A share of the crop belonging to the cultivator (My.); ವಾರು— (vâru-) a share of the crop due to the landlord by the tenant (My.).

ಕೌಲು **kaulu.** An agreement, *also* ಕೌಲಕರಾರು; 2, a mode of granting waste-land at a nominal assessment until it is brought into full cultivation; —ಆಚಾರ (-âčâra) quit-rent.

ಖಮಾವಿಷಿ **khamâvishi.** Land cultivated directly under the superintendence of government.

ಖರ್ಡಾ **khardâ.** An account-book; ಕಚ್ಚಾ— (kaččâ-) an account-book kept by the village-accountant, of payment of revenue by the cultivators of a village, as opposed to ಪಕ್ಕಾ— (pakkâ-) which is only a fair copy of the same, *see also p.* 2.

ಖಸ್ತು ಮಾಡು **khastu mâḍu.** To dun, as for payment of assessment.

ಖಾತೆದಾರ **khâtedâra.** A holder or proprietor of land, a vargadâr; *for the difference between* ವರ್ಗದಾರ *and* ಖಾತೆದಾರ *see* ವರ್ಗ.

ಖಾನೆಷುಮಾರಿ **khâneshumâri.** Census.

ಗಾಮಗಾನೆ ಲೆಖ್ಖ **gâmagâne lekhkha.** The revenue account of a district containing several villages.

ಗ್ರಾಮತೆರಿಗೆ **grâmaterige.** Village cess (S. C.); 2, a fine levied on the ryots who have left their own villages and settled in others (My.).

ಗಿಡಗಾವಲು **giḍagâvalu.** Tax on forest produce (My.).

ಗುಂಜಾಯಷು **guñjâyashu.** In fiscal language, the capability of a village, particularly with reference to a proposed increase of revenue; 2, excess of worth over the assessment; —ಮಾಡು (-mâḍu) to outbid another in a sale or contract.

ಗುಜಸ್ತಾ, ಗುದಸ್ತಾ **guzastâ, gudastâ.** Past; —ಬಾಕಿ (-bâki) past balance.

ಗುತ್ತಿಗೆ, ಗುತ್ತೆ **guttige, gutte.** A monopoly, a contract; —ದಾರ (-dâra) a contractor; ಕಾವಲಿ—, ಕೊಂಡ— (kâvali-, konḍa-) a contract for collecting and selling forest produce. *For the many obsolete* ಗುತ್ತಿಗಳು *of Mysore, see Mr. Rice's Mysore and Coorg,* vol. I. p. 486.

ಗೌಡ ಆಯ **gauḍa âya.** Proportion of the crop formerly set apart for the headman of a village and now resumed by the government (My.).

ಚಡ್ಸಾಲ್ **čaḍsâl.** A year in which the maximum amount of revenue was derived from a village (My.).

ಚಪಾವಣಿ, ಛಪಾವಣಿ čapâvaṇi, čhapâvaṇi. Clandestine concealment of land to defraud revenue collections, malversation.

ಚಪ್ಪೆ, ಛಾಪಾ čappe, čhâpâ. A stamp made on goods at a custom-house.

ಚರಪೈರ, ಚಾರಪೈರ čarapaira, čârapaira. A tax of various items on villages (My.).

ಚರಾದಾಯ čarâdâya. By-gains or occasional taxes or profits; duty levied on all sorts of goods and commodities, transit and town dues (My.).

ಚಿಟ್ಟಾ, ಚಿಟ್ಟೆ čiṭṭâ, čiṭṭe. A rough daily account of particulars; 2, an account of all the lands in a village, showing the quantity of land under cultivation, the kind of cultivation and the name of the cultivator; ಜಮಾಬಂದಿ- (jamâbandi-) a record showing the additions or reductions of assessment on a ryot, made annually at each ಜಮಾಬಂದಿ (*infra*, s. c.); ದುರ್ಮತಿ- (durmati-) a seed-statement of lands under cultivation in the year Durmati (1801 A. D.) or in the second year of the "Company's Government" (C.).

ಚೆಕ್ಕು, ಚಕ್ಕು čekku, čakku. A portion of land divided off, as the detatched fields of a village or patch of rent-free land. In old revenue accounts the term was applied to lands taken from the residents of a village and given to a stranger to cultivate (W.); —ಬಂದಿ (-bandi) determination of the boundaries of a land or estate (W.); the limits of a revenue jurisdiction (C.).

ಚೆರಾದಾಯ čerâdâya. Profits by sale of unclaimed cattle; *see* ಚರಾದಾಯ *supra*.

ಚೌತ್ čaut. An oppressive tax, originally a fourth of the standard assessment; —ಕಾಯಿ (-kâyi) (or ಚೌತಿಕಾಯಿ? compulsory contribution of cocoanuts for the Gaṇêša čaturthi festival?) a tax in kind—of cocoanuts—said to have been extorted in S. Canara before 1820 and subsequently included in ಧಾರಾ (*p.* 152).

ಜಂಗುಲಿ jaṅguli. The cattle of a whole village.

ಜಕಾತಿ, ಜಕಾಯತಿ jakâti, jakâyati. Custom-house duty.

ಜಮಾಬಂದಿ jamâbandi. Annual settlement of assessment (C., My.); 2, a revenue registry, a paṭṭâ (Cg.); ಅಸಾಮಿವಾರ್- (âsâmivâr-) account of revenue settlement settled with each individual cultivator; ಕುಳವಾರ್— (kuḷavâr-) the annual tour of a revenue officer, village by village, for the settlement of assessment; ಕಿಸಮವಾರ್— (kisamvâr-) a statement of revenue assessed at certain rates, according to the quality of the soil; ಚಡ್ಸಾಲ್— (čaḍsâl-) the maximum amount of revenue derivable at some former period from a village (My.).

ಜಮೀನ್ ಶಿಸ್ತು **zamin šistu.** Land-tax (C.).

ಜರೀಬು **jaribu.** Mensuration of land; measurement.

ಜಾದಿ **jâdi.** Land-tax, assessment of land (My.).

ಜಾರಿ ಭೂಮಿ **jâri bhûmi.** A land once attached or sequestered by government; ಜಾರಿ ಚೀಟು (jâri čîṭu) a written grant of such land; ಜಾರಿ ಜೋಡಿಗೆ (jâri jôḍige) quit-rent.

ಝಾಡೆ **jhâḍe.** Final settlement; —ಪಟ್ಟಿ (-paṭṭi) the final demand of government for house or land tax; ದೇಹ— (dêha-) the census of cattle and houses in a village; ಸಾಲ್— (sâl-) accounts of annual income and expenditure.

ಠೇವಣಿ **ṭhêvaṇi.** An advance; 2, a deposit; *also* ಠೇವಣಾತಿ.

ತಕಾವಿ **takâvi.** Advances, made by the government, of money at a low interest to farmers to help them in cultivation; recoverable advances made to ryots to enable them to cultivate.

ತಕ್ರೀರದಾರ **takriradâra.** The claimant in a kuḍtale case, 'objection-petitioner' (S. C.); *also* ದಾವೆದಾರ.

ತಖ್ತು, ತಖ್ತೆ **takhtu, takhte.** An abstract statement, a summary or total.

ತಗಾದೆ **tagâde.** Dunning for payment; —ಪತ್ರ, —ಚೀಟು (-patra, -čîṭu) a notice of demand, a distraint order, an order for distraint of property for failure to pay assessment (C.).

ತನಖಾ **tanakhâ.** An assignment (*see p.* 52); an assignment on the revenue (My.).

ತನಿಖಿ **tanikhi.** Examination or comparison of a statement; 2, inspection, enquiry, investigation.

ತರಂ **taram.** The term of land-tax (My.); survey (N. C.); class.

ತರದೂದಪಟ್ಟಿ **taraddûdapaṭṭi.** An account showing the species and quantity of seed sown, the extent of land under cultivation and the quantity remaining fallow (My.).

ತರವಳೀ ಲೆಖ್ಖ **taravaḷi lekhkha.** An account of the amount of taxes levied.

ತಸದೀಕು, ತಸ್ತೀಕು **tasadiku, tastiku.** The annual allowances made by government to temples (C., My.).

ತಹರೀರು **taharîru.** The allowances made to a superintendent of public works.

ತಹಸೀಲು **tahasilu.** Collection of land-revenue; —ದಾರ (-dâra) the head revenue officer of a tâluk.

ತಾರೀಫ್ **târiph.** A tariff rate, table of rates; duty on exports and imports (S. C.).

ತಾಳಾಬಂದ್ **tâḷâband.** (*see p.* 2) An account of receipts and disbursements; a treasury account showing the correspondence between the balance in hand and that which should be left on a comparison between the receipts and disbursements (W.).

ತಿರುವಳ್ಳಿ **tiruvaḷḷi.** A temporary assessment (S. C.); *see under* ವರ್ಗ.

ತೀರ್ವೆ, ತೀರ್ವಾ **tirve, tirvâ.** Land-tax; —ಜಾಸ್ತಿ (-jâsti) an additional assessment on inferior land when made to produce crops, usually limited to land of superior quality, as garden crops or those raised from irrigated land (W.); —ದಾರ್ (-dâr) a person paying assessment (S. C.); ಒಳ— (oḷa-) assessment paid to government through the person directly liable to government for the assessment, sub-assessment (S. C.).

ತ್ರಿಜಾಯಿ **trijâyi.** A mode of cultivation in which the farmer pays a third of the produce to government.

ತೆರಿಗೆ **terige.** Cess, assessment; ಘರ್— (ghar-) an obsolete assessment on house-sites in town (S. C.); ನೆಲ— (nela-) a temporary assessment for the site of a shop erected on a government *unassessed* waste-land, the assessment being remitted on the occupant giving up the building (S. C.); ಭೂ— (bhû-) land-cess; ಮನೆ— (mane-) house-tax; ಗ್ರಾಮ— (grâma-) *see p.* 145.

ದರ್ಖಾಸ್ತ **darkhâsta.** A tender; a proposal or offer for renting out government waste-land; ಕ್ರಯ– (kraya-) buying up of lands at a public auction; –ಪಟ್ಟೆ (-paṭṭe) a document given by the revenue officer to the person leasing out government land, and specifying the extent, assessment, etc. (S. C.); 2, a sale-certificate given by a Civil Court to the purchaser of a land in the execution of a decree (S. C.).

ದರ್ಚಡಾವ್, ದರ್ಜಾಸ್ತಿ **darčaḍâv, darjâsti.** An extra assessment realized by delivering the government share of the crop to farmers at a price higher than the selling price.

ದಫಾತೆ ಜಮಾ **daphâte jamâ.** Extra or miscellaneous collections.

ದಸ್ತು **dastu.** The money collected; –ಬಾಕಿ (-bâki) *see p.* 151.

ದೊಡ್ಡಿ **doḍḍi.** A cattle-pound, a pound; –ಹಣ (-haṇa) poundage (S. C.).

ಧಡೆವಾರಪಟ್ಟಿ **dhaḍevârapaṭṭi.** An account showing the total assessment due by a kuḷa or individual ryot for his several holdings within the division of a Mâgaṇe Šânabhâg or Paṭêl, and is as such opposed to ಕುಳವಾರಪಟ್ಟಿ which shows the amount due by each individual for his separate holding (S. C.).

ಧ್ರುವಫಲ **dhruvaphala.** 'Stable-crop produce'; one-half of the produce of cocoanut and arecanut trees given to the Sarkâr by farmers holding gardens on the vâram tenure (*p.* 96), the payment being made only in case of the trees bearing fruit, but not otherwise (My.).

ನಂಜಾ **nañjâ.** Wet soil fit for—or under—cultivation as opposed to ಪುಂಜಾ; *cf.* ಬೈಲು (S. C.).

ನಗದು ಗುತ್ತೆ **nagadu gutte.** Money assessment, *also* ನಗದಿಯಾತೆ (My.).

ನಜರಾಣಾ, ನಜರ್‌ಬಂದಿ **nazarâṇâ, nazarbandi.** Unjust taxation (C.).

ನಷ್ಟ **nashṭa.** A term which seems to have been applied to land periodically wasted away by the sea in creeks or rivers, to land torn up and rendered uncultivable by the action of rivers, to land never cultivated since the time of the Vijayanagara government, and which from its situation amongst hills and jungles was withdrawn from the general assessment of the country;

for ತೇಜಾ–, and ತುರ– *see under the respective words;* ಚಿತ್ರಭಾನು– (čitrabhânu-) a tax imposed in 1792 A. D. to meet the expenses of the 3rd Mysore war (S. C.); ಸಳಿ– (snăi-) a tax imposed on account of the devastation of a plantation (?) (S. C.).

ನಾದಾರ್ ಮುನಾಸಬ್ **nâdâr munâsab.** An item of remission of revenue on account of the poverty of the cultivators.

ನಿಗದಿ **nigadi.** An instalment; periodical payment of government assessment on an estate, or of tax on property; the net surplus proceeds of an estate paid to the farmer or owner by the occupant (W.); government demand, assessment (S. C.).

ಪಟ್ಟೆ **paṭṭe.** A paṭṭâ, a document given by the Collector of a district to the landholder specifying the extent and description of the land, the conditions of the tenancy, the rate and amount of assessment he is liable to pay; ಬೇರಿಜ್– (bêriz-) an annual receipt granted by government to each ryot showing the nature of his tenure and the rent received from him (S. C.); ಮೂಲ– (mûla-) a document by which former governments conferred on individuals mûli or permanent rights in the land (C.).

ಪಹಣೆ **pahaṇe.** Inspection by sight; estimates from mere inspection without actual measurement or survey; *also* ನಜರ್– (nazar-).

ಪಯಕಾರಿ **payakâri.** A temporary cultivator; one cultivating the land of another for a stipulated term and a given share of the crop (W.); a ryot living in a different village from that he resides in.

ಪಾರ್ಕಣೆ, ಪಾರ್ಖಾವಣಿ **pârkaṇe, pârkhâvaṇi.** Paying into the treasury the revenue collected from village officers (S. C.).

ಪಾಯಮಾಲಿ **pâyamâli.** Remission of taxes owing to the depredation of enemies.

ಪಾಳುಕಂದಾಯ **pâḷukandâya.** Assessment on land left fallow or untilled, ಪಾಳು being a waste land (My.).

ಪುಂಜಾ **puñjâ.** Dry soil unfit for the cultivation of rice.

ಪೈದಾಸ್ತು **paidâstu.** Crop, produce.

ಪೈಮಾಶಿ **paimâši.** Land-survey; ಕೋಲ್– (kôl-) regular survey or measurement by the kôl or rod.

ಪ್ರಹಾರಪಟ್ಟಿ **prahârapaṭṭi.** Tariff tables (My.).

ಫರ್ಮಾಯಿಷ, ಫರ್ಮಾಯ್ಶಿ **pharmâyisha, pharmâyši.** Petty articles of provisions formerly exacted from the villagers by the government; produce *payable* to the government in kind or at an undervaluation (W.); 2, voluntary presents of curiosities, rarities made to official superiors (S. C.).

ಫಸಲ್, ಫಸಲಿ **phasal, phasali.** *Lit.* Crop or time, the current revenue year commencing from July to June; –ಕಮ್ಮಿ (-kammi) deductions made in a cess owing to the scantiness of crops; –ಜಾಸ್ತಿ (-jâsti) an extra cess imposed on land bearing more than a single crop.

ಫುರೋಕ್ತು **phurôktu.** *Lit.* Sale, sale of stamps or stamp-papers; 2, sale-endorsement on stamps or stamp-papers.

ಬಟ್ಟಿ **baṭṭi.** A distillary; –ಸುಂಕ (-suṅka) still-head duty.

ಬರಾವರ್ದ **barâvarda.** A monthly statement of the revenue and village establishments, of the sums payable to each; a pay-abstract; a memo. of payments of salaries to government servants made every month; a list of an establishment.

ಬಾಂದು **bându.** Survey (N. C.); –ಕಲ್ಲು (-kallu) land-marks placed by the survey officers.

ಬಾಕಿ **bâki.** Balance (*see p.* 2); ಗುಜಸ್ತಾ– (guzastâ-) past year's balance; ಫರಾರಿ– (pharâri-) balance due from revenue defaulters; ಫೌತಿ– (phauti-) balance due to government from deceased persons; ದಸ್ತು– (dastu-) the balance realised and held by a revenue officer and not sent to the treasury; ಶಿಸ್ತು– (šistu-) the balance of šist or land-tax still due by, and outstanding against, the farmers themselves; ಬೇಸುಮಾರ್– (bêsumâr-) a hopeless, irrecoverable balance; ಶಿಲಶಿಲಾ– (šilašilâ-) balance due by renters, but carried to the next jamâbandi and collected with the following year's rent (My.).

ಬಾಣೆ **bâṇe.** Land adjoining the rice-fields, and covered with jungle and used for the same purposes as a ಕುಮ್ಮಿ (*p.* 143) (Cg.).

ಬಾಡಿಗೆ **bâdige.** Quit-rent, a low rent on inâm lands.

ಬಾಬ್ **bâb.** *Lit.* An item, an item of revenue; ಪಂಚ– (pañča-) revenue derived from five things—tobacco, betel-leaf, gâñjâ, arrack, and toddy (My.); ಬಾಜೆ– (bâje-) miscellaneous items (S. C.); 2, revenue derived from small farms and licenses (My.); –ವಾರ್ (-vâr) classified, arranged; –ವಾರಿ (-vâri) classification.

ಬಾರಾಮಾರ್ಗ **bârâmârga.** Transit-duties (My.).

ಬಾರಿಕೆ **bârike.** Low swampy portions of land adjacent to, or below, the paddy-fields and used for grazing purposes (Cg.).

ಬಿರಾಡ **birâḍa.** Land-tax (My.); ಬಾಗಾಯತ್ ಜಾಸ್ತಿ– (bâgâyat jâsti-) an extra cess charged on garden cultivation (My.).

ಬುಕ್ಕು **bukku.** A revenue registry, corresponding to the ಮುಸ್ತೆದ ot S. Canara (My.); –ದಾರ (-dâra) a person in whose name the revenue registry stands, a paṭṭâdâr (My.).

ಬೇರಿಜು **bêrizu.** The assessment or amount of revenue fixed in ancient times to be drawn from villages, assessment on land. The various assessments imposed in Canara and Mysore, in the order of time are:—1, ಶಿಸ್ತು (śistu) the standard rental introduced by Hurry Hur Roy of Vijayanagar (1334-37 A. D.); 2, ದಾಸೋಹ (dâsôha) an addition to the above, imposed by Chinnammâji (1700 A. D.) for the support of an establishment for providing food *gratis* to all who applied; 3, ಪಗಡಿ (pagadi) imposed by the wife of the Râja of Bednore on the occasion of the marriage of her son Basavappa Naik; 4, ಪಟ್ಟಿ (paṭṭi) imposed by the Râja of Sonda for discharging the tribute to the Mogul princes; 5, ಚಕ್ರ (cakra) imposed in 1720 A. D. instead of the interest paid to the sâvakârs (merchants), who advanced kists earlier on behalf of the ryots; 6, ಶಾಮಿಲ್ (śâmil) assessments of Hyder and Tippoo over and above the ಶಿಸ್ತು; 7, ಕದೀಮ್ (kadîm) the total of ಶಿಸ್ತು and ಶಾಮಿಲ್; 8, ಠರಾವ್ (ṭharâv) the assessment of 1819-20 A. D.; this assessment was fixed on the average of the assessment for the 17 years following the Company's rule (1802 A. D.)—ಸಕ್ರಾಸಾಲ್ ಸರಾಸರಿ (q. v.)—and included all imposts and taxes imposed in the preceding years—some of which are ಶಿಸ್ತು, ಶಾಮಿಲ್, ಚಿತ್ರಭಾನುನಷ್ಟ, ಸಿಕಿನಷ್ಟ, ಕರ್ಣೇಕ ವರ್ತನೆ, ಚೌತಿಕಾಯಿ, ಅಸುವರಿ, ಬಸಪ್ಪನಾಯಕನ ಶಿಸ್ತು (*explained elsewhere*); 9, ಶಾಸ್ವತ (śâsvata) the permanent assessment after 1820 A. D.

ಭರ್ತಿವರ್ಗ **bhartivarga.** Lands paying the full demand fixed at the ṭharâv settlement (1819-20), estates subject to and paying the ṭharâv bêriz; ಕಂ— (kam-) lands the assessment of which was below the average when the ṭharâv bêriz was introduced; these vargs were divided into: 1, ವಾಯಿದೆ (vâyide) or those to be brought up to the full bêriz by annual instalments, 2, ಬೋರ್ಡ್ ಶಿಫಾರಸ್ (bôrḍ śiphâras) or those recommended to the Board of Revenue for permanent remission of the assessment, and 3, ತನಖಿ (tanakhi) or those remaining under investigation (Ch.).

ಮಚ್ಛಿಕಾರಕ **maččhikâraka.** A tax on fishermen (S. C.).

ಮದಗಡ **madagaḍa.** Recoverable advances to cultivators to enable them to cultivate, *see* ತಕಾವಿ.

ಮದ್ದತು ಕೊಡು **maddatu koḍu.** To advance money to cultivators to help their cultivation, *see* ತಕಾವಿ.

ಮನೆಹಣ **manehaṇa.** House-tax (My.); *also* ಮನೆತೆರಿಗೆ.

ಮರಂಮತ್ **marammat.** The entire operations of any art, as in agriculture, ploughing, manuring; *see also* ಮರಹಂಮತಿ *p.* 31.

ಮಹಾಲು **mahâlu.** Revenue.

ಮಹಾಸಲು **mahâsalu.** Octroi, toll; public income from any source as land, custom, etc.

ಮಾನ್ಯ **mânya.** A grant (My.); *see* ಇನಾಮು, *p.* 91.

ಮಾಲಿಕಾನಾ **mâlikânâ.** Allowance paid to the representatives of zamindars removed by government from the management of their estates.

ಮಾಹೆ **mâhe.** A month; ಗುಜಸ್ತಾ— (guzastâ-) last month; ಚಾಲತಿ— (čâlati-) current month; —ಬಾಕಿ (-bâki) balance of the month.

ಮಿನಹು **minahu.** The fractional parts obtained in measuring lands, but not entered in the account (Cg.).

ಮುಂಗುತ್ತಿಗೆ **muṅguttige.** Contract-money for taxes paid in kind; —ಹೊಲ (-hola) a field the assessment of which has been paid in advance.

ಮುಗ್ಗೊಲಿ, ಮುಗ್ಗೊಳಿ **muggoli, muggoḷi.** An oppressive tax or contribution—of the nature of an extortion, or which gave rise to extortion at least—levied at the time of Hyder and Tippu (S. C.).

ಮುಚ್ಚಳಿಕಾ **muččaḷikâ.** A counterpart covenant on the part of proprietors of land agreeing to the rates of assessment fixed by the government (W.).

ಮುಜರಾಯಿ **mujarâyi.** A department for the control of temple funds and other religious property (My.).

ಮುಜ್ರೆ **mujre.** Remission of revenue; ಚಾಗೆ— (čâge-) remission on account of failure of rains.

ಮುದ್ರಾಪಣೆ **mudrâpaṇe.** *Lit.* Stamping, marking or branding the house of an individual who during Hyder's time refused to meet the demands of petty revenue officers—such as ಮುಗ್ಗಲಿ. The house was besieged by the army and the individual yielded.

ಮುಲ್ಕಿ **mulki.** Revenue; ದರ್ಬಾಬ್— (darbâb-) pertaining to revenue.

ಮೂಲಸಾಧನ **mûlasâdhana.** An acknowledgment given by the principal cultivator to the government, a grant or assignment to an original occupant, a title-deed.

ಮೇಲ್‌ವಾಸಿ **mêlvâsi.** Additions made to the rate of the government assessment.

ಮೊಹತರ್ಫೆ, ಮೊಹತರ್ಫಾ **mohatarphe, mohatarphâ.** Taxes which are not to be included in land-tax or assessment; profession-tax; ಆರಂಬಡ— (ârambaḍa-) tax paid by the zamindar himself (Cg.); ಬಿದುಕುಳದ— (biḍukuḷada-) tax paid by others than the zamindars (Cg.).

ಮೋಗುಮ್‌ಜಾಸ್ತಿ **môgumjâsti.** Out-bidding; a fruitless enhancement; offering a higher rent for land than is necessary.

ಮೊಹಸ್ಸಲು **mohassalu.** Restraint placed on a person to enforce the payment of a demand, or to prevent his escape.

ಮೋಜಣಿ **môzaṇi.** Land-survey (N. C.).

ಮೌಜೆ **mauze.** A village and all the land belonging to its inhabitants.

ರಸ್ತಮುಹೂರ್ತ **rastamuhûrta.** A ceremony performed in tâluk katchêris with which begins the collection of assessment, from the vargadârs, for the current Fasli (S. C.).

ರಹದಾರಿ **rahadâri.** A passport; 2, a permit; 3, an intimation to village officers of the programme of the movements of a traveller, to whom supplies are to be furnished; ಮಾಫಿ– (mâphi-) a passport granted for the conveyance of goods from one place to another for which duty has been already paid (My.).

ರಹಿಯತ **rahiyata.** A subject, a cultivator, a ryot; *also* ರಹಿತ.

ರಿವಾಜ್ **rivâz.** The ancient rate of assessment on each particular field or its produce.

ರೇಖಾ **rêkhâ.** The fixed standard assessment of lands in Kanara under Raja Hurryhur Roy of Vijayanagar; *otherwise called* râya-rêkha or rêkhi-mâr; –ಝಾಡ್ತಿ (-jhaḍti) an account, prepared in 1802 by Sir Thos. Munro, of the total of the land cultivated in Kanara, the assessment in kind or money and the proportion due to the government; –ನಷ್ಟ (-nashṭa) government waste-lands which are without assessment, unassessed government waste-land.

ಲಗ್ತಿದಾರ **lagtidâra.** The owner of land adjoining government unassessed waste-land, and who as such has prior right to get the government land on assessment, the nearest vargadâr (S. C.).

ಲಾಗುಜಾರಿ **lâgujâri.** Rent-free land.

ಲಾವಣ **lâvaṇa.** A village account showing the total assessment, and by whom it is paid (W.); 2, the registered right of paying land revenue. The word is used in the Udipi and Kundapore tâluks (S. C.); *see* ಕುದ್ದಲೆ.

ವರ್ಗ **varga.** The literal meaning of this word is 'account'. Long before the British rule in Kanara, several detached plots in one village, often lands in more than one village, and sometimes even in more than one sub-division of a district, were enjoyed by—rather the holding was put down to the name of—a single individual, so that, at an early stage of the British rule the word came to mean 'a holding or an estate', and the holder called ವರ್ಗದಾರ (vargadâra); "this word corresponds to ಖಾತೆದಾರ (*p.* 145) of the 'settled' districts with this difference that if a ವರ್ಗದಾರ takes up fresh land from government or by agreement or purchase, obtains the transfer of another ವರ್ಗ, the additional land is not entered in the original ವರ್ಗ, but a new one is made". The word ವರ್ಗದಾರ is also applied to the permanent assignee under the original proprietor and known as ಒಳವರ್ಗದಾರ (oḷavargadâra) a sub-proprietor; —ವಾರ (vâr.) a settlement made with each proprietor of an estate upon his entire holding, and not with reference to that portion only which may be actually under cultivation (Ch.). The different varieties of vargs are:—1, ಗೇಣಿ ವರ್ಗ (gêṇi varga). During the latter part of the 18th century, under Hyder and Tippu, the country was depopulated, in consequence of which and other causes, lands formerly cultivated reverted to government. They were subsequently offered to the highest bidder, and thence went by the name of ಸರ್ಕಾರ ಗೇಣಿ ವರ್ಗ (sarkâra gêṇi varga), the word therefore means "lands originally waste or which had devolved upon the state by escheat or abandonment and let to a tenant by the state". Since 1834 the distinction between ಗೇಣಿವರ್ಗ and ಮೂಲಿವರ್ಗ (*see infra*) ceased and the government was looked upon in both cases as the original proprietor to whom the vargadârs were to pay assessment. The two names are still retained in revenue accounts, although this distinction is made without any difference (C.); 2, ತಿರುವಳ್ಳಿ ವರ್ಗ (tiruvaḷḷi varga) a land the assessment of which has not been fixed but is to be raised as the trees standing thereon come to bearing (S. C.); 3, ಬನಾಮೆ ವರ್ಗ (banâme varga) the word ಬನಾಮೆ—not to be confounded with ಬೇನಾಮಿ—comes from the Persian and means "nominal, with name", so that ಬನಾಮೆ ವರ್ಗ means a varga standing in the name of a certain person, as opposed to government waste-land that is not entered in the accounts as a varga; 4, ಮೂಲಿ ವರ್ಗ (mûli varga) the derivation of the word ಮೂಲಿ is still a matter of speculation. Sir Thos. Munro's derivation from ಮೌಲ್ಯ (maulya, price) favors the theory of these vargs having been bought from the government for a price called ನಜರಾಣಾ (nazrâṇâ); others however derive it from ಮೂಲ (mûla, permanent). Whatever these philological differences may be, all are agreed that the word means "a holding of a permanent nature, land held on permanent rights" (C.); 5, ಮೇಲ್ವಾಸಿ ವರ್ಗ (mêlvâsi varga) "a varga or holding bearing an assessment exceeding the amount properly leviable according to its produce" (Vaikunta Bâpuji *v.* the Government of Bombay); 6, ವಾಯಿದೆ ವರ್ಗ (vâyide varga) vargs for which a limited period was fixed for bringing them up to the ಠರಾವ್ (ṭharâv) standard (Ch.); 7, ಹೊಸಾಗಮೆ ವರ್ಗ (hosâgame varga) vargs made on account of lands newly brought into cultivation; "the term hosâgame is confined to the re-occupation of government waste-land which is either ಕುಳನಷ್ಟ (q. v.) or ರೈಬನಷ್ಟ (q. v.) as distinguished from government waste estates, and does not include lands which are registered as distinct estates, however long they may have been abandoned or left waste by the holders or proprietors." Often a varga has an auxiliary unassessed plot of ground connected with and forming a part of it; and these plots go by different names in different parts: ಕುಮ್ಕಿ, in Kanara (*p.* 143); ಹಂಕಲು, ಹಾಡ್ಯ in Mysore (*pp.* 159, 160); ಕಟ್ಟಿನ ಹಂಕಲು in the Malnad (*p.* 159); ಬಾಣೆ, ಬಾರಿಕೆ in Coorg (*pp.* 151, 152).

ವರ್ತನೆ **vartane.** Fees or perquisites, generally in kind, paid to the public servants of a village; ಶಾನಭಾಗ– (śânabhâga-) a percentage of ¼ fanam per pagoda paid to Šânabhâgs.

ವರಿ **vari.** Tax, assessment.

ವಾಯಿದೆಚೀಟು **vâyideciṭu.** Notice of demand fixing the date within which assessment should be paid, and in default of which a distraint is to be made (S. C.).

ವಾರಾವಾರಿ **vârâvâri.** Settlement, assessment.

ಶರ್ತಬಂದಿ **šartabandi.** Conditions, terms (S. C.).

ಶರ್ತಿ **šarti.** A contract made by the Amildar that he would realize for government a certain amount of revenue, that if his collections should fall short of the amount, he would make good the deficiency, and that if they exceeded it, the surplus should be paid to government. This system, which had its origin under Pûrṇaiya's regency, was a source of oppression to the people (My.).

ಶಿಕಂ, ಶಿಕಮಿ **šikam, šikami.** A subordinate tenure under which the holder pays his revenue to government through some other person (My.); *cf.* ಒಳವರ್ಗ.

ಶಿಕಸ್ತು šikastu. Deficit in the collections; loss on the rent or farm of an estate.

ಶಿವಾಯಿ šivâyi. Any addition to the standard or customary revenue, whether as an increase of the amount or in the shape of a new or additional impost (W.); –ಕಿಸ್ತು (-kistu) miscellaneous items of revenue not included in the kistbandi; –ಜಮಾ (-jamâ) receipt of extra revenue items not included in the demand or ಜಮಾ (S. C.); 2, escheats, the effects of a person dying heirless, which descended to government (My.); 3, miscellaneous receipts of revenue credited to government (Cg.).

ಶಿಸ್ತು šistu. The fixed standard rate of land exclusive of other imposts, assessment or tax; 2, a register of lands compiled in the time of the Coorg Rajas and containing the class of soil of each field, its area, and a list of bâṇe lands attached to it (Cg.); ಸ್ಥಳ–, ರಿವಾಜ್– (sthaḷa-, rivâz-) the ancient rate of assessment on each particular field (My.); ಕಾಣ– (kâṇ-) assessment on kâṇs (*p.* 130).

ಶೇಮ šêma. Hidden treasure.

ಶ್ರಯ šraya. Waste land granted to ryots undertaking to reclaim it from jungle and bring it under permanent cultivation, upon progressively increasing leases.

ಸಂಚಾಯಿತ, ಸಂದಾಯಿತ sañčâyita, sandâyita. Lands not let but farmed by the government or the proprietors themselves.

ಸರ್ಕಾರ sarkâra. Assessment payable to government (S. C.); –ಸಾಗು (-sâgu) land held directly under government or cultivated by government, but differing from ಸೀರ್ಸಾರ್ (*p.* 156) in being temporary and not alienable.

ಸರಾಸರಿ sarâsari. *Lit.* Average; sarâsari settlement is a name given to Mr. Harris's settlement, which was fixed (1819 A. D.) with reference to the average collections of the first 17 years of the "Company's government"; also termed ಸತ್ರಾಸಾಲ್– (satrâsâl-) or the average of 17 years (C.); –ಚಿಟ್ಠಾ (-čiṭṭhâ) a čiṭṭa prepared in 1819.

ಸ್ಥಳ sthaḷa. Spot, site or place; 2, a portion of land comprising several fields; –ಕಮ್ಮಿ (-kammi) part of a field left waste (S. C.); –ಭರ್ತಿ (-bharti) duty on goods levied at the place of production in contradistinction to ಕರಗಪದಿಹಾಸಲ್ (*p.* 160) (My.); —ವಾರ್ (-vâr) a record showing the particulars of each field or parcel of land; —ವಾರ್ ಚಿಟ್ಠಾ (-vâr čiṭṭhâ) an account according to the fields, fieldvâr account.

ಸಾಗುಸಂತು **sagusantu.** An account showing the species and quantity of seed sown, the extent of land under cultivation, and the quantity remaining untilled (Cg.) *cf.* ಕರಡೂದ್ಪಟ್ಟಿ.

ಸಾಗುವಳಿಚೀಟು **sâguvaḷičiṭu.** A written permission given to a ryot to cultivate land, on his application to take it being accepted (Cg.).

ಸಾಯರ್ **sâyar.** Customs, tax; ಅಳ್ವೆ—, ದರ್ಯಾ— (aḷve-, daryâ-) sea customs.

ಸಿದ್ದಾಯಾ **siddâyâ.** The fixed assessment recorded in ರಾಯರೇಖ (q. v.).

ಸುಂಕ **suṅka.** Toll, custom; —ದ ಕಟ್ಟೆ (-da kaṭṭe) a custom-house; ದಾರಿ— (dâri-) transit duties.

ಸೋಡಿ **sôḍi.** Remission, abatement of a charge or demand (My.).

ಹಂಕಲು **haṅkalu.** A tract of land for which no assessment is paid, but which is said to be included in a varga and is set apart for grazing purposes, although of late used for dry cultivation (My.); ತಟ್ಟಿನ— (taṭṭina-) dry land attached to each gadde or wet field, unassessed but said to be included in a varga (Malnad, My.); —ತೆರಿಗೆ (-terige) a stubble-tax, tax on stubble on which cattle of the ryots is allowed to graze (My.).

ಹಂಚುಗೋಲು **hañčugôlu.** A wooden seal used by government officers when farmers divide their corn on the threshing floor.

ಹಕ್ಲುಸಾಗುವಳಿ **haklusâguvaḷi.** A kind of dry cultivation carried on during the monsoon in spots detached from estates and differing from kumri in not requiring to be cleared of large trees (Ch.).

ಹಡ್ಲುಮಾನ್ಯ **haḍlumânya.** Fees from ryots who have taken up waste-land on progressive tenure—šraya—and who resign the lands before they become liable to the full rate of assessment, the amount of the fee being one year's full assessment (Cg.).

ಹತ್ತೆಟ್ಟಿ **hatteṭṭi.** Tax levied on clearings of forest or kumris.

ಹಪ್ತಾ **haptâ.** A period at which a portion of assessment is due (S. M.); —ಬಂದಿ (-bandi) settlement for payment by instalments, kistbandi (S. M.).

ಹಸಗಿ **hasagi.** One of the equal portions of a rice-field in each of which one or more khaṇḍis of paddy can be sown (N. C.).

ಹಾಡ್ಯ **hâḍya.** Lands covered with low brush-wood and small trees, from which firewood, leaves, etc. are taken for manuring the fields of a varga (My.).

ಹಾಸಲ್ **hâsal.** Duty or tax; 2, postage; ಆಮದ್— (âmad-) import duty (My.); ಕರಗಪಡಿ— (karagapaḍi-) consumption-duty, or duty on goods sold (My.); ಭರ್ತಿ— (bharti-) export-duty (My.); ಭಾರಾಮಾರ್ಗ— (bhârâmârga-) transit duty (My.).

ಹಾಳತ್ **hâḷat.** Export duty or excise on goods (My.); a term by which the high duties on pepper, betel-nut, cardamoms, etc. paid at certain stations to which these commodities are brought previous to leaving the district, are termed (Sir Thos. Munro).

ಹುಟ್ಟುವಳಿ **huṭṭuvaḷi.** The produce of a land, out-turn; ಗೇಣಿ— (gêṇi-) rent-produce (S. C.); ರಿವಾಜ್— (rivâz-) nett produce, full rack-rent; 2, customary produce (S. C.); 3, attainable rent-produce calculated at ½ the gross produce on cultivable land; ಹಾಜರ್— (hâzar-) actual rent-produce derived from land actually under cultivation and calculated in the same manner as ರಿವಾಜ್—; 2, the present produce (S. C.).

ಹುಲ್ಲುಬನ್ನಿ **hullubanni.** A tax paid by the gollas or cow-keepers for liberty of grazing their flocks on public lands (My.).

ಹೆಚ್ಚಿಗೆ **heččige.** The increase in the assessment of Mysore, made in the two years Krôdhi and Dundubhi, and respectively called ಕ್ರೋಧಿ ಹೆಚ್ಚಿಗೆ, ದುಂದುಭಿ ಹೆಚ್ಚಿಗೆ.

ಹೇಮಸಾಯ **hêmasâya.** (From Hindustani, ಹಮ್‌ಸಾಯಾ neighbouring) The rate of assessment paid on neighbouring lands taken as the standard in assessing lands newly cultivated (Cg.).

ಹೊಗೆತೆರಿಗೆ **hogeterige.** Tax paid by those who do not pay land-tax to government; mohatarphâ (My.).

Weights, Measures, etc.

Note: **The Weights and Measures of different places have been reduced to a uniform standard, the Tola or Rupee weight, to facilitate comparison.**

ಅಂಗುಲ aṅgula. A lineal measure for wood, 24 making a ಗಜ or ಕೋಲು (S. C.); a finger's breadth, 4 of which make a ಮುಷ್ಟಿ or fist's breadth.

ಅಂಡಿಗಿ aṇḍigi. A dry measure of 8960 tolas in Mundagod (N. C.).

ಅಗಲ agala. Breadth, width.

ಅಚಿತ ačita. A weight of 10 khaṇḍugas (q. v.); a cart-load.

ಅಟ್ಟೆ aṭṭe. A lump of tamarind (S. C.); 2, muḍis of rice stored one on another (S. C.).

ಅಡಿ aḍi. A footstep of 10½ inches.

ಅಡ್ಡ aḍḍa. A gold or silver weight of about 5·68 grains (Avoirdupois) (S. C.); 2, a fractional part denoting ½ and written || (ಅರ್ಧ).

ಅಡ್ಡಣ addaṇa. Half a pint.

ಅರ್ವಳ arvaḷa. A dry measure of 18 tolas in Kumta and Honawar (N. C.).

ಅಳಕ aḷaka. An old measure of capacity for salt, and equal to 15 tolas (S. C.).

ಅಳತೆ aḷate. Measure, capacity, dimension; ಅಗಲ— (agala-) breadth; ಉದ್ದ— (udda-) length; ಘನ— (ghana-) cubic measure; ಚೌಕ— (čauka-) square measure; ತೀಕೆ— (tȇke-) struck measure (S. C.); ರಾಶಿ— (râśi-) heapmeasure (S. C.); ಸುತ್ತು— (sutta-) circumference.

ಆಜ್ಲೆ âjle. A dry measure of 4 kaḷasis or 56 šerus (S. C.).

ಆಟ್ವಾ âṭvâ. A dry measure of 32 tolas in Karwar and Ankola (N. C.).

ಆಣೆ âṇe. An anna, $\frac{1}{16}$ of a rupee; 2, $\frac{1}{16}$ of a gunṭe, a square land-measure of 7 $\frac{9}{16}$ square yards, *also* ಆಣಿ; 3, a gold weight equal to $\frac{1}{16}$ of a tola (N. C.); 4, an old measure of salt, equal to 100 ಫರೆ (Bel.); ಅರ್ಧ—, ನೀಮ— (ardha-, nîma-) half anna; ಪಾವ— (pâv-) quarter anna; ದೋನ— (dôn-) two annas.

ಆಳ âḷa. The height of a person, roughly about 5½ feet (S. C.).

ಉದ್ದ **udda.** Length; —ಅಗಲ (-agala) length and breadth.

ಎಂಟೆ **eṇṭe.** A secure band of straw put round muḍis of grain.

ಎಕ್ರೆ **ekre.** An acre, a land-measure containing 4840 square yards.

ಎಣ್ಣಾ **eṇṇâ.** A bundle containing 40 to 50 betel leaves, and equal to two ಕವಳಗಳು (S. C.).

ಒಕ್ಕಳ **okkaḷa.** A dry measure of 6144 tolas in Haliyal and Supa (N. C.), and of 10240 tolas (Bel.).

ಕಂದಾಯ **kandâya.** A space of three months, a quarter (My.).

ಕಟ್ಟಿಗೆ **kaṭṭige.** A land-measure of 34 $\frac{1}{36}$ square cubits (Bel.).

ಕಡಿಮಟ್ಟು, ಕಡೆಮೆಟ್ಟು **kaḍimaṭṭu, kaḍemeṭṭu.** A measurement by which horses are measured.

ಕಬಾಡ **kabâḍa.** A beast's burden of wood or straw.

ಕರೆ **kare.** A call or shout's distance (S. C.).

ಕಲ್ಲು **kallu.** A mile, a milestone (S. C.); 2, a weight equal to 14 lbs.

ಕವಳಿ **kavaḷi.** A bundle of 20 to 25 betel leaves (S. C.).

ಕಳಸಿ **kaḷasi.** A dry measure of 1120 tolas (S. C. and Bhatkal in N. C.), although $\frac{1}{3}$ of a muḍi in S. C., and $\frac{1}{4}$ in Bhatkal.

ಕಾಟಿ **kâṭi.** An obsolete dry measure of the 14th century, containing four hânis of 80 tolas each; 2, a land-measure of 484 square feet (W.;

ಕಾಡಿ **kâḍi.** A measure of capacity; ಸಣ್ಣ— (saṇṇa-) a capacity measure of 10 khaṇḍugas; ದೊಡ್ಡ— (doḍḍa-) of 20 khaṇḍugas.

ಕಾಣಿ **kâṇi.** A fractional part denoting $\frac{1}{64}$ and written ।; 2, $\frac{1}{640}$ of a pagoda; 3, a land-measure of 57,600 square feet, a cawnie.

ಕಾಲ್, ಕಾಲು **kâl, kâlu.** A fractional part denoting a quarter; ಅರೆ— (ar-) an eighth; ಗಿರೆ— (gir-) a sixteenth; ಮುಕ್ಕಾಲು (mukkâlu) three-fourths; 2, a quarter anna (S. C.).

ಕಾಲಾಡ **kâlâḍa.** A fluid measure of 448 tolas, and $2\frac{1}{2}$ of which make a maṇa (S. C.).

ಕಾಸು **kâsu.** $\frac{1}{384}$ of a rupee, half a pie (S. C.); 2, a pie, or $\frac{1}{192}$ of a rupee (My.).

ಕುಂಬ kumba. A dry measure of 20 khaṇḍis or 76800 tolas in Karwar and Ankola (N. C.).

ಕುಡು kuḍu. A dry measure of 672 tolas, also called ಕೊಳಗ (My.).

ಕುಡುಪ kuḍupa. A measure of grain containing 12 handfuls.

ಕುಡುವ kuḍuva. A dry measure of 192 tolas in Karwar, Ankola, and 216 tolas in Kumta and Honawar (N. C.).

ಕುಡುತೆ, ಕುಡ್ತೆ kuḍute, kuḍte. A dry measure of 12⅓ tolas and a fluid measure of 12 tolas (S. C.).

ಕುತ್ತಿ kutti. A fluid measure of 112 tolas and made up of 9 kuḍtas (S. C.).

ಕೂಗು kûgu. The distance of a call or a shout, *also* ಕೂಗಳತೆ (S. C.).

ಕೂರಿಗೆ kûrige. The space occupied by 4 acres.

ಕೈ kai. A set of 5, as loose sticks of firewood (S. C.); 2, a cubit (S. C.).

ಕೊಂಡೆ koṇḍe. A *dry* measure of 20 tolas and a fluid measure of 12 tolas (S. C.).

ಕೊಂಬುಸೊನ್ನೆ, ಕೊಂಬುಸಣಿ kombusonne, kombusaṇi. The distance occupied by the sound of a horn, about two miles.

ಕೊತ್ತು kottu. A mark showing the limit of a liquid measure (S. C.).

ಕೊಯಿಲು koyilu. A measure of seed-corn containing 4 hânis of 100 tolas and reckoned to be as much as a man can sow in a proportionate space of ground in a day (W.); 2, a dry measure of 5 nâḍis, 12 of which make a muḍi seed-area; in some parts it is made up of 10 nâḍis, 6 of such going to make up a muḍi seed-area (Udipi, S. C.).

ಕೊಳಗ koḷaga. A dry measure of 768 tolas in Yellapore, 384 tolas in Sirsi, 72 tolas in Siddhapore, and 224 tolas in Bhatkal (N. C.); 2, a dry measure of 672 tolas (My.). In Mysore there are 3 varieties of koḷagas: the ಸುಲ್ತಾನಿ (sultâni) established by Tippu Sultan containing 16 šêrus, the ಕೃಷ್ಣರಾಜ (krishṇarâja) containing 8 šêrus. and ಖರಾರ (kharâr) containing 10. As a land-measure a koḷaga of seed requires 3200 square yards of dry and 500 of wet land (My.).

ಕೋಡಿ kôḍi. A score of uncut "stones" (S. C.); 2, a wood measurement of 240 kôl × 12 aṅgula × 2 aṅgula, by which sawyers are paid and by which *felled* trees are sold (S. C.).

ಕೋರ್ಜಿ **kôrji.** A set of 42 muḍis of grain, equal to 141120 tolas (S. C.), and to 127008 tolas in Kumta and Honawar (N. C.); —ಕಟ್ಟಳೆ (-kaṭṭaḷe) by kôrjis (S. C.

ಕೋಲು **kôlu.** A pole or rod; a wood measurement of 24 fingers' breadth (S. C.); ಇಕ್ಕೇರಿ— (ikkêri-) a pole 2 feet 7 inches long. An Ikkêri cubic pole is 1 kôl × 12 aṅgula × 2 aṅgula; 240 of these make a ಕೋರಿ, by which felled trees are sold (S. C.); ಮಲೆಯಾಳಿ— (maleyâḷi-) a pole 2 feet 4 inches long; a Malayali square pole is 1 kôl × 12 aṅgula, the cubic being 1 kôl × 12 aṅgula × 1 aṅgula; 24 of the latter make a ಖಂಡಿ by which sawn trees are sold (S. C.); ಹೊಕ್ಕಳು— (hokkaḷu-) a pole as high as the navel. This is taken as a standard for breadth and depth of a pit for planting cocoanut palms (S. C.); ಕದ್ರೆ— (kadre-) a pole, an aṅgula less than Ikkêri kôl (S. C.); ವೀರರಾಜೇಂದ್ರ— (vîrarâjêndra-) a pole 18 feet 8 inches long (Cg.); ಲಿಂಗರಾಜೇಂದ್ರ— (liṅgarâjêndra-) a pole 16 feet long (Cg.).

ಖಂಡಿ **khaṇḍi.** A word applicable to weight, dry and fluid measure, etc.: 1, *metals*—22400 tolas or 5 cwt. (S. C. and Bhatkal in N. C.); 23040 tolas in Honawar, Yellapore and Ankola (N. C.), 20000 tolas in Mundagod, 22400 tolas in Sirsi (N. C.); 2, *timber*—38 ft. 10¾ inches (N. C.); 24 kôl × 12 aṅgula × 1 aṅgula (S. C.); 3, *sugar*, *ghee*—16000 tolas (Bel.), 19200 tolas (Cg.); 4, *jaggory*—19200 tolas (S. C.); 5, *dry measure*—3840 tolas in Karwar and Ankola, 4320 tolas in Kumta and Honawar, 122880 tolas in Haliyal and Supa, 15360 tolas in Yellapore, 1440 tolas in Siddhapore, and 71680 tolas in Mundagod (N. C.); 6, *fluid measure*—11200 tolas (S. C.); 23040 tolas in Sirsi, 20000 tolas in Mundagod (N. C.); ದೊಡ್ಡ—, ಹಿರೆ— (doḍḍa-, hire-) a grain measure of 153600 tolas in Sirsi (N. C.); ಫಾಟಾ— (phâṭâ-) a khaṇḍi of 25 maṇas, only used in Virarajendrapett (Cg.).

ಖಂಡುಗ **khaṇḍuga.** (*cf.* ಖಂಡಿ) A *dry* measure of 409600 tolas (Bel.); 12800 tolas (Cg.); 13440 tolas (My.); 2, a *salt* measure of 64000 tolas (Bel.); 3, a *weight* of 19200 tolas for silk, sugar, drugs and cotton

(My.); 4, a *land* measure requiring 64000 square yards of dry 10000 of wet land (My.); 5, a synonym for a muḍi in Bhatkal (N. C.).

ಖಣ **khaṇa.** A piece of cloth for petticoats of women, and containing a cubit or 18 inches (S. C.).

ಖಪ್ಪತ **khappata.** A bale of dried Arabian dates weighing from 5 to 5½ maṇas (S. C.).

ಗಜ **gaja.** A yard of 3 feet; 2, a wood measurement of 24 aṅgulas (S. C.).

ಗಡಿ **gaḍi.** 10 quires of paper, half a ream.

ಗದ್ಯಾಣ **gadyâṇa.** A weight of a ruvi or farthing; 2, a small gold coin (Bel.); 3, a pagoda (Abbr. ಗ.).

ಗಾರ್ಸು **gârsu.** An old measure for salt, containing 120 maṇas or 384000 tolas (S. C.).

ಗಿದ್ದಾಣಿ **giddâṇi.** $\frac{1}{256}$ part of a fanam (W.).

ಗಿದ್ದನ **giddana.** A fourteenth part of a maṇa (W.).

ಗಿದ್ನ **gidna.** A dry measure, 4 of which make a solige (My.).

ಗಿರೆ **gire.** $\frac{1}{16}$th part of a yard (Bel.).

ಗುಂಟೆ **guṇṭe.** A land measure containing 121 square yards, and 40 of which make an acre.

ಗೂಳಿ **gûḷi.** A land measure of 576 square feet, and 100 of which make a kâṇi or cawnie.

ಗೇಣು **gêṇu.** A lineal measure denoting a span.

ಗೊಣಸು **goṇasu.** A link of a chain measuring 33 feet (S. C.).

ಘಳಿಗೆ **ghaḷige.** An Indian hour of 24 minutes; ವಿ— (vi-) $\frac{1}{60}$ of the preceding, 24 seconds.

ಚಂಬು **čambu.** A fluid measure of 132 tolas in Ankola, 60 tolas in Haliyal and Supa, and 120 in Yellapore (N. C.).

ಚಕ್ರ **čakra.** A four anna piece (S. C.).

ಚಚ್ಚೌಕ **čaččauka.** Square; —ಅಳತೆ (-aḷate) square measure.

ಚಟಾಕ್ **čaṭâk.** A dry measure of 20 tolas (Bel.); 2, a liquid measure

ಚವಲ **čavala.** An eighth of a pagoda, $\frac{1}{2}$ a rupee (My.).

ಚವಲಿ **čavali.** A two anna piece, $\frac{1}{8}$ of a rupee (S. C.).

ಚಾಪ **čâpa.** A piece of 4 Madras handkerchiefs (S. C.); *also* ಝಾಪ.

ಚಾಹೂರ **čâhûra.** A land-measure of 120 bighas, $1\frac{1}{5}$ acres (Bel.).

ಚಿಟ್ಟೆ **čiṭṭe.** A dry measure of 384 tolas in Yellapore, Haliyal and Supa, 280 tolas in Mundagod (N. C.), and 640 tolas (Bel.).

ಚಿಟ್ಣಿ ಖಂಡಿ **čiṭṇi khaṇḍi.** A dry measure of 1440 tolas in Siddhapore (N. C.).

ಚೋಟು **čôṭu.** A span from the tip of the thumb to that of the fore-finger (S. C.).

ಝಾಮ, ಯಾಮ **jhâma, yâma.** A space of 3 hours, $\frac{1}{8}$ of a day.

ಟಕ್ಕೆ **ṭakke.** A weight equal to $\frac{4}{55}$ of a rati by which pearl and precious stones are sold (Bel.).

ಟಾಕ **ṭâka.** A weight of 62 grains Troy by which pearl and precious stones are sold (Bel.).

ಟಾಕೆ **ṭâke.** A piece of cloth containing 20 to 40 yards (S. C.), *also* ಠಾಕೆ.

ತಸು **tasu.** A lineal measure of $1\frac{1}{2}$ inches, 12 of which make a cubit (Bel.).

ತಾತಿ **tâti.** A fluid measure of 20 tolas (Bel.).

ತಾರ **târa.** Two pies or $\frac{1}{6}$ of an anna (S. C.).

ತಾವು **tâvu.** A sheet of paper, $\frac{1}{24}$ of a quire (S. C.).

ತಾಸು **tâsu.** An English hour of 60 minutes.

ತಿಪ್ಪಿ **tippi.** A toddy measure of 2 ounces (Tulu, S. C.).

ತೂಕ **tûka.** Weight; 2, a gold weight equal to 51 grains (Av.) and 82 of which make 1 tola (S. C.); ಗುರಗುಂಜಿ– (guragunji-) gold weight equal to $1\frac{5}{12}$ grains (S. C.) and to 6 grains of rice (N. C.); ಮಂಜೂಟಿ– (mañjûṭi-) a weight of 2 of the preceding (S. C.); ದಾಮ್– (dâm-) a weight equal to 2 of the preceding or to $5\frac{2}{3}$ grains, $\frac{1}{9}$ of a tûka (S. C.); ಸಂತಮಿ– (santami-) a gold weight *practically* equal to 10 tûkas (S. C.); ವರಹ–, ವರ್ತೂಕ (varaha-, vartûka) a weight equal to $\frac{4}{15}$ tola;

ತರಹು, ಸೂಟು (tarahu, sûṭu) tret; ನಿಕ್ಕಿ— (nikki-) suttle weight (S. C.); ಬಾರದಾನ್ (bâradân) tare (S. C.).

ತೊಡೆಮಟ್ಟ **toḍemaṭṭa.** Knee-deep.

ತೊಲೆ **tole.** A weight equal to a rupee or 6·4 drachms (Av.); a gold weight equal to $\frac{1}{24}$ of a šêru (S. C.).

ಥಾನು **thânu.** A piece of cloth containing from 20 to 40 yards (S. C.); *cf.* ಟಾಕೆ.

ದಮ್ಮಡಿ **dammaḍi.** A pie, $\frac{1}{12}$ of an anna.

ದಸ್ತು **dastu.** A quire of paper; a set of 4 cards, a trick.

ದುಗುಲ **dugula.** $\frac{1}{16}$ of a pagoda or varaha (My.).

ದುಗ್ಗಾಣಿ **duggâṇi.** Two pies or $\frac{1}{6}$ of an anna.

ದುಡ್ಡು **duḍḍu.** Four pies (S. C.); three pies (My., Bel.).

ಧಡೆ **dhaḍe.** A *weight* of 7 lbs. or 280 tolas (S. C.), 200 tolas (Bel.), 275 tolas (Cg.), 240 tolas (My.), 280 tolas in Sirsi and Bhatkal, 250 tolas in Mundagod and Supa, and 288 tolas in Honawar, Yellapore and Ankola (N. C.); 2, a *fluid* measure of 320 tolas in Karwar, 288 tolas in Kumta, Sirsi, and 250 tolas in Mundagod (N. C.).

ಧರಣ **dharaṇa.** A fourth of a pagoda, a rupee (My., C.).

ನಾಗ **nâga.** A fluid measure of 8000 tolas in Mundagod (N. C.).

ನಾಡಿ **nâḍi.** A dry measure of 8 kuḍtâs, and 3 of which make a Mangalore muḍi.

ನಾಣ್ಯ **nâṇya.** Coin; —ವಾರ್ (-vâr) according to coin, arranged according to coins (vlg. ನಾಣೆವಾರ್).

ನಿಜ **nija.** A dry measure of 6 maṇas; 2, a dry measure of 20736 tolas in Sonda and 17280 tolas in Bilgi (N. C.).

ನೌಟಾಂಗ **nauṭânga.** A fluid measure of 4 tolas in Karwar (N. C.).

ಪಂಚಕ **pañčaka.** Five or 6 sheets of paper (S. C.); 2, a dry measure of 5 koḷagas (My.).

ಪಂಚೇರು **pañčêru.** A word meaning literally five šerus, although practically not so; 1, a *weight* of 140 tolas (S. C.); 125 tolas in Supa, 144 tolas in Honawar, Yellapore and Ankola (N. C.); 137½ tolas for potatoes, butter, etc. (Cg.); 100 tolas for sugar and ghee (Bel.);

120 tolas for sugar, silk, drugs (My.); 2, *fluid* measure 100 tolas (Bel.), 144 tolas in Kumta and Honawar (N. C.).

ಪಡಿ **paḍi.** An old measure of 120 tolas for salt (S. C.); 2, a dry measure of 192 tolas in Haliyal and Supa (S. C.), of 320 tolas (Bel.), of 10½ tolas (My.).

ಪಡುವಣಿ **paḍuvaṇi.** Testing or comparing a measure with another.

ಪಯಿಲಿ **payili.** A dry measure of 10¼ tolas (My.); *also* ಪಡಿ. As a land measure a payili of seed wants 200 square yards of dry and 31¼ of wet land (My.).

ಪಲ್ಲ **palla.** A dry measure of 8400 tolas (Cg.).

ಪಲ್ಲೆ **palle.** A weight of 6400 tolas for sugar, ghee, *also* ಹೇರು (Bel.).

ಪಕ್ಷ **paksha.** A fortnight, 15 days.

ಪಾಂಡು **pâṇḍu.** A square land measure of 20 ಕಟ್ಟಿಗೆ (*p.* 162) (Bel.).

ಪಾವ್, ಪಾವು **pâv, pâvu.** A weight and capacity measure; 1, *weight:* 6 tolas for gold and silver (S. C.), and for arecanut, sugar, drugs (My.); 2, a *grain* measure, of 20 tolas (S. C.), 140 tolas in Mundagod, 192 in Yellapore (made up of 2 šêrus) (N. C.); ಗಿರ– (gir-) a dry measure of 40 tolas (Bel.).

ಪಾವಲಿ **pâvali.** A four anna coin (S. C.).

ಪುಳಿ **puḷi.** Hundred bundles of grass or hay (N. C.).

ಪ್ರತಾಪ **pratâpa.** A pagoda, a hoon, and symbolised by ೱ.

ಪ್ರಹರ **prahara.** A time of 3 hours.

ಫರೆ **phare.** A salt measure (Bel.); 2, a dry measure of 800 tolas (Cg.).

ಫಾಡು **phâḍu.** A fluid measure of 4 kâlâḍa or 1792 tolas (S. C.).

ಫಾಸಿಲೆ **phâsile.** Distance.

ಬಳ್ಳ **baḷḷa.** A grain measure of 8 kuḍtâs (S. C.); a dry measure of 168 tolas (My.); 2, a land measure requiring 800 square yards of dry, and 125 square yards of wet, land (My.).

ಬಿಲ್ಲಿ **billi.** Three pies or a quarter anna (Bel.); *also* ದುಡ್ಡು.

ಬೀಘೆ **bighe.** A square land measure of 20 ಪಾಂಡು, $\frac{1}{160}$ of an acre (Bel.).

ಬೆಳ್ಳಿ **beḷḷi.** Three annas (S. C.).

ಬೇಳೆ **bêle.** A fractional part denoting an eighth.

ಬೊಟ್ಟು **bottu.** One-sixty-fourth of a hoon or pagoda (My.).

ಭಟ್ಟಿ **bhatti.** A dry measure of 6400 tolas; 2, a land measure of about 176 square yards —roughly 3 acres are equal to 100 bhattis—(Cg.).

ಮಕಾರ **makâra.** The distinguishing 'mark' of a fanam, the sign ⌐.

ಮಜಲು **majalu.** A stage or halting place in a journey; 2, nine miles (S. C.).

ಮಣ **mana.** A maund, applicable to weights and fluid measures; 1, *weight:* 1120 tolas (S. C.) in Bhatkal, Karwar, Kumta, and Haliyal (N. C.), 1000 tolas in Mundagod, and 1152 tolas in Honawar, Yellapore, Siddhapore and Ankola (N. C.); 960 tolas for sugar and ghee (Cg. & My.); 1100 tolas for sweetmeat and butter (Cg.); 800 tolas (Bel.); 2, *fluid:* 1120 tolas (S. C. here a mana is $\frac{1}{10}$ of a khandi), 1280 tolas in Karwar. 1152 tolas in Honawar and Sirsi, 960 tolas in Haliyal and Supa, 1920 tolas in Yellapore, 1000 tolas in Mundagod, 1120 tolas in Bhatkal (N. C.), and 800 tolas (Bel.); 3, salt measure: 3200 tolas (S. C. & Bel.).

ಮಧ್ಯಾಹ್ನ **madhyânha.** Noon; ಒಳ– (ola-) fore-noon (S. C.); –ತಿರುಗುವಾಗ (-tiruguvâga) just after midday (S. C.); –ದ ಮೇಲೆ (-da mêle) afternoon.

ಮರ್ಕಾಲು **markâlu.** A measure of salt equal to 960 tolas (S. C.).

ಮಾನ **mâna.** A *fluid* measure of 18 tolas (Cg.), and a *dry* of 32 tolas (My.).

ಮಾನಗಿ **mânagi.** A Kundapore word for ಮುಡಿ (*infra*, S. C.).

ಮಾರು **mâru.** A fathom, made up of 4 cubits.

ಮಾಸಿ **mâsi.** A weight for gold used by Goa goldsmiths, and 11½ of which go to make up a tola or rupee weight, although theoretically 12 (N. C.).

ಮುಂಡ **munda.** Neck-deep—a standard by which coolies are paid for digging wells and tanks (S. C.).

ಮುಟ್ಟಿ **mutti.** A toddy measure equal to a pint (Tulu, S. C.).

ಮುಡಿ **mudi.** A dry measure of 3 kalasis in Canara, except in Bhatkal (N. C.) where it is 4 kalasis. The equivalents are 3360 tolas (S. C.),

3024 tolas in Kumta and Honawar (N. C.), and 4480 tolas in Bhatkal (N. C.); ನಗ– (naga-) a quantity of grain *tied up* in a bundle of straw, as opposed to ಸುರಿ– (suri-) which is loose (S. C.). The different kinds of muḍis are the following: ಕಾಯಿದೆ– (kâyide-) a government standard muḍi containing 42 šêrus of grain, 3360 tolas (S. C.); ನಿಜ– (nija-) a Mangalore muḍi of 42 šêrus (S. C.); 2, the *estimated* number of muḍis of seed for sowing a field with in contradistinction to the actual number (W.); ಅಜಲ್–, ಆಜ್ಲೆ– (ajal-, âjle-) a muḍi containing from 56 to 60 šêrus (C.) although in S. C. it is invariably 56 šêrus; ಕಂಚಿನ– (kañcina-) containing 63 šêrus (Kundapore, S. C.); ಕಿಮ್ಜಾ– (kimčâ-) 60 šêrus; ಸ್ಥಳ– (sthaḷa-) a local muḍi and therefore varying almost in every village, also termed ಸ್ಥಳರಿವಾಜ್– (sthaḷarivâz-); ಸಣ್ಣ– (saṇṇa-) a muḍi containing 30 to 32 šêrus; 2, a muḍi containing 52½ šêrus in Kundapore and 48 in Bramhavar (S. C.); ವಕ್ಲು– (vaklu-) a tenant's muḍi and *supposed* to contain a little more than ಕಾಯಿದೆ– (S. C.); ಹೊಲಿಕೆ– (holike-) a local standard muḍi, differing for different grains and in different villages. The muḍi is supposed to contain a certain number of šêrus, the deficiency being termed ಕುಂಡ್ಲು, ಕುಂಡೇಲ್ (kundlu, kundêl) (S. C.). The holike or standard for a muḍi of rice in different parts of S. C. are:—Mangalore 42 šêrus, Padubidre 50, Manjeshwar 36, Kumbla and Karkal 37½, Mulki 48.

Generally 100 muḍis of unhusked rice are considered equal to 50 of husked rice, but in Honawar and Kumta (N. C.), equal to 42 of husked rice.

The word also denotes the extent of land that can be sown with a muḍi of grain—about an acre (S. C.) and 3414 sq. yards (Padinalknad Taluk, Cg.).

ಮುಷ್ಟಿ **mushṭi.** A fist; 2, a fist-breadth; 3, handful.

ಮುಹೂರ್ತ **muhûrta.** A time of 48 minutes.

ಮೊಳ **moḷa.** A cubit, roughly equal to 18 inches; ಗುದ್ದು– (guddu-) a cubit from the elbow to a closed fist (S. C.); ಗಿಡ್ಡ– (giḍḍa-) a short cubit (S. C.).

ರತಿ **rati.** A weight for precious stones and equal to about 1⅝ of a grain.

ರಾತ್ಲು **râtlu.** One lb.; one-twenty-eighth part of a maṇa. The râtlu of S.C. is made up of 1⅓ šêrus of 24 tolas, and that in N.C. of 2 šêrus; 2, a fluid measure of 40 tolas in Yellapore (N. C.).

ರೇಜಮ್ **rêjam.** A corrupted form of "ream", a ream of paper (S. C.).

ವಡ್ಡಿ **vaḍḍi.** A set of four.

ವಡ್ಡೆ **vaḍḍe.** A multiplication table.

ವರಹ **varaha.** A pagoda, a hoon, and denoted by the symbol ೱ.; —ತೂಕ (-tûka) a gold weight of 9 fanams or 1·92 drachms (Av.) (S. C.) and $\frac{4}{15}$ tola (N. C.).

ವಾರ **vâra.** A day; 2, a week of seven days (S. C.).

ವಾರು **vâru.** A yard of 3 feet (S. C.).

ವಾಸ್ **vâs.** A wood measurement of 20 ವಿಶ್ವ or 23⅓ inches (N. C.).

ವಿಶ್ವ **višva.** A wood measurement of 1⅙ inches (N. C.).

ವೀಸ **visa.** A wood measurement, $\frac{1}{16}$ of an aṅgula (S. C.); a gold weight of 1·21 grains (Av., S. C.); a fractional part denoting $\frac{1}{16}$; ಅರೆ— (are-) $\frac{1}{32}$ part; ಮುರು— (muru-) $\frac{3}{16}$ part.

ಸಿದ್ದೆ **siddhe.** A *dry* measure of 36 tolas in Kumta, Honawar and Siddhapore, and 28 tolas in Bhatkal (N. C.); 2, a *fluid* measure of 33 tolas in Ankola and 28 tolas in Bhatkal (N. C.).

ಶೇರು, ಸೇರು **šêru, sêru.** A seer, a word applicable to weight, dry and fluid measure; 1, *weight*— 24 tolas for metals and jaggory (S. C. and Sirsi in N. C.), and for sugar, ghee and jaggory (Cg.); 20 tolas in Karwar, Kumta, Haliyal, Siddhapore and Mundagod (N. C.), and for sugar, ghee and jaggory (Bel.); 2, *dry measure*— 80 tolas (S. C., Cg.), 72 tolas in Kumta and Honawar, 96 tolas in Yellapore and Sirsi (N. C.), 160 tolas (Bel.), and 84 tolas (My.); 3, *fluid measure*— 24 tolas (S. C.), 32 tolas in Karwar, 24 tolas in Kumta and Sirsi, 36 tolas in Honawar, 20 tolas in Haliyal, Supa and Mundagod (N. C. & Bel.); 4, *salt measure*— 80 tolas (S. C. & Bel.), 5, *for potatoes and butter*—27½ tolas, and known as the "local šêru" (Cg.); 6, a *land-measure* requiring 400 square yards of dry and 62½ of wet land (My.); ಕಚ್ಚಾ- (kaččâ-) a šêru of 20 to 30 tolas; ಪಕ್ಕಾ- (pakkâ-) of 80 to 100 tolas; ಅಡೈ- (aḍai-) a weight of 60 tolas for sugar, drugs, silk (My.); 2, a weight of 70 tolas for metals in Sirsi (N. C.).

ಸಂಕ್ಲಿ saṅkli. A chain 33 feet long used in measuring land or in survey (S. C.).

ಸಮಯ samaya. Time; ಕೋಳಿ ಕೂಗುವ- (kôḷikûguva-) at cock-crow; ಗೋಧೂಳಿ- (gôdhûḷi-) time at which cows return home from grazing, *i. e.* about 5 p. m. (S. C.).

ಸಲೆ sale. Extent; 2, a year (from ಸಾಲ್, S. C.); -ಗಜ (-gaja) square yard (S. C.).

ಸಾಸು sâsu. An obsolete salt measure equal to 16 ಅಸ (q. v., Bel.).

ಸೂಡಿ sûḍi. A sheaf of hay, 1000 of which make a ಸಲಾಯಿ (salayi) or a truss (S. C.); 2, a bundle of 80 to 100 betel leaves (S. C.).

ಸೊಲ್ಗಿ, ಸೊಲಿಗೆ solgi, solige. A dry measure of 9 tolas in Kumta and Honawar (N. C.), of 640 tolas (Bel.) and of 8¼ tolas (My.).

ಹಣ haṇa. Money; 2, a fanam or four-ninths of a rupee; -ತೂಕ (-tûka) a gold weight of ·213 drachm (Av., S. C.).

ಹಪ್ತೆ hapte. A week of seven days.

ಹರದಾರಿ haradâri. A distance of 2000 fathoms; 2, a league or 3 miles (S. C.).

ಹಾಗ hâga. A fractional part denoting a quarter and symbolized by | ; -ತೂಕ (-tûka) a gold weight of 4·84 grains (Av., S. C.).

ಹಾನೆ, ಹಾನಿ hâne, hâni. A word applicable to dry and fluid measure: 1, *dry*—133 tolas (Manjeshwar, S. C.), 112 tolas in Bhatkal (N. C.), and 160 tolas (Cg.); 2, *fluid*—144 tolas (Cg.); 2211 tolas in Ankola (N. C.).

ಹಾಳೆ hâḷe. A sheet of paper, a leaf of a book.

ಹೇಡು hêḍu. A *fluid* measure of 2304 tolas in Honawar (N. C.).

ಹೇರು hêru. A word applicable to weight, and dry and fluid measures: 1, *weight*—8000 tolas for metal in Mundagod (N. C.) ...

6400 tolas for sugar and ghee (Bel.); 2, *dry measure*—12288 tolas in Haliyal and Supa, 17920 tolas in Mundagod (N. C.), and 20480 tolas (Bel.); 3, *fluid measure*—8000 tolas in Mundagod (N. C.).

ಹೊತ್ತು hottu. Time; ಒಂದು—, ಒಪ್ಪತ್ತು (ondu-, oppattu) half a day (S. C.); ಎಲೆ ಹಾಕುವ— (ele hâkuva-) time requisite for a 'chew' (S. C.).

ಹೊನ್ನು-honnu. Half a pagoda, 2 rupees.

ಕ್ಷೇತ್ರಫಲ kshêtraphala. The area of a piece of land, superficial area.

Supplemental List of Words.

Accounts and Book-keeping.

ಅಂತುಕ, ಅಂತುಗ **antuka, antuga.** A total (S. C.).

ಊಳಿಗ **ûliga.** *see p.* 1. —ದ ಚಟ್ಟು (-da čaṭṭu) the entries of a day continued on the following page of a day-book for want of space (S. C.); —ದ ವಿಂಗಡ (-da vingaḍa) entries made in the ledger without being entered in the day-book, *also* —ಕ್ಕೆ ತಟ್ಟದೆ (-kke taṭṭade) (S. C.).

ಕಡ **kaḍa.** *see p.* 1. —ನಾದಾಯ (-nâdâya) temporary loans from others entered in a day-book or journal, the repayment of which being entered as —ಪಿಡಿತ (-piḍita) (S. C.).

ಖತಾವಣಿ **khatâvaṇi.** Posting figures under different heads to find out the totals under each (S. C.).

ನಗದಿಯಾತ್ **nagadiyât.** Cash account.

ನಿಕ್ಕಿ **nikki.** Nett balance; what remains after deductions (S. C.).

ಬಾಕಿ **bâki.** *see pp.* 2 & 151; ಬಾದು— (bâdu-) cash balance at the end of a day (S. C.); ವಸೂಲ್— (vasûl-) collections and outstanding balances.

ಮೊಬಲಗು **mobalagu.** Amount; ಖುಲ್ಲು— (khullu-) gross amount.

ಸಲ್ಲಾ **sallâ.** Cancelled—said of a settled-up account (S. C.).

Affinity and Relationship.

ಕುಟುಂಬ **kuṭumba.** A family consisting of one's parents, brothers, sisters and wife; among Aḷiyasantâna people ಕುಟುಂಬ means a family consisting of one's uncles, sisters and all but one's wife and children; —ದವ (-dava) one related in the family; —ಸ್ಥ (-stha) a family-man.

ತಾತ **tâta.** A grand-father (My.); ಮುತ್ತಾತ (muttâta) a great grand-father (My.).

ಬೀಗಬಿಜ್ಜ **bigabijja.** Relation by marriage.

ಸಂತಾನ **santâna.** Race, line, clan; —ದವ (-dava) a clans-man, *also* —ಗಾರ (-gâra) (S. C.).

Agricultural and Rural.

ಅಂಡ್ಲೆ aṇḍle. Lowest paddy-fields where waters stand abundantly in rainy season.

ಆಲೆಹಗ್ಗ âlehagga. A grazing-rope, a rope for cattle when grazing; *cf.* ಮೇಹಗ್ಗ (S. C.).

ಒಮ್ಮಣ್ಣು ommaṇṇu. Land yielding one crop of rice (S. C.).

ಒಮ್ಮಯು ommaya. Compact, lying together—said of property or land (S. C.).

ಕಜೆಸ್ಥಳ kajesthaḷa. A site near a river where grass grows; swampy ground near salt-water rivers (S. C.).

ಕರಹೈನ karahaina. Hiring a cow for milking purposes.

ಗದ್ದೆ gadde. *see p.* 11: XIII; ಕಂಪ–, ಗಂಪ– (kampa-, gampa-) a very fertile field; a field producing three crops, although there is some difficulty owing to excess of water (S. C.); XIV, ಕೊಟ್ಟಪುಂಜೆ– (koṭṭa-puñje-) a field where suggi or the second crop can be raised with great difficulty (S. C.); XV, ಮುಗುಳಿ– (muguḷi-) a field at the very top of a hill and depending entirely on rain-water (S. C.); *see* ಬಾಣ ಬೆಟ್ಟು (*p.* 11).

ಜೋಡಿ jôḍi. A plucking hook.

ತೋಡು tôḍu. A water-channel, a drain (S. C.); ಕೈ– (kai-) a small drain (S. C.); ಚನ್ನೆ– (čanne-) a drain for water of one field to go into another, *also* ತೆಂನೆ– (tenne-) (S. C.).

ದಣಪೆ daṇape. A turn-stile; *also* ತಡಮೆ.

ದರಳೆ, ದರ್ಕಿ daraḷe, darki. Dried or dead leaves (S. C.).

ಪುಣಜಿ puṇaji. Paddy growing on dry land (My.).

ಪೈರು pairu. *see p.* 14; ಧ್ರುವ– (dhruva-) trees grown in garden lands (My.).

ಬರಬಡ್ಡಿ barabaḍḍi. *see* ಮುಗು (*p.* 17) (S. C.).

ಬಿತ್ತನೆ bittane. Sowing of seeds (My.).

ಬೇಲಿ bêli. A fence (S. C.); ತಡಲು (tadalu) a gate of thorns in a fence.

ಮುಮ್ಮಣ್ಣು mummaṇṇu. A land yielding 3 crops of rice (S. C.).

ಸಪ್ಪುಶದೆ sappuśade. Different sorts of leaves (My.).

Architecture, Carpentry, etc.

ಉತ್ತರ **uttara.** A wall-plate, *also* ಉತ್ರಿ (Cg.).

ಉತ್ತರಾಸು **uttarâsu.** A lintel (Cg.).

ಕವಕೋಲು **kavakôlu.** Rafters (Cg.).

ಕೋಳು **kôḷu.** The ridge of a roof; –ಕಂಭ (-kambha) the main beam supporting a thatch.

ತೀರು **tiru.** Rafters (My.).

ತುರಾಯಿಕಂಭ **turâyikambha.** A pillar tapering at the top (Cg.).

ಪಟವರಸೆ **paṭavarase.** The rafters of a roof.

ಬಾರಿಪಟ್ಟಿ **bâripaṭṭi.** Laths (Cg.).

ಬಿಟ್ಟ **biṭṭa.** A cross-beam (Cg.).

ಬೆಂತೊಲೆ **bentole.** The ridge-pole.

ಬೆಂಮರ **bemmara.** The ridge-pole, the beam over a king-post; *also* ಹೊದೆಮರ (Cg.).

ಬೆಲಗು **belagu.** A rafter, a joist; ತಲೆ– (tale-) a rafter on the ridge of a roof.

ಭಂಟ **bhaṇṭa.** The supporter of a roof.

ಮುಂಜೂರು **muñjûru.** (from ಮುಂ+ಸೂರು?) Eaves (My., Cg.).

ಮಂಡಿಗೆ **maṇḍige.** A pillar, part of which is inside a wall (Cg.).

ಮೊಳೆಕುತ್ತಿ **moḷekutti.** The pivot hole of a native door (Cg., S. C.); *cf.* ಗುಬ್ಬಿಗೂಡು (*p.* 31).

ಹಂಜರ, ಹಂದರ **hañjara, handara.** Laths (My.).

ಹಣತಲೆ **haṇatale.** The upper part of a king-post to support a beam (Cg.).

ಹಲಿಗೆಶಿಂಬಿ **haligeśimbi.** The capital of a pillar (Cg.).

ಹಾರು **hâru.** A roof (My.); ಕವಳಿಗೆ– (kavaḷige-) a cupolaed roof (My.).

Civil and Judicial.

ಅಂತರಾಯ **antarâya.** Estoppel.

ಅಲಬುಸಲಬು **alabusalabu.** A word used with ಸವಾರ್ಧ (*p.* 57) and the meaning of which is not very clear: receipts and charges? (S. C.).

ಉರಿಸಿರಿ **urisiri.** *Lit.* Fire and wealth; participation and liability in things good and bad (S. C.).

ಊರಾಳ **ûrâḷa.** A guardian or manager of a temple whether singly or jointly with others (W.).

ಕಾಣ **kâṇa.** A mortgage; —ದ ಹಣ (-da haṇa) mortgage-amount (S. C.).

ಕಾಸಿ, ಕಿಲಿ **kâsi, kili.** Money or land given by the relations of a Mopla female to the man she is about to marry, to be enjoyed by the latter during the continuance of the marriage but reverting to the woman's family on dissolution of marriage either by divorce or the death of either party (S. C.).

ಜಂಟಿ **jaṇṭe.** Partnership (My.); —ಪಟ್ಟೆ (-paṭṭe) a deed in the name of two persons (My.).

ತೆರವು **teravu.** The price paid for a wife, present of money made to a wife.

ದಸ್ತೇವಜು **dastêvaju.** *see p.* 53; ಒಳ— (oḷa-) supplemental documents, documents included in, and forming a part of, another document (S. C.).

ನಷ್ಟಕಷ್ಟ **nashṭakashṭa.** Loss and damage, the bad consequences of an act (S. C.).

ಪಂಚನಾಮೆ **pañcanâme.** An award by an arbitration.

ಬದಿ **badi.** Gifts to a bride by her relations, and not reverting to the grantor as in ಕಾಸಿ (Tulu, S. C.).

ಬರ **bara.** Divorce, dissolution of marriage according to the Aḷiya-santâna law (S. C.); —ಹೇಳು (-hêḷu) to divorce, to dissolve a marriage, by the wife returning the tâḷi, mûguti, and teravu money given her by the husband, and by the husband disowning his wife before an assembly of the gowḍas and the relations of the parties (S. C.).

ಬಾಧ್ಯಸ್ಥ **bâdhyastha.** The trustee or manager of a temple (S. C.).

ಬಾಳಿಕೆ **bâḷike.** Enjoyment, possession (S. C.); —ಸಾಧನ (-sâdhana) a document which empowers one to freely enjoy property, an absolute deed of sale (S. C.).

ಬಿಡುಮಾನ್ಯಳು **biḍumânyaḷu.** A wife divorced by her husband according to the Aḷiyasantâna law. Bhûtâḷapâṇḍya defines ಬಿಡುಮಾನ್ಯಳು as a woman who (1) has become pregnant through a person socially lower than herself, (2) after puberty, has eloped with a person of an inferior caste, (3) has eloped with a person of an inferior caste after a divorce from her husband (S. C.).

ಬುಡವಳತಿ **buḍavaḷati.** A widow according to the Aḷiyasantâna law, a woman who has lost her husband (S. C.).

ವಾಕ್ರೂಪಿ, ವಾಗ್ರೂಪಿ **vâkrûpi, vâgrûpi.** Declaratory (S. C.); –ವಿಧಿ (-vidhi) a declaratory decree (S. C.).

ವಿಭಕ್ತ **vibhakta.** Divided; ಅ– (a-) undivided (S. C.).

ಸರ್ತಿಸಾಮ್ಯ **sartisâmya.** Fees due to priests and temples (N. C.).

Commercial.

ಆಣಿಕೆ, ಆನಿಕೆ **âṇike, ânike.** A contract under which a trader advances money to the ryots to secure the saleable produce of the latter to himself; hence an advance under a contract (S. C.).

ಕಡಗಟ್ಟು **kaḍagaṭṭu.** An arrangement (S. C.); –ಮಾಡು (-mâḍu) to arrange, as for a loan or a payment (S. C.).

ಪಡಮೂಲೆ **paḍamûle.** Wholesale dealings.

ಪಡಾವು **paḍâvu.** A great deal of profit.

ಬಡ್ಡಿ **baḍḍi.** *see p.* 64; ನಿ– (ni-) without interest (S. C.); ಧರಣ– (dharaṇa-) 12 per cent interest (dharaṇa being a rupee, S. C.); ನಫೆ– (naphe-) an enhanced rate of interest (S. C.); 24 per cent interest (S. C.); ಮುಚ್ಚಾಲು– (muččaulu-) 18 per cent interest, though 18¾ per cent in theory (S. C.); ಅಡ್ಡ– (aḍḍa-) 5 per cent interest (S. C.); ಹಣ– (haṇa-) 10 per cent interest (S. C.); 2, principal and interest.

ಬಿಡುಗಟ್ಟು **biḍugaṭṭu.** Interest in excess of the usual or customary interest, usury (S. C.).

ಭರಾಮನ್ **bharâman.** Letters of credit (S. C.).

ಮೊದಲು **modalu.** The capital of a firm; 2, the cost price.

ರೂಢಿಗೆ **rûḍhige.** Laying out money in profitable investments.

ವತ್ಸಾದ **vatsâda.** An agent, a consignor, a consignee (S. C.).

ಹವಾಲೆಕಾಗದ **havâlekâgada.** An order of payment; a letter asking another to pay a sum to a third party—differing from a huṇḍi in not stating the time within which to make the payment (S. C.).

Land Tenures.

ಕಟ್ಟುಗುಡಿ **kaṭṭuguḍi.** A permanent leasehold, mûlgêṇi (S. C.), *also* ಕಟ್ಟುಗುತ್ತೆ (kaṭṭugutte).

ಗೇಣಿ **gêṇi.** *see p.* 93; ಬಾಳು— (bâḷu-) the meaning of this word, *once* used exclusively in Kundapore, is by no means clear or definite. Some define it as a permanent tenure lasting during the life-time of the tenant after which it reverted to the proprietor, thus partaking of the nature of both ಚಾಯಿದೆ—, ಮೂಲ—; others define it as a tenure to last for ever, a permanent tenure (from ಬಾಳು to last) (S. C.)

ಪಾಲುಪಟ್ಟಿ **pâlupaṭṭi.** Lands left for cultivation on the condition that the lessor and lessee share the produce of the lands between them (N. C.); *see also* ಅಧೇಗಲಿ *p.* 91.

ಶಾಸನಭೂಮಿ **śâsanabhûmi.** Waste lands for which a ನಜರಾನಾ or price was paid to the Sarkâr, in consideration of which they were made over to the purchaser for the simple śist or standard rent, exempt for ever from all extra assessment, *also* ಸನದ್‌ಭೂಮಿ (sanadbhûmi) (Sir Thos. Munro).

Nautical.

ಅಖೋಟ್ **âkhôṭ.** Hire for a ship or vessel, charter (S. C.); --ಕರಾರ್ (-karâr) charter-party (S. C.).

ಕುಟ್ಟೆ, ಕುಟ್ಟಿ **kuṭṭe, kuṭṭi.** Anchorage, tonnage.

ಕೊರಟು **koraṭu.** The forepart of a ship or boat.

ಜಾಗ **jâga.** High tide at full or new moon.

ಹಂಕಾರಿಸು **haṅkârisu.** To set sail, to weigh anchor (S. C.).

Revenue.

ಕಾಕಿಶಾ ರುಸುಂ **kâkiśâ rusum.** An oppressive impost levied by Hyder Ali for the support of a fakir of that name (Rd. S. C.).

ಕಾಣಿಕೆ **kâṇike.** Subscription; 2, a present; ಕಟ್ಟಿ– (katti-) a present from certain Moplas in the village of Ullal to the former reigning governments (Rd. S.C.); ಬುಟ್ಟು– (buṭṭu-) a tax levied upon the merchants of the town of Mulki (S. C.), being a gift formerly agreed by them to be paid to the pagoda, but which was usurped by the former government (Rd. S. C.); *see* ಕುಟ್ಟಿ– (*p.* 143).

ಕಾರಕ **kâraka.** *see p.* 142; ಬಿಲೆ– (bile-) a vexatious and unjust tax, originating formerly in voluntary alms given to a fakir, and from long continuance considered as a fixed revenue, though the object in which it took its rise no longer existed (Rd.); ವರ್ಗ– (varga-) a tax levied as a compensation for customs on the produce of ryots' estates brought to market for sale (Rd. S. C.).

ಕಾಸಿನ ಚಡ್ತ **kâsina čaḍta.** An ancient tax levied in the Râṇi of Bednore's reign on shroffs and bazaarmen to cover the loss on the exchange of 'copper' sent from Nagar to the lower country to be returned in silver and gold coins (Rd. S. C.).

ಜಾಸ್ತಿ **jâsti.** An increase or addition made to the assessment; ನಗರ– (nagar-) additions made to the ಶಾಮಿಲ್, under Hyder, by Sheikji, Dewan of Nagar, and some of which were afterwards reduced and the remainder finally added to the šâmil under 'Sheikji Jâsti'.

ಧರ್ಮ **dharma.** Charity; ಹೊರ– (hora-) charities paid directly by cultivators to temples, without control of government; ಒಳ–, ಕೈ– (oḷa-, kai-) presents of money to temples; these were subsequently added to the bêriz, and tastik granted instead (C.).

ಫಲಗುತ್ತೆ **phalagutte.** An assessment on the produce of fruit gardens (N. C.).

ಸವಣೂರ್ವಟಾವ್ **savaṇûrvaṭâv.** Discount of Savanur coins, under the government of the Raja of Bednore.

INDEX.

ಅ.

ಛ

ಜ

ಝ

ಥ

ದ

ಧ

ನ

ಪ

ಫ

ಬ

ಭ

ಮ

ಯ

ರ

ಹ